Studies in American Popular History and Culture

Edited by
Jerome Nadelhaft
University of Maine

A Routledge Series

Studies in American Popular History and Culture

Jerome Nadelhaft, *General Editor*

Popular Culture and the Enduring Myth of Chicago, 1871–1968
Lisa Krissoff Boehm

America's Fight over Water
The Environmental and Political Effects of Large-Scale Water Systems
Kevin Wehr

Daughters of Eve
Pregnant Brides and Unwed Mothers in Seventeenth-Century Massachusetts
Else L. Hambleton

Narrative, Political Unconscious, and Racial Violence in Wilmington, North Carolina
Leslie H. Hossfeld

Validating Bachelorhood
Audience, Patriarchy, and Charles Brockden Brown's Editorship of the Monthly Magazine and American Review
Scott Slawinski

Children and the Criminal Law in Connecticut, 1635–1855
Changing Perceptions of Childhood
Nancy Hathaway Steenburg

Books and Libraries in American Society during World War II
Weapons in the War of Ideas
Patti Clayton Becker

Mistresses of the Transient Hearth
American Army Officers' Wives and Material Culture, 1840–1880
Robin Dell Campbell

The Farm Press, Reform, and Rural Change, 1895–1920
John J. Fry

State of 'The Union'
Marriage and Free Love in the Late 1800s
Sandra Ellen Schroer

"My Pen and My Soul Have Ever Gone Together"
Thomas Paine and the American Revolution
Vikki J. Vickers

Agents of Wrath, Sowers of Discord
Authority and Dissent in Puritan Massachusetts, 1630–1655
Timothy L. Wood

The Quiet Revolutionaries
How the Grey Nuns Changed the Social Welfare Paradigm of Lewiston, Maine
Susan P. Hudson

Cleaning Up
The Transformation of Domestic Service in Twentieth Century New York City
Alana Erickson Coble

Feminist Revolution in Literacy
Women's Bookstores in the United States
Junko R. Onosaka

Great Depression and the Middle Class
Experts, Collegiate Youth and Business Ideology, 1929–1941
Mary C. McComb

Great Depression and the Middle Class

Experts, Collegiate Youth and Business Ideology, 1929–1941

Mary C. McComb

Routledge
Taylor & Francis Group
NEW YORK AND LONDON

Routledge
Taylor & Francis Group
711 Third Avenue
New York, NY 10017

Routledge
Taylor & Francis Group
2 Park Square
Milton Park, Abingdon
Oxon OX14 4RN

Routledge is an imprint of Taylor & Francis Group, an Informa business

First issued in paperback 2012

International Standard Book Number-13: 978-0-415-97970-2 (Hardcover)
International Standard Book Number-13: 978-0-415-64813-4 (Paperback)

Library of Congress Cataloging-in-Publication Data

McComb, Mary C.
Great depression and the middle class : experts, collegiate youth and business ideology, 1929-1941 / Mary C. McComb.
p. cm. -- (Studies in American popular history and culture)
Includes bibliographical references and index.
ISBN 0-415-97970-6 (alk. paper)
1. Middle class--United States--History--20th century. 2. Middle class--United States--Social conditions. 3. College students--United States--Attitudes. 4. Depressions--1929--United States--Psychological aspects. 5. United States--Social conditions--1918-1932. 6. United States--Social conditions--1933-1945. I. Title. II. Series: American popular history and culture (Routledge (Firm)) III. Series.

HT690.U6M37 2006
305.5'509730904--dc22 2006006497

Visit the Taylor & Francis Web site at
http://www.taylorandfrancis.com

and the Routledge Web site at
http://www.routledge-ny.com

Table of Contents

Acknowledgments

These acknowledgments, much like the book itself, are organized thematically and chronologically. Thank you first of all to my parents, Sharon and Ken McComb, siblings Pat, Dan, Eileen, Kathy, Tara, Mike and niece Victoria for shaping my sensibilities and teaching me to see humor and fun in almost any situation. Thanks to the University of Michigan faculty including Corey Dolgon for letting me know that I'm an American Studies person and to David Scobey and Carol Karlsen for teaching me dedication to the research and writing process.

Many thanks to the George Washington University graduate students Brian Finnegan, Stephen Kidd, Kate Kruckemeyer, Sara Romeyn, Michele Gates Moresi and Lisa Davidson for reading multiple drafts of the early chapters of this book. Much appreciation to Kirsten Swinth who prompted me to work on this topic and to faculty members Barney Mergen, Melani McAlister, James Horton and my advisor Phyllis Palmer. Thank you to the George Washington University for providing fellowships and always managing to come through with funding just when I needed it most.

Norma Angel, you have my undying gratitude for your support, inspirational words and Sunday evening pizzas at Café Luna. Jan Albert and John Murray Albert, thanks for both being fun, smart and super cute. Paulette McElwain, muchas gracias for always providing wise counsel. Thank you to the Society for Neuroscience posse of cool chicks including Elissa Petruzzi, Allison Kupferman and Terri Morauer who listened to me kvetch about the writing process.

Alexis Long, thanks for being there from the beginning, from sitting up all night on the co-op couches in Ann Arbor talking about postmodernism and social movements to letting me stay with you, Chris and Robert after finishing my Ph.D. I appreciate and love you guys more than you'll ever know.

Thank you to the Greensboro group of Diane Levine, Sarah and Rob Jones, Cheryl Greenberg and Julie McKnight for all of your support during the final phases of writing this book.

My lasting and profound gratitude to Elizabeth McDonnell; thank you for being there for me through the ups and downs of the creation process, for spurring me onward and for never allowing me to lose faith in myself.

Chapter One

Great Depression and the Middle Class: Experts, Collegiate Youth and Business Ideology, 1929–1941

> It has been rightly said that no man is broke who has kept a sense of values. . . . A sense of value usually is the one thing that you have to cling to when everything else is gone. A sense of values creates a new horizon for which you can set your new course when the financial winds have deserted you.[1]
>
> "A Sense of Values" *The University of Michigan Daily*, July 3, 1932.

Young people and experts alike raised questions about what to value during the harsh years of the Great Depression. The crash of the stock market in 1929 and the ensuing years of financial hardship represented an emotional and economic earthquake that shook the foundations of established social, cultural, political and economic institutions to the core. The impact of the crash displaced people, both literally and figuratively, with many Americans losing their homes, jobs and savings. Others endured less dire material setbacks, yet experienced an extreme sense of psychic dislocation, feeling that they had lost their footing and established place in the world.

Writings from the Depression era portray an initial sense of mass befuddlement at the beginning of the crisis, followed by a collective sorting through the psychic rubble left in the crash's wake. The Depression proved particularly harrowing for middle-class Americans who were raised to embrace the ideal of competitive individualism and the notion that hard work and individual striving would lead to material and emotional security. The pecuniary and psychic crises assaulted people's sense of identity, often creating the notion that if one's personal worth could be measured in dollars earned, so too could one's personal worthlessness.[2] Middle-class college students and expert authors participated in the sifting process by writing articles and books that raised questions about what to value, what to discard, how to define success and how to rebuild some concrete foundation on which young people could construct their futures.

Members of the middle class expressed a range of fears about the impact that the Depression might have on them. They worried that the destabilizing reverberations from the stock market crash had the frightening potential of acting as a leveler of social class distinctions or, worse yet, being the harbinger of a class-based revolution. The effects of the stock market crash in 1929 had affected the poorest people first, but by 1932 members of the professional middle class began to feel the repercussions of the financial fallout.[3] People who were fortunate enough to have jobs still experienced financial setbacks, with the amount of money paid out in salaries decreasing by 40% and wages dropping by 60%.[4] These rapid economic and social changes prompted questions about where things had gone wrong in the past, how to fix them in the present and how to prepare for the future. Middle-class youths who had grown up during the prosperous 1920s learned from their parents and teachers that if they worked hard, saved their money and planned wisely they would be guaranteed access to the American Dream, which usually included a salaried job, marriage, children, a house, a car, mass-produced consumer items and household appliances.[5] The Depression robbed young members of the middle class of this sense of security, challenged their belief systems and raised the question of why they should value hard work and ambition when so many dedicated workers were fired and people who wanted jobs could not find them.[6]

In the early years of the Great Depression politicians repeated the promise that prosperity was "just around the corner," yet with strikes, marches and rallies occurring around the country on a regular basis the potential for a mass class-based uprising hung heavy in the air. As the Depression wore on with little relief in sight, radical notions began to circulate in the national discourse. Many Americans feared that a proletarian uprising could occur at any time; journalists and politicians alike began predicting that revolution, not prosperity, might be lurking just around the corner.[7] American citizens from all age groups and socioeconomic backgrounds responded discursively to the pecuniary and psychic repercussions from the stock market crash. Some people wrote letters to the editors of their local papers suggesting ways to deal with the Depression. Students, parents, unemployed people, social workers and scientists generated theories about how the government and individuals could best cope with the crisis. Most of these suggestions for solutions did not make it into the upper echelons of national governmental policy making, yet the politicized writings of Americans created a national discourse that played out on the pages of daily newspapers, magazine columns and student campus newspapers during the early years of the Depression.

Much has been written about working-class people organizing around a shared socioeconomic-political identity as a means to empower themselves during the Depression era, but little has been written about the middle-class retrenchment process. Historians examine the political, economic, social and cultural currents of the Great Depression, but their work often ignores the lives of middle-class youths and the particular gender and racial dynamics of the middle class.[8] Some images of the Depression include working-class employees engaging in sit-down strikes, masses of forgotten men standing up to a faceless bureaucratic government, Dorothea Lange's haunting images of the Dust Bowl and married women workers quietly trudging off to their jobs under the harshly-critical eyes of the larger society. Historians have done an excellent job of portraying the dynamics of these large-scale struggles. Many studies of Depression-era American culture have explored the plight of these forgotten men and the backlash against married women workers, but few have focused on the struggles that young, college-aged, unmarried middle-class women and men faced.[9]

Michael Denning argues in *The Cultural Front* that during the economic disruptions of the Depression, people in the United States took a communal turn to the left, which resulted in the "laboring of American culture." This process, like earlier social struggles for the abolition of slavery and suffrage for women, reshaped American culture and promoted a profound and lasting transformation of American mass culture.[10] Denning's excellent text reads working-class cultural productions including songs, manifestos and dramatic performances as a means to explore working class organizations, movements and cultural productions generated during the Depression era and beyond. While Denning's work provides provocative insight into the laboring of American culture, it fails to elucidate how middle-class youths of the 1930s coped with the Depression and how gender and race issues figured into the process. Denning's contention that during the 1930s many Americans, including people from both working class and middle class, embraced the rhetoric and ideals of the labor movement, including collective bargaining, joining unions and supporting solidarity among their ranks, overlooks a tenacious defense of middle-class exclusivity. Middle-class people who grew up in the competitive, individualistic, capitalist system of the United States often favored preserving their individual freedoms and pursuits, more than they valued collective organizing.[11]

My intervention is to look at the class-based discursive formation that occurred on college campuses during the 1930s, by examining the discourse produced by middle-class collegiate youths at Amherst College, Mount Holyoke College, George Washington University, Howard University and the University of Michigan and middle-class experts including sociologists, psychologists, professors, etiquette writers and mass-market manual authors who produced written texts between January 1930 and January 1942.[12] This book explores how expert authors and college students articulated their middle class status during the crisis of capitalism in the 1930s. It examines how students struggled to define themselves in an uncertain world where a college degree no longer guaranteed immediate employment after graduation and how students learned to use the language of the marketplace to cope with the crisis of capitalism. During the stressful years of the 1930s, experts and students formed symbiotic relationships in an attempt to articulate and define a middle-class position appropriate to the national crisis. The successful reproduction of the taken-for-granted American standard of living was disrupted by the economic, social and political dislocations generated by the Depression, so collegiate youths and experts banded together to create a discursive rationale for the downturn in their economic and social status.

Even in the face of an extreme crisis of capitalism, Americans wanted to maintain the level of well-being they had before the crash of the stock market as well as a certain level of respectability within their community.[13] At the simplest level, during the first few decades of the twentieth century, many members of the middle-class had attained an "American Standard of Living," meaning that middle-class Americans enjoyed a sense of material comfort, security and abundance on a daily basis.[14] In this paradigm, consumerism became a primary mode for pursuing individual happiness and prestige.[15] Middle-class consumer-citizens who had felt solidly self-aware of their positions on the social, political and economic fields of the 1920s were thrown off balance by the market upheaval and began to question their place in the larger hierarchies.[16]

Middle-class experts and collegiate youths of the 1930s coped with the emotional and economic dislocations of the Great Depression by creating discourses that relied on the language of the marketplace as a means to shape their individual senses of identity while creating a collective set of middle-class standards and norms to which they could abide. They collaboratively created a vision of a stable future that drew largely from the past and used the language of business and commerce as a retrograde solution to a current problem.[17] Experts and students effectively pieced together bits of the scientific-management and business rhetoric of the 1920s and combined them with the gender norms of the pre-feminist era with the hope that the mixture of ideologies would provide them with a sense of stability that the Depression had greatly disrupted. Middle-class youths and experts appeared to embrace the notion that if they aligned themselves with the corporate order they would be protected from the worst effects of the Depression. The language of the marketplace and business ideology bled over into the realms of fraternity and sorority life, rating and dating and marriage and family life because the economic crisis was so ongoing, far-reaching and seemingly endless that it made an impact on all areas of culture. Depression-era students and experts attempted to make sense of their situation by using the tools they had on hand, including the language of business efficiency, scientific expertise, normative values and adjustment that were popularized by prominent sociologists, psychologists and business people of the 1920s.

Expert authors and middle-class collegians alike espoused the tenets of liberal individualism and methods of self-commodification as key tools with which to navigate their way through the economic and emotional quagmire created by the Great Depression. Liberal individualism places primacy on the individual person; individuals are encouraged to "think only about themselves, about their shares and about whether their rights have been respected or violated and whether they have received or failed to receive their fair share."[18] People who embrace the ideology of liberal individualism often believe that people can be the most effective agents when they are allowed to carve out for themselves "the most extensive set of rights and the largest bundle of commodities" that they can obtain.[19]

Students of the 1930s who were struggling to obtain the symbolic capital of a college degree definitely had interests in obtaining as many privileges, rights and commodities as they could in a time when economic capital was in short supply. Symbolic capital encompasses diverse elements including prestige, recognition and power in one's social circle.[20] In this system, economic and symbolic interests are deemed equally viable since the accruing of symbolic capital often is intrinsically intertwined with reaping real social and material benefits.[21] Agents seeking prestige draw on their educational, cultural and material resources as they attempt to seize the dominant culture in an acceptable manner. If agents' legitimate attempts to appropriate culture fail, they will question the grounds on which legitimacy was bequeathed. These competitions and conflicts regarding the legitimate culture create hierarchies of what is seen as possessing social worth and prestige.[22]

By contrast with labor union emphasis on the collective and on the need to unite to get better wages and treatment in the workplace, the middle class embraced individualism and a seemingly selfish set of values. The experts and the students both upheld individual agency as the key for coping with the systemic crisis. Both groups agreed that *nonmaterial* qualities including personality, charm, frame of mind and values should be the criteria used to calibrate the social standing of young people.[23] During the Depression era these evanescent symbolic goods became, for many people, more valuable than material assets. At the same time, the language of competitive striving and the constant evaluation of self and others mimicked the calculations of profit-oriented businesses. The parlance of emotions and economics intermingled in a discursive domain where investing financially and emotionally, taking stock, calculating one's worth, reading the price tags of life and performing personality inventories all were depicted as viable means to reap profits in the social world. In addition, the concept of confidence, or lack thereof, appeared in countless advice books about monetary and mental malaise. During the 1930s, many economists posited that a lack of consumer confidence caused the Depression to continue unabated. Meanwhile, psychologists repeatedly informed young people that their lack of personal confidence, in the form of the dreaded Inferiority Complex, created the conditions for an ongoing bout of emotional depression.

The young people who grew up in the 1920s and attended college in the 1930s were privy to an ongoing cultural discourse rife with commercial messages and business terminology that had emerged full-force during the first decades of the twentieth century. Middle-class Americans of the 1920s and 1930s regularly utilized the concepts of markets, customers, suppliers, laws, trends, schedules, timetables, statistics, grades and profit margins to make sense of their daily lives.[24] College students and expert authors of the 1930s relied heavily on the language of the marketplace to express themselves, and planned on using self-commodification to find a job, score a date, or seek out a marriageable mate.

Self-commodification processes functioned differently depending on a person's gender. Young white women were encouraged to commodify and sell themselves on the dating and marriage marketplaces. Experts and peers often advised females to fashion themselves into marriageable mates who were attractive, appealing and willing to submit to the leadership of their husbands. Women in the dating and marriage marketplace competed against one another for male attention. Men were expected to compete in the commercial marketplace to attain jobs. These gender-based forms of competition and self-commodification became a bit skewed in the 1930s because women, often out of financial necessity, began competing against men in the commercial marketplace for jobs. Self-commodification required self-promotion, marketing oneself just like any other product. In 1931, writer Henry Adams explained that men needed to recognize themselves as commodities that were up for sale on an open market and they needed to use business methods to compel their elders to buy them as investments.[25]

Conceptualizing humans as investments both reduced people to commodities while simultaneously valuing them as commodities, so the concept could be read in differing ways depending on an observer's vantage point.[26] Some youths embraced the principles of self-commodification to present themselves in the best light to marriageable mates or potential employers. Other college students resisted the standards of self-commodification as an affront to their personal dignity and struggled to find other values to sustain them through the Great Depression.

Some might question why middle-class experts and youths clung so tenaciously to the language of the marketplace in a time when the market had obviously failed. Denning contends that during the 1930s discourse in America took a leftward turn and that many people embraced the rhetoric of the labor movement. I argue that students and experts organized themselves around their shared middle-class identity in a similar manner to the way that working-class people organized themselves in the labor movements of the Great Depression. The material conditions of members of the working-classes inspired them to band together to demand their rights as workers. Members of the middle class organized around their material circumstances as well, but did so in a conservative effort to consolidate and preserve the privileges that had been passed down from previous generations. Middle-class experts and youths protected their social, economic and cultural capital by clinging to the tenets of the marketplace because they understood the language and their fluency with market concepts appeared to offer them a safe harbor in which to anchor their hopes and dreams until the maelstrom of the Depression passed.

EXPERT AUTHORS & STUDENT WRITERS

During the Depression era a remarkable number of expert-authored advice books flooded the marketplace, offering young people counsel about whether to stay in school or try to find a job, how to score dates and points with their peers, how to modulate their sexuality enough to gain popularity without getting themselves into trouble, how to succeed academically in order to achieve professionally after graduation and how to find a life mate and marry.[27] While the validity of using prescriptive literature like expert-penned advice books to glean what was going on during a particular cultural moment has been questioned by some historians, I believe that these texts prove invaluable because they expose the publicly-embraced conventions of the era as well as the rules that provided the "context for concrete acts and individual experience."[28]

The experts who wrote advice literature to young people in the 1930s possessed disparate levels of education, credentials and expertise in their fields; many had advanced degrees in sociology, psychology and education, while others boasted of first-hand experience working with young people as teachers, administrators or traveling lecturers.[29] Some expert authors were more of the self-appointed variety and included advice columnists from magazines and newspapers, etiquette writers and individuals who wished to share their unique wisdom with the youth of the nation. All of the experts bore the distinction of belonging to a relatively new professional niche.

Student newspapers provide fascinating sources of information, especially when read in contrast to the expert writings of an era. Newspapers from college campuses represent cultural sites where the tensions, trends, fashions and passions of the day play out in vivid form.[30] Student publications contained serious stories, heartfelt editorials, advertisements, cartoons and jokes that bring the era to life in a way that monographs cannot. Student newspapers illuminate the inner workings of the student bodies of the 1930s giving resonate voice to the concerns and controversies that mattered most to them. In reading these texts one feels bestowed with the gift of being able to peer into the collective psyche of a puzzled generation and to gain some insight into the ways they struggled to make sense of the fate that had befallen them.

The articles in college newspapers provide excellent complementary evidence and valuable counterpoints to the content in the expert-penned texts. Still, it is important to recognize that neither set of sources provides a social mirror that simply reflects the reality of the era. Roland Marchand notes that using advertisements as primary documents more often exposes the hopes and aspirations of the copy writers rather that the daily lives of the ad readers; the same could be said of the more fanciful writings by both experts and students.[31] Factual newspaper articles that focus on international, national and government affairs provide historians with a sense of temporality, grounding and atmosphere for the era. More subjective pieces including editorials and letters may not provide purely accurate depictions of the social realities of the day, but they can help to illuminate the inner life of their writers in this particular historical moment. Following the stream of thoughts, images and ideas generated by scholars, intellectuals, writers and opinion-makers assists in accessing the sense-making processes that middle-class people utilized during the Depression era.

Student newspapers functioned as sites where campus communities were solidified and cross-campus cultural discourses took place. Middle-class college students wrote letters to the editors of their student newspapers, contributed essays to campus publications and attended lectures presented by experts, raised questions in the national discourse about the place of college graduates in the larger world. The students' humanity, intelligence and humor come across clearly in their writings. The geographic, economic, gender and racial location of the students in the 1930s made a huge difference in the ideals that they held close to their hearts and the ideas that they expressed in their writings. Each newspaper, like each institution of higher learning, had its own unique "personality" that came across on its pages.[32]

In the 1930s Amherst College was a small, private, all-male liberal arts college located in the small town of Amherst in Western Massachusetts. Most of the students at the all-male college came from privileged backgrounds, lived on campus and attended school full-time with very few working outside jobs to support themselves. Amherst students appeared to be pretty proud of their sheltered status. One student described the campus as a peaceful haven where student life was rarely disrupted by the "muddy currents of grim reality."[33]

If a twenty-first century reader was unaware that a huge economic crisis occurred in the 1930s, reading *The Amherst Student* would offer few clues that something had been amiss. The men of Amherst College did not appear too concerned with their job prospects but expressed much concern about their campus social life, facilities and activities. *The Amherst Student* came out twice a week during the school year on Mondays and Thursdays and typically had eight to ten pages of copy including advertisements for local diners, movie theaters, travel agencies and shops. The front page sometimes carried stories about issues happening outside the college, but for the most part *The Amherst Student* editorial content centered on collegiate sports, social events, fraternity life, college administration and campus rules. Two of the most hotly-contested issues during the 1930s centered on rules for fraternity rushing and the unpalatable food served on campus. Articles in *The Amherst Student* that mentioned the outside world usually referred to weekends spent on other college campuses, movies, Broadway shows and other recreational issues.[34]

Undergraduates who attended The George Washington University, a private coeducational, urban university located in Washington, DC explored a wider range of issues than their Amherst peers including national and international politics, post-graduation job prospects, campus dances, extracurricular activities and student elections in the pages of *The George Washington University Hatchet,* which was published on a weekly basis from September to June with one issue in July. In the 1930s the George Washington University had an all-white student body. While there was no racial diversity at the school, students came from a wider variety of socioeconomic backgrounds than students from Amherst and Mount Holyoke. Many George Washington University students attended school full-time, lived on campus and participated in extracurricular activities. A small percentage of students attended night classes on a part-time basis so that they could work full time at jobs in Washington, DC.[35] By the mid-1930s more than half of the undergraduates at the university worked part time in offices, private homes or on campus to help pay their way through school. Students attending the university during the 1930s appeared very career-focused and seemed to worry about the potential payoff for attaining a college degree. Throughout the 1930s many students wrote editorials questioning why they should spend years of their lives taking classes when they could probably get jobs of the same caliber without having a degree. This perspective arises more often in the *Hatchet* than in any other student publication, most likely because there were full-time positions available in Washington, DC for middle-class white youths. Students living in small college towns lacked access to full-time employment while students from Howard University were shut out of many professional opportunities because of their race.

The young men and women who attended Howard University, a private, coeducational, urban school with an African-American student body appeared more serious, mature and politically conscious than their counterparts at other colleges and universities.[36] Howard students expressed great interest in issues of racial uplift, race prejudice and economic conditions for African-Americans, lynching and civil liberties.[37] Howard University and the George Washington University are located within a few miles of each other in Washington, DC, but in the 1930s the two schools may have as well existed in separate universes. Unlike the interplay between students and potential marriage partners at Mount Holyoke and Amherst that shows up in the headlines and editorials in the newspapers, Howard University and George Washington University students showed no interest in breaching the racial barrier.[38] In the early 1930s *The Howard Hilltop* was issued every Thursday from October until May, except during school holidays. In the autumn of 1935 the paper switched to biweekly production schedule during the school year, but by the fall of 1936 *The Howard Hilltop* was published on a bimonthly basis. Their advertisers included local restaurants, coffee shops and hair salons; often a reminder to patronize the advertisers' establishments appeared on the masthead.

An intriguing aspect of *The Howard Hilltop* is that like *The Amherst Student,* the Depression was rarely mentioned in its pages. This is for very different reasons; most students from Amherst knew that their financial futures were secure, while for most African-Americans in the United States in the 1930s facing an uncertain financial future was the norm. The students at Howard, unlike their peers at other schools, did not spill much ink fretting about the future. They realized that it would be difficult to find jobs after graduation, but they remained sanguine in the face of adversity. Students from Howard appeared to have realistic, but not fatalistic, visions for the future. The editorial pages of *The Howard Hilltop* demonstrate this in that they were consistently filled with articles about racial uplift, African-American role models and the achievements of students, alumni and faculty and the future prospects for Howard graduates.

Mount Holyoke College, located a few miles from Amherst College in the small town of South Hadley, Massachusetts, was a small, private, women only, liberal arts college founded in 1837 by Mary Lyon. Lyon championed the progressive concept that young women should have the opportunity to be educated like young men. During the 1930s the students resided in the somewhat insular world of the campus. Some officials at women's colleges wanted to demonstrate that their students were respectable, and, to this end, often "placed numerous social restrictions on their students."[39] Mount Holyoke appears to have fallen into this category during the 1930s. Judging by the news articles, most young women's lives consisted of attending classes, studying, going to chapel services, taking walks, keeping up extracurricular schedules of sports, volunteer work and social clubs. Women's colleges like Mount Holyoke took great pride in offering an academically-rigorous curriculum that rivaled the best men's colleges including Amherst. [40]

The Mount Holyoke News was issued weekly during the school year, except during holidays, vacations and exam periods. The debates that appear in *The Mount Holyoke News* centered around mandatory chapel attendance, smoking on campus, fears about scholastic standing and worries about future careers. This newspaper definitely had the most articles about the importance of academic success, all-night study sessions and getting good grades. The women of Mount Holyoke were not, to use the popular vernacular of the 1930s, merely "grinds" that cared only about grade point averages and future career prospects. Many articles and editorials focused on dances at men's colleges, social events on campus, field trips and debates about the hazing of first year students. Even during the worst years of the Depression, it was rare for students from Mount Holyoke to work for wages while attending school. Articles from *The Mount Holyoke News* reveal that many students experienced tension and guilt about being in a fairly privileged position when so many people were suffering from economic and emotional hardship. Several writers duly noted that their working-class "sisters" were struggling to make ends meet and offered support through volunteer work and consciousness-raising articles in the paper.

The University of Michigan Daily was published every morning except Monday during both the school year and the summer session. Most students who attended this large, Midwestern, public, coeducational university lived on campus and took courses full time. During the Depression many students also held part time jobs at restaurants, cafes or on campus to help pay their way through school. Most University of Michigan students in the 1930s haled from the Midwest and came from families where the parents were owners of small businesses. Many were first or second generation college students. Letters from the Dean's office show that for many students, attending college was seen as an enormous privilege for the young person, often a burden for the rest of the family and something taken quite seriously by all parties. The student body at the University of Michigan was so large that an extremely wide range of opinions were expressed on the pages of *The Michigan Daily.* Some undergraduates were most interested in fraternity and sorority life, campus events, dances and gossip. Other students embraced political activism and wrote long essays about the benefits of communism and socialism. The gender tensions at this coeducational school ran much higher than they did at either Howard or George Washington University. Part of this could be that Howard students felt united by a shared racial identity while students at George Washington University felt less threatened than Michigan students about their chances for getting jobs after graduating. Clearly, the geographical locations of the schools had some impact on the editorial content of the newspapers. More importantly, the social, economic, racial and gender compositions of the student bodies attending the schools created distinctive fields for actors to play out their struggles within the microcosm of campus life and the macrocosm of the larger world.

WHY LOOK AT COLLEGES?

College campuses of the 1930s functioned not only as sites where cultural capital was *distributed,* but also as the locations where cultural capital was *valorized.*[41] Attending college was popularly understood as a four-year time span that bridged the gap between adolescence and adulthood. College campuses functioned as social spaces, or fields, where students were encouraged to experiment with new roles, ideas and experiences in order to enrich their lives. In the course of their college careers students were expected to become self-reliant, self-directed, motivated, individualistic, opportunistic, dedicated, reliable, educated individuals who would be prepared to face the world of work, business, politics, home and family life. The middle-class discourse about college life upheld the tenets of striving for individual success, competing with peers for accolades and honors and accruing the symbolic capital of a college degree as viable methods for proving that youths had transformed themselves into adults who were worthy of inheriting access to professional careers and the middle-class lifestyle. Students were encouraged by experts and one another to put their resources including money, leisure time and their intellects to the best uses to attain these forms of symbolic and economic capital. Young middle-class people willingly engaged in the defining process of attending college in order to prove themselves as valuable commodities who were worthy of earning academic honors, pledging to Greek organizations, taking on leadership roles on campus or becoming popular with their peers.

Students from most schools agreed that college attendance was meant to be used as preparation for the world after graduation. Most middle-class male students, from both African-American and white backgrounds, were seeking white collar professional positions after graduation. Undergraduate males from Amherst College, Howard University, George Washington University and the University of Michigan prepared to become doctors, lawyers and business men. White middle-class young women who attended coeducational schools during the 1930s appeared to be divided about what life after college would look like. Many female students admitted that they were enrolled in school so that they enjoy the college experience, make friends and find husbands; most of these women were preparing themselves for post-graduate careers as wives, mothers and members of social clubs. Young women who attended school to prepare for a life of domesticity expressed different concerns from female undergraduates who were in college to ready themselves for paid employment. Middle-class females who looked forward to marriage and family life wanted college to furnish them with home economics curricula, marriage and family courses and extracurricular activities that would teach them how to use their leisure time wisely and train them to become pillars of their middle-class communities. The young undergraduates who attended all-female schools colleges like Mount Holyoke often were pursuing education to train for lifelong careers as teachers, social workers, medical professionals, department store managers, journalists and advertisement writers. A large percentage of Mount Holyoke women continued on with graduate studies. Female students of African-American descent, like those attending Howard University, readied themselves for dual careers involving marriage and family life coupled with wage-earning professions. Even though students at Howard were from solid middle-class and elite backgrounds, they understood that their families would probably need to have two wage earners if they wished to live a middle-class lifestyle.

The middle-class lifestyle, as defined by the standards of the 1920s and 1930s, included being married, having children, enacting proper gender roles, owning a home, belonging to local groups and clubs and participating vigorously in the worlds of business and politics. College students recognized that they would be called upon to be leaders in the future. Some students accepted this privilege and power as a birthright that did not need to be expanded upon through individual effort. Most students, however, embraced the responsibility of becoming productive adults and envisioned their four years in school as an important time to ready themselves to take on the roles of middle-class pillars of their communities. These serious students embraced the ethos of hard work, independent initiative and constant self-evaluation. They attempted to ascend hierarchies by participating in extracurricular activities, joining clubs, getting involved in campus politics and making connections with people who would likely benefit them in the future, either as marriageable mates, well-connected friends or business colleagues.

College students of the 1930s understood that their future class status depended on having both capital and power. They realized that their financial, social and emotional futures were tied in with their ability to access symbolic capital, especially since access to material capital proved so uncertain. While material capital like gold, land, buildings and cash can be stockpiled, stashed away and passed on to future generations, symbolic capital must be earned by individuals and cannot be saved or transferred to others.[42] People earn symbolic capital by completing "defining experiences" that usually require mental labor and garner credentials and prestige instead of wages. Defining experiences include attending college, graduate school, law school or medical school.[43] Individuals who wish to complete defining experiences most often have to embrace the all-American qualities of rugged individualism, solitary striving and delayed gratification in order to earn the symbolic rewards.[44] The notion of individual striving as the key for gaining symbolic rewards makes it sound as if access to the professional middle class was based on merit, talent and hard work.[45] This denies that other factors, including an individual's race, gender, class background and ethnicity definitely come into play. The fact that most people could not afford to partake in the defining experiences necessary to accrue symbolic capital demonstrates how the unequal power relations play out on the social plane. This denial erases the constructed nature of middle classness while naturalizing and justifying economic inequality by relying on the ideology of meritocracy.

This study of middle-class formation draws on Pierre Bourdieu's theories about the creation of social space through a group's categorizing itself by measuring itself against others. Bourdieu contends that all endeavors in which humans engage occur in social fields which function as spaces where people compete for resources. In these fields, individuals, institutions and other agents attempt to distinguish themselves from others and to accrue whatever has been deemed useful or valuable in that particular arena. Two dominant forms of hierarchy exist in capitalist societies; the first being economic hierarchies, where power and social positions are determined by having access to money and property. The second form of hierarchy is based in social, cultural and symbolic realms where individual status is measured by how much cultural or symbolic capital one possesses.

It is important to make the discursive machinations of the middle-class retrenchment process visible, because the reproduction of the social order can appear so subtle, ordinary and mundane that it is often overlooked. This can lead to middle-class ways of perceiving reality to be taken for granted by the public.[46] The paradox of the process is that the dominant cultural norms—in this case those of the middle class—become naturalized to such an extent that domination is achieved by negating itself. Certain practices are legitimized as inherently superior to others, which makes the practices seem superior even to those on the margins, thus making the entire process of normalization, naturalization and domination less visible.[47]

The discursive formations created by middle-class students and experts differ greatly from the connections made by young people in labor unions. Labor unions were built on a basis of a shared material position and interests, where working-class people banded together in great numbers to fight against management for fair treatment and decent pay. Middle-class students believed that being treated well and paid decently for their work were part of their birthright. They were not bonded together in a collective struggle, but rather were part of a large field where they used gender, race and social status to differentiate among themselves. For many middle-class students, college was about striving to earn the best grades, to score the most prestigious dates, to join social organizations like fraternities, sororities and campus clubs and to win positions of power including being editor of the school paper, class president, student council member or leader of clubs. These defining experiences not only prepared students for futures of competitive individualistic striving in the workplace, but also determined students' social status on campus. Even within the relatively elite field of the college campus, hierarchies within hierarchies existed. The hierarchies were based on different criteria depending on people's social locations and the colleges they attended.

At Amherst, the all-male student body valued young men who proved to be leaders, but who also, somewhat conversely, managed to mix well with the other fellows and not stand out too much. They liked men who exhibited confidence and self-assuredness in academic and social situations.

The qualities that Amherst men upheld as valuable were the very qualities that would help their graduates succeed in future careers in business and politics. Female undergraduates at Mount Holyoke College also believed in competitive striving, but mostly for grades and for preparing for futures as missionaries, teachers and business professionals. In 1931 a large number of recent graduates from Mount Holyoke pursued graduate study in the humanities, attended secretarial schools, schools of social work, nursing and medicine. [48] The numbers were similar in 1938 with a majority of Mount Holyoke alum taking graduate or secretarial courses. Those who held down full-time jobs mostly were in teaching professions. Several female graduates of the 1930s studied law and social work, while some worked as research assistants in labs and hospitals.[49] Graduates from the class of 1939 pursued diverse options, with ten students marrying right after graduation, fifteen teaching and several pursuing graduate studies in philosophy, English, psychology, physiology, Latin and French. The female graduates who worked for wages right after graduation took jobs in New York and Boston doing statistics work, laboratory work and executive training at large department stores.[50]

The women of Mount Holyoke bonded together in sisterhood, yet each individual woman appeared to want to prove herself as an intelligent, strong, capable person who could forge paths into careers and compete with men for jobs, positions of power and accolades. In the early 1930s, one student explained that marriage was "no longer women's only responsibility," and that since 1920 females "had a wider obligation."[51] College students, especially young women who had so recently been granted the right to vote, were urged to recognize and embrace the obligations that came with the advantage of going to college. Many serious students believed that they should learn to form practical and well-founded opinions, express and defend their opinions with confidence and ease and take an active role in democratic government. They encouraged one another to take active roles in campus government, learn to speak up in class discussions in order to train themselves for future duties as middle-class American citizens.

Young men attending coeducational schools including the University of Michigan and the George Washington University seemed less assured that they would be inheriting power, privilege and prestige or a world that embraced them as leaders of the future. Many male students at George Washington prepared themselves for careers in white collar government work, while white males attending the University of Michigan, the largest of the schools examined herein, readied themselves for a variety of careers. Some white male graduates of the University of Michigan expected to become doctors, lawyers and political leaders, but other white male students had less illustrious strivings to become teachers, shopkeepers and members of the managerial class in small Midwestern towns. The female students at both of these schools also appeared ambivalent about what their futures held. About half fully expected to get married soon after college, so their time on campus was spent striving for popularity, dates and opportunities to engage with future mates. The other fifty percent of the women wanted careers but recognized that their options were limited by traditional gender norms regarding women's professions. Many women prepared to become teachers, social workers and nurses, all of which were commonly viewed as proper "female" professions.

The men and women at Howard University who were of African-American descent faced economic circumstances that were greatly shaped by the economic and political circumstances of the 1930s. Middle-class female students prepared for dual careers of being wives and mothers while also earning paychecks. Even though most African-American women planned on working after graduating from college, their views about what future careers were available to them were very limited.[52] Lucy D. Slowe, the Dean of Women from Howard University commented that the curricula at many African-American colleges seemed pointed at training "teachers and preachers," while focusing on little else.[53] In 1932 she sent a questionnaire to 76 institutions that were teaching college-level courses to African-American female students. The responses culled from the forty-four institutions that answered the questionnaire, showed that out of 14,843 women enrolled almost all were training to be teachers, social workers or nurses. Of those students surveyed, only four percent were studying political science and economics and only seven percent studied psychology. Slowe feared that the African-American women who were attending college during the 1930s were preparing to be intelligent heads of homes and strong members of their communities, but that they were missing out on opportunities to prepare themselves for well-paying careers.[54] One student from Howard University shared Slowe's concerns stating that it was "absolutely ridiculous in the present economic and social status of the country," for students to study teaching because they would have an almost impossible time finding jobs in a professional field that was already overcrowded.[55] The student admonished his peers to study engineering, botany, economics and architecture if they wished to have careers in the private or governmental sectors of society. The situation was especially precarious for African-American students, one of whom stated that, "Negroes are losing out in many of the trades and pursuits which they formerly had a monopoly, simply because they have not kept up with the changes of the modern world."[56] African-American men feared that with the economic crisis, jobs that they may have had access to in previous years would be taken by white males in the competitive Depression-era job market.

Members of the middle class experienced both economic and psychological setbacks during the 1930s. The rising costs of living hit white-collar workers especially hard in the years of 1933–1936 because most salaried employees did not experience the same increase in weekly earnings that wage-earners did.[57] Researchers of the 1930s found that while working-class families experienced the greatest economic hardships during the Depression, it was deprived middle-class families who often suffered equal or greater psychological distress because of their loss of prestige.[58] Trends in popular psychology, when coupled with the ethos of rugged individualism, manufactured the widely-held belief that failure was personal, not social, and that success could be achieved by making adjustments to one's individual personality rather than by challenging the social order.[59] Young people, according to some of the literature of the 1930s, were less traumatized by downward mobility than were their parents. Even if young people felt less shame than their elders about economic setbacks, they had still been raised in a capitalist culture where poverty was often perceived as a sign of personal failure. Many experts responded to these assumptions by repeatedly informing young readers that if they exerted enough effort, they would be able to attain the symbolic capital—popularity, peer esteem, good grades and college degrees—they desired.

MEANING OF CLASS

Most expert authors and college students of the Depression era shared the distinction of being from middle-class backgrounds. Class is a notion that is "inherently fuzzy around the edges," but generally a person's class status is determined by their possession of money, authority, influence and power.[60] Recent historical works have defined class in a number of ways. Denning points to the division between performing either manual or mental labor as the defining factor of whether someone is part of the working class or middle class. In a similar vein, historian Warren Susman posits that members of the middle class, including managers, salespeople and engineers received salaries while working class employees earned hourly wages.[61] Some argue that class standing is not solely determined by how much monetary capital a person possesses; it can often be about where a person stands on the spectrum of power.

It is important to remember that a class is "defined as much by its being perceived and by its being," both of which have little to do with an actor's position in the relations of production.[62] While Karl Marx and Max

Weber's perspectives on production, consumption and classification provide starting points to analyze the cultural texts of the 1930s, using a purely economic model overlooks the power dynamics inherent in the production of cultural texts. Bourdieu's discussions of actors moving through cultural fields and empowering themselves by accruing symbolic capital provide an extremely useful analytical framework for examining how experts and college students articulated their middle class status. Competition for monetary capital usually occurs in the marketplace, but struggles for symbolic capital play out in fields, which are abstractly-constructed spaces with their own laws of functioning. The concept of fields proves more inclusive than the concept of the marketplace when explicating exchanges between youths and experts in the 1930s. This holds true because with Bourdieu's field theory people's interests and investments "can be analyzed with terms of economic logic without reducing them to economics."[63] The familiar realm of economic exchange is complicated by this supposition because the "goods"—in this case mostly discursive goods—are produced and circulated throughout the fields with highly fluctuating exchange rates. A symbolic cultural commodity that is valued on one day might be cast aside the next. Youths and experts both acted as producers and consumers of knowledge in the fields and often reinscribed previously existing systems of power.[64]

To be a successful player in the field one had to possess "a feel for the game" with the rules usually being picked up through a combination of formal education and informal exposure to various elements of culture. Actors who have a feel for the game tend to, in specific situations, act and react "in ways that are not always calculated and not always about conscious obedience to rules."[65] The fields themselves represent arenas where goods, knowledge and ideas are produced, circulated and appropriated by the actors, who engage in contests to acquire symbolic capital. One of the key rules for successful play in the fields involves consciously or unconsciously denying one's interest in gaining political, social or economic power, especially since often the practices of players in the fields served to "reconstitute preexisting power structures." Therefore, symbolic capital is often "denied capital" because players on the field must assume a stance of disinterestedness in attaining power, prestige or acclaim if they wish to stay in the game.

Bourdieu's concept of symbolic capital differs from Thorstein Veblen's descriptions of emulatory societies in his groundbreaking *Theory of the Leisure Class: An Economic Study of Institutions*. Veblen argued that people used aggressive tactics to obtain material trophies as proof of their power, because in an emulatory society, the possession of material capital conferred honor. In an emulatory society the possession of wealth is conflated with the inherent goodness of the person who possesses it, so people were encouraged to accumulate material goods in order to maintain their social standing in the community.[66] In Veblen's rendering, the possession of property becomes the basis for esteem. Even so, most people living in an emulatory society continue to live in a constant state of dissatisfaction. In order to gain some semblance of happiness, people construct pecuniary boundaries between themselves and their peers. In constructing these boundaries, people of all classes are encouraged to accumulate as many material possessions as they possibly can, because that is the way in which power and status are conferred. Bourdieu's analysis differs from Veblen's because Bourdieu construes distinction as happening outside of any conscious intention or deliberate search for distinction."[67]

Higher education often serves to reinforce social differences, transmit the cultural values of the dominant class and naturalize the existing social hierarchies of the larger world.[68] By the 1930s higher education had taken on the role of gatekeeper to the professions and to the middle class. Many college students of the 1930s readily admitted that their principle motivation for attending college was to improve their chances for class mobility and attain middle-class privileges.[69] In the predominantly agrarian society of the nineteenth century, college represented one of many pathways to financial success and social privilege, but in the industrialized and bureaucratized 1920s and 1930s, a college degree became more important for those who wished to attain or maintain middle-class status.[70]

Debates about the part that schools played in instilling values in the nation's young people while fulfilling the *in loco parentis* role had raged since the early nineteenth century when local country schools began cropping up on the rural landscape. While the common-schools of the nineteenth century were run by part-time educational evangelists who had a stake in guarding the morals and manners of minors, by the first decades of the twentieth century, "a new breed of professional managers who made education a life-long career and who were reshaping the schools according to the canons of business efficiency and scientific expertise" emerged as the vanguard of the educational elite.[71] This new professional-managerial educational elite utilized corporate decision making models for running the schools and attempted to develop programs that would prepare youths for life in the modern work force.[72]

GENDER & RACE ISSUES

One feminist scholar wrote in the late twentieth century that, "only men are 'persons' and there is no gender but the feminine."[73] Distributing and assigning gender roles and race positions was part of the middle-class process of self-definition. Groups that are involved in creating cultural meanings must address matters of "how to organize their survival, how to represent themselves, how to resist and where to accommodate and who within the group has rights to what valued goods."[74] Where women fit into the picture and how gender would be organized in the middle class had been under negotiation for decades by the 1930s. The trend of middle-class females attending college and working in clerical and professional positions began in the mid-to-late nineteenth century, but during 1930s women students and workers were perceived as larger threats than they had been in previous and more prosperous decades. College enrollment figures show that in 1870, 21 percent of all students enrolled in college were female. In 1890 the number of female students increased to 35.9 percent and by 1920 the female enrollment figures were 47.3 percent.[75] Caroll Smith-Rosenberg noted that many "new women" of the early twentieth century pursued college degrees and careers and decided to forego marriage.[76] The new women of the earlier decades of the twentieth century received a fair share of scorn, but the increased numbers of young women in school coupled with competition for jobs made female college students of the 1930s more suspect than their predecessors.

The numbers of women in the professional work force had risen in tandem with the numbers of women enrolled in colleges. In 1870 the number of females in the work force was about 16 percent; by 1900 it had reached 20 percent. By the 1920s about forty percent of paid workers were female.[77] In the 1930s women made up about 50% of the professional work force.[78] Many business offices became "feminized" in the early years of the twentieth century; for example, in 1870 only 5% of stenographers were female, but by 1930 96% were women.[79]

In the white middle class, ambitious women were popularly perceived of as a problem, but within the African-American middle class the need for two incomes for families to survive and thrive mitigated much of the criticism about women attaining higher education. Education for women, in fact, was understood as a key component to racial uplift. African-American families who were in a position to provide their daughters with access to higher education that would allow them to achieve professional status were encouraged to do so by other members of the African-American community; the "desire to protect and uplift young black women was shared across classes."[80] By 1930 four out of every ten graduates from Black colleges were women and there were over 63,000 African-American female professionals in the work force.[81] Many working-class whites in the southern United States were ill at ease about providing access to education to African-American youths because they feared that education would enable them to compete for better-paying jobs that used to only be accessible to whites. Even though middle-class white university students did not explicitly voice similar sentiments about competition from college-educated African-Americans, there still existed an environment of extreme competitiveness between college-trained graduates from diverse ethnic, racial and gender positions.

Economic historian William A. Sundstrom examined unemployment patterns of African-American and white workers in urban areas during the 1930s, arguing that much attention has been paid to the effects of the Great Depression and New Deal policies for African-American agricultural workers, but less attention has been given to urban workers during the same time period.[82] African-American men and women, especially those living in northern sections of the United States, experienced much higher rates of unemployment than their white counterparts. In the early years of the Depression, in this case April 1930, the unemployment rate for white men in northern sections of the United States was 8%, while the unemployment rate for African-American men in the north was 14.3%. In the South both African-American and white men faced unemployment rates of 4.1%. White women who lived in the north during 1930 experienced an unemployment rate of 4.6% while African-American women workers in the North had an 8.2% unemployment rate.[83]

As the Depression wore on, the unemployment rates for African-American women living in urban areas ranged from twice as high to four times the rates of unemployment for white women. African-American women participated in the paid workforce more often than white women during this time, meaning that many urban African-American families experienced "dramatic welfare losses" when compared to whites. [84] In the later half of the 1930s, a National Health Survey collected information regarding unemployment from heads of households in 83 cities during the winter of 1935–1936. The study showed that 10.8% of white male heads of households were seeking work, while 17.9% of African-American male heads of households were looking for employment. A total of 11.5% of white female household heads were seeking employment during the winter of 1935–1936, while 24.4% of African-American female heads of households were trying to find jobs. The unemployment figures in 1937, when many Americans believed that the Depression had passed, show that in the north, 14.1% of white men were seeking work, while 27% of the African-American men living in northern cities sought employment. The numbers of white and black women seeking work in 1937 were much higher than the numbers of men, with 20.7% of white women and 38.3% of African-American women looking for jobs. [85] These statistics demonstrate that

African-American workers, especially African-American female workers, were especially hard-hit by the effects of the Depression.

White men had a keen interest in preserving a middle-class formation process that maintained male dominance. On coeducational college campuses with mostly white student bodies, male students and administrators erected policies that barred women from entering certain buildings or attaining positions of power. White male students of the Depression era also created a steady stream of "humorous" articles that denigrated female students and reminded them that they were outsiders on the college campus. Ruth Feldstein's description of "gender conservatism" makes the process of defining boundaries based on gender more comprehensible. Gender conservatism involves the eclipsing of organized feminism coupled with the glorification of traditional strictly-demarcated heterosexual gender roles.[86] These notions siphoned down from the national discourse to be distilled into ideologies that prevailed on college campuses in the 1930s. Alice Kessler-Harris argues that during the 1930s most American men and women shared a similar set of "gendered habits of mind" that shaped their ideas about what culture should look like. For example, most men and women in the United States conceptualized women as nurturing and men as competitive.[87] The gendered imagination conditioned people's expectations of what women and men were capable of doing, which often served either to limit or to expand an individual's vision about his or her potential in the world. During the early twentieth-century most young women expected to get married and have families while most young men anticipated holding down jobs and supporting wives and children. Kessler-Harris notes that "since women and men shared the same expectations of family life, it made sense to allocate the better jobs to men."[88]

Gender conservatism and the gendered imagination definitely played roles in shaping the boundaries of the college experience for young women of the 1930s. At the same time, discourses generated on coeducational college campuses contributed to the ideology of gender conservatism and created a no-win situation for young women attending school during the Depression era. Many student newspapers throughout the 1930s touted the beliefs that intellectual women who were attending school to train for future careers suffered from the "masculine protest," where females desired to compete with men and even become manly as part of their intellectual pursuits. The intelligent and driven "greasy grind" women on coeducational campuses often were socially shunned by their peers, both male and female. Female students who followed traditional gender norms of being acquiescent, docile and passive were deemed intellectually inferior to men and were accused of coming to college to find husbands from whom they could gold dig for the rest of their lives.

On college campuses, gender divided along lines of schools, majors and geographic regions of campus. An article from *The University of Michigan Daily* proves illustrative as it describes "The Man's World" and "The Woman's World" in contrast to one another. The man's world was located in the East Engineering building where "quiet, peace and order" prevailed; men stood and pondered pieces of machinery, puzzling over important solutions to technological problems while down the hall the author came across the "usual scene of a woman at a typewriter."[89] The woman's world, according to the writer, was centered in the nursery section of the University Elementary School, where "tots play, romp, draw, eat and sleep." [90] The male author described a scene where chaos broke loose; children began screaming and crying, while the reporter made a quick dash for the door, because the noisy, frenzied world filled with irritable children, spilled food and broken crayons, "is a woman's world."[91] These brief descriptions explicate some of the implicit expectations about what roles men and women should plan to play after graduation, what their four years college of training would be used for and what types of careers options would await them.

Middle-class and elite African-American women also bore the brunt of gender-based ideological shifts during the Great Depression. During the 1910s and 1920s, middle-class and elite African-American women embraced what Evelyn Brooks Higginbotham calls a "politics of respectability." African American women adopted values of industriousness, thrift, piety, temperance, good manners and sexual restraint and spread the messages to newly-arrived urban dwellers that were part of the Great Migration northward for jobs. In her text about the politics of respectability in Detroit during the inter-war years, Victoria Wolcott finds that there was a "significant shift in racial discourse from a focus on bourgeois respectability in the 1910s and 1920s to a more masculine ideology of self-determination during the Great Depression."[92] This ideological shift appears to have taken place at Howard University as well. Especially toward the later years of the Depression, articles in the campus newspaper encouraged women to support male initiative and to take a backseat in making decisions or letting their voices be heard in public forums.

CONSUMERISM & CONSUMPTION

The ideals of consumerism and consumption helped to shape a marketplace-style discourse regarding social lives of young people. Using the language of economics to describe oneself, one's position in the social structure and one's social status became completely normalized during the Depression era. By the 1930s students had learned from expert and peer discourse how to fashion themselves into products that would compete for attention in a social marketplace. During the 1920s, when most Americans were more affluent than they were during the 1930s, the boundaries separating commerce from culture fell away.[93] At the same time, religious and moral prohibitions regarding envy, social striving and status seeking that existed before World War I slowly faded and were replaced by a tacit acceptance of competitive consumerism and conspicuous consumption.[94] The new corporate order that emerged in the early decades of the twentieth century focused on creating large national markets and encouraging expanding consumerism. During the 1910s and 1920s a wide array of secular experts including psychologists, doctors, economists and advertisers gained an influential foothold in the United States urban industrial order, and promoted consumerism, social striving and emulative spending as ways to achieve happiness.[95] The corporate economic sector encouraged individuals to identify their physical, social and psychological needs with various commodities.[96]

Expert writings from the 1930s encouraged middle-class to empower themselves by becoming well-educated and selective consumers. Edward Filene, founder of the Boston-based department store chain, explained in 1931 that women would soon discover that their "economic well-being comes not from the organization of the family but from the organization of industry."[97] Filene promised that women who aligned themselves with the new industrial order would stop looking to their fathers for guidance, but instead would turn to expert scientists who could show them the "truth which science is discovering."[98] White corporate heads of industry were not the only advocates for middle-class women empowering themselves by becoming savvy consumers. African-American activists like Mary McLeod Bethune believed that educated African-American women could help the race as a whole by earning money, controlling the purse strings and using purchasing power to open doors for African-Americans that had previously been closed to them.[99]

For many working-class men, aligning themselves with the new corporate order proved to be a painful process that involved a loss of independence in the work world and weakened their foothold in their previous patriarchal position in the home and family. Middle-class men, on the other hand, had a stake in reconciling their allegiance to the corporate order because they had been trained to value ascending hierarchies by using intelligence, skill and business acumen to outdo their competitors and to outperform their peers in order to garner accolades and monetary rewards in the business world. The ascendance of big business in the 1920s and 1930s forced young men to reconceptualize their ideas of success and security.[100]

As the United States became more urbanized, modernized and bureaucratized middle-class men who would have once embraced the idea of being independent entrepreneurs instead took on roles as white collar employees who worked for wages in anonymous settings.[101] White collar employment offered the benefits of being non-manual labor that paid a salary rather than hourly wages and provided a decent income and the chance to advance up the corporate ladder.[102]

The corporate white-collar work world of the 1920s may have felt suffocating and stupefying to many of its members, but white collar jobs still had the benefit of being somewhat safe havens for educated men who lacked the entrepreneurial spirit or capital to venture out on their own.[103] Yet, even large corporations were still dependent on larger market forces. For many males, both working-class and middle-class, being dependent on market forces and having the market collapse proved to be a devastating blow. The deprivations of the Depression affected people from various social strata, and neither age nor educational level predicted whom the effects would strike.[104] During the Depression era unemployment rates were particularly high for white-collar employees and unskilled workers, and lower for skilled and professional workers. Self-employed workers including small business owners generally kept their positions but experienced large income losses.[105] During the Depression years social inequality was defined not as a flaw in the undergirding of societal structures, but as an individual failure.[106]

CONSUMPTION, MASS CULTURE & NORMATIVE VALUES

Consumption and consumer practices proved important for creating social hierarchies in the Depression era. Pierre Bourdieu explores the social patterning of consumption and taste in *Distinction: A Social Critique of the Judgment of Taste*. Bourdieu explains that family patterns and educational experiences work together to determine individuals' tastes for cultural goods including food, clothing, art work and home decor. Bourdieu argues that class status can be lost, gained or reproduced through acts of consumer behavior. People can obtain access to social circles, land jobs and build business relationships by enacting proper tastes, manners and culture. Conversely, individuals who dress incorrectly or display "vulgar" manners can lose chances to attain jobs and social status.

Experts of the 1930s including sociologists, psychologists and government officials expressed an interest in discriminating and classifying people and objects, because they were concerned that the rise of mass culture and the mass man would destroy previously-erected social and class hierarchies thereby creating social mayhem. Experts, as defined by Bourdieu, are people who are appointed to produce points of view which are recognized as transcendent over other, common, points of view.[107] A report on the state of America's youth that was issued in the late 1930s explained that the walls that had divided the American population into groups and classes had been broken down by the ascendancy of common culture. People from all socioeconomic classes, regions, ethnicities and races could tune in to the same radio programs and read the same newspapers, provided they had the means to own a radio and the literacy necessary to read the paper. Bureaucrats bemoaned the emergence of the mass man stating that "the common life comes whether or not we will it."[108]

Prominent intellectuals of the 1930s countered that the "mass organization of the mind" that had occurred during the first few decades of the twentieth century represented a process of social domination not social empowerment for the masses.[109] They argued that nationally-distributed newspapers, magazines and periodicals informed the public about current events, but also produced a public discourse that insured "collective readjustment by consent."[110] Intellectuals feared that mass culture functioned as a means of social control where the values of the cultural producers impressed themselves on the collective unconscious of the members of the reading public. Many believed that the mass organization of the mind would lead to standardization of knowledge, norms and mores to such an extent that individual initiative and character would be squelched in the process. Some expressed fears that "a regimentation of opinion" would come about because newspapers and magazines, by their very nature, gathered together their "own group(s) and . . . proceed to work out some sort of standardizing of opinion and information upon these presumably helpless creatures."[111]

Experts in some fields had an interest in promulgating normative values. During the 1930s psychologists and sociologists collected empirical data and used the data to construct a normative model of the theoretical average abstract American. As the concept of the "average American" became more accepted, many citizens felt pulled in two directions—wanting to emulate the average normative theoretical citizen, yet also struggling to maintain "the distance separating them from such a fictitious character."[112] Many solutions to systemic problems were focused on assisting the abstract average American. Unfortunately, since this theoretical citizen was indeed an abstraction, often groups and individuals who failed to fit the normative construct were overlooked.[113]

During the years of 1908–1916 psychologist Edward L. Thorndike and his graduate students at the Teachers College at Columbia University created scales of achievement—commonly referred to as norms—in a wide variety of subjects including math, reading and handwriting. Educators could compare their students' performance against the average achievement of a representative sample of children to see if they measured up to Thorndike's norms.[114] These norms provided school administrators with the first tools to compare the knowledge and abilities of their students against an average.[115] Two other researchers who contributed to the widely-embraced ideas about normative intelligence were Lewis M. Terman and Robert M. Yerkes. Until 1935 Terman functioned as an active proponent of the eugenics movement and used IQ tests to study the link between intelligence and heredity.[116] Yerkes' was a psychologist at the Johns Hopkins University who is widely credited for leading his team of peers in creating the Alpha-Beta tests that measured the intelligence of young Army recruits. The data, now widely discredited by academics including Stephen J. Gould, suggested that African-American men and Southern and Eastern Europeans scored the worst. Even though the authors recommended a restrained reading of the results, policy makers in the United States cited the results in 1921 and 1924 as reason for restricting immigration from such countries as Italy, Poland and Russia.[117] Teachers and administrators also pointed to Yerkes' findings to justify their racist beliefs that African-Americans were innately intellectually inferior.[118]

The shapers of normative values played large roles in shaping the fields of sociology, economics and political science during the first two decades of the twentieth century.[119] The men and women of academe who created IQ testing, pioneered the frontiers of applied psychology, acted as proponents of the Eugenics movement, worked in the forefront of advertising and honed polling techniques all held a great amount of power and prestige in the public's imagination. These purveyors of norms played a large part in shaping public expectations about gender roles, racial roles, class roles and appropriate behavior for people who inhabited various roles. Shapers of normative ideals helped to create images of how society should look and what persons should fulfill each role available, whether it was that of a college student, professional business man, housewife, porter, elevator operator or domestic servant. It made sense for expert authors and middle-class college students to emulate the people who shaped normative models of behavior, because the shapers of norms had a lot of symbolic, social and cultural capital at their disposal.

The following chapters bring into sharp relief some of the discursive skirmishes in which Depression-era expert authors and college students engaged in order to make sense of the cultural and social upheavals of the 1930s. Experts and youths trudged through the figurative fields of college campuses, fraternity and sorority houses and the realms of the dating and marriage marketplaces in discursive attempts to create a sense of middle-class retrenchment, stability and normalcy in a time of crisis. The next four chapters, which are arranged both chronologically and thematically, explore distinct areas where experts offered advice to collegiate youths about how to accrue symbolic capital, attain accolades and maintain middle-class privileges. The themes and the chronology are based on the issues that arose most predominantly in the writings of students and experts in the 1930s. Throughout the Depression era, youths and experts alike expressed strong interests in using the language of the marketplace and the logic of capitalism to make sense of the current situation and to plan for a more prosperous future.

Chapter Two

Why Are We Here? How Do We Sell It?: Life on Campus, 1930–1934

> To the deeply mystified American public, college life is a fabulous sort of thing, strangely beautiful in its sentimentality and detachment, mostly rousing and rowdyish in its outward manifestations, always gay and eminently social within. Always it is dramatic, never drab like life outside the magic pale.[1]
>
> –*The University of Michigan Daily*, November 20, 1934.

> The present-day college generation is fatalistic . . . It keeps it shirt on, its pants buttoned, its chin up, and its mouth shut. If we take the mean average to be the truth, it is a cautious, subdued, unadventurous generation, unwilling to storm heaven, afraid to make a fool of itself, unable to dramatize its predicament . . . Security is the *summum bonum* of the present college generation.[2]
>
> –*Fortune Magazine*, 1934

Depression-era undergraduates matriculated during a particularly interesting historical juncture, when fears about the present and the future permeated the economic, political and social realms of society. During the early 1930s college students were anything but deeply mystified about their lives on campus and their prospects for the future; they had many reasons to be wary, restrained, unadventurous seekers of security. In 1932, the most brutal year of the Depression, the average number of unemployed people in the United States reached 12.5 million.[3] The middle-class expectations of the 1920s that a college degree would open the door to an affluent, stable and predictable world fell apart in the early 1930s.[4] Undergraduates feared that they would join the ranks of the millions of unemployed upon graduation.

Undergraduate concerns about impending joblessness were based on hard data: studies conducted in the Northeastern and Midwestern United

States that found that young people who had graduated from high school between 1931 and 1934 had searched for jobs for six months to two-and-a-half years, yet in some towns up to 58% of the young people looking for work had still not obtained a position. The numbers were predicted to escalate because over two and a quarter million youths finished their schooling each year and about two million of them would be seeking gainful employment.[5] A study released by The Employment Stabilization Research Institute in November 1930 assured students that only 1% of those unemployed were college graduates, but one undergraduate pointed out that students should not conclude that a degree would immunize 99% against unemployment, since one could cite statistics that "less than one one-hundredth of one percent of the unemployed were one-eyed cobblers."[6] The studies failed to provide an accurate index of college graduates' ability to avoid unemployment.[7] Countless students were watching or playing a part in "a drama which is being played in an atmosphere of uncertainty. . . . Unemployment, actual or threatened, has produced not only a nation-wide but a world-wide crisis and consequent anxiety and insecurity."[8]

Even with the onerous economic circumstances in place, undergraduates understood that a college degree still represented a "very real social symbol" that could be bartered for "rights to certain social positions."[9] Depression-era undergraduates and experts alike created multiple discourses that utilized the language of the marketplace to protect and defend their stakes in preserving middle-class status and primacy during the economic crisis. Crafty students puzzled over how best to commodify and market not only themselves, but college life as a whole, to their advantage in order to attain accolades while in school and win jobs after graduation.

Students attending college in the 1930s recognized what French sociologist Pierre Bourdieu would proclaim fifty years later: that a "school credential or diploma is a piece of universally recognized symbolic capital that is good on all markets."[10] Although the social prestige and monetary benefits once linked to having a college degree were diminished by the dearth of jobs available for college graduates, accruing symbolic capital in the present often led to attaining material capital in the future.[11] In the earlier part of twentieth century, schooling had replaced breeding as the key means for attaining access to middle-class social standing.[12]

Many students attending college in the 1930s explained that their dominant motivation was the desire to rise to a higher social class.[13] Young white men who graduated from college could expect to earn more than men of the same age who did not graduate. A longitudinal study showed that female college graduates of the Depression era could count on reaping symbolic rewards for earning a degree. For young women, a college degree "did not guarantee personal happiness or a beneficent personality, nor was it the only entry into a career;" in fact, many women who lacked college degrees reached higher career levels than their peers who had graduated.[14] The effect of having a college education for young women was subtle yet powerful, in that it "facilitated movement toward favored social status" and provided young women of the 1930s with social perks including happier marriages, better health and fewer daily stresses than women who left college or never attended.[15] While these social perks cannot be measured in dollars and cents, the symbolic capital women accrued by graduating from college definitely proved life-changing. African-American students attending college in the 1930s had even fewer guarantees of finding employment after graduating, but having access to a college education represented a chance to gain prestige and to elevate the status of the race as a whole. In the 1930s material and social gains were both embraced as a means to an end—the progress of the race.[16]

If symbolic capital was the only capital available, middle-class students were eager to get their hands on it. During the first few years of the Depression, the number of students enrolling in college actually increased. Enrollment figures grew steadily between 1900 and 1930, and they continued to rise into the Depression. A report issued in 1931 revealed that enrollment figures for American colleges and universities were 12 percent higher than those of five years before.[17] In 1900 about 224,000 young men and women were enrolled in colleges and universities in the United States. By 1930 the numbers grew to more than 900,000, meaning that one-eighth of the country's population between the ages of 18 and 21 were attending institutions of higher learning.[18] The growth was partially attributed to the fact that there were few jobs available to tempt students to leave school.[19] In the early 1930s some experts posited that students were attending college "in spite of, or perhaps, *because* of the Depression."[20] In previous years students might have left college when their families faced reduced financial circumstances, but with the dramatic effects of the Depression being so widespread, students decided it was safer to stay in school. From a middle-class parental perspective, higher education might be quite expensive but often it was not as costly as supporting children who wanted to live on their own; parents may have been sending their children to school to save money. A study conducted by the journal *Schools and Society,* published in April 1930, argued that the greatest expense for college students was the loss of potential earnings during the four years that they attended college.[21] The journal estimated that youths would earn about $100 a month if they were employed, but the lack of employment opportunities for young people during the 1930s made attending college a viable option for middle-class youths.

Youths writing for campus newspapers in the early 1930s expressed concerns that were plaguing most Americans at the time: the perilous economic situation, unwelcoming job market and shifting gender roles. Undergraduates from college campuses across the country shared similar anxieties about the Depression, yet dissimilar forms of symbolic capital were at stake for various players in the fields. Access to symbolic rewards was often determined—or at least shaped—by an individual student's race, gender or both. Middle-class students consolidated around their shared middle-class identity, but the competition for symbolic and material capital was so fierce that youths tended to erect social barriers against their contemporaries, especially in regard to gender and race. White middle-class men, who benefited from the social hierarchies that were crafted and maintained through years of laws, customs and culture cashed in on their privilege and used it as an edge to maintain dominance in college classrooms, on-campus employment, student offices and positions of power.

Depression-era students who had come of age in 1920s "Era of Prosperity" had a firm grasp on the concepts of business, capitalism, commodities and advertising. The bleak job market frightened many middle-class collegians, but inspired them to draw on their knowledge of business practices of the 1920s to work their way through the economic and psychological crises. Youths of the 1930s held a capitalist world view and envisioned themselves as commodities. Students incorporated their business savvy to further their interests, raise their caches of symbolic capital, shape themselves into desirable commodities for future employers, and move themselves—much like merchandise—into the job marketplace. This process involved taking stock of their situation, performing an analysis of the costs and benefits of attaining a degree and weighing the amount of labor necessary for accumulating capital that was purely symbolic. Once students surveyed usefulness of a college degree in a dismal job market, they utilized the information available to craft themselves into marketable commodities. Youths adopted some cutthroat marketing practices during the early years of the 1930s. White males, especially, attempted to gain monopoly over access to "the set of actually usable resources and powers" including college degrees, that helped agents move into powerful positions in a field.[22]

This chapter explores how students navigated the rocky terrain of determining prestige and hierarchies on campus based on gender, grades and race. Once students had sorted out why they were there and why Others were there, they turned their attention to advertising college life to the public in order to secure jobs for themselves after graduation. Aspiring female students and professionals were perceived as threats by white middle-class men who were already experiencing the dislocations of the Depression.[23] College women who attended coeducational schools competed with men in the classroom and would likely compete with them for jobs after graduation.[24] In the early decades of the twentieth century college life prepared young men to compete in the world of business, while it prepared serious female students for unknown futures. Women who took on roles as leaders on college campuses broke the previous molds of femininity and challenged the ideas of what women could achieve.[25]

When white females attempted to tread on previously all-white-male domains, the young men responded by defending the boundaries of gender, utilizing anti-female rhetoric and constructing policies of exclusion to keep females from accessing the privileges of middle-class manhood.[26] Many young white males jealously guarded what they saw as their birthright to higher education, a college degree and a good job. The most visible targets for their outrage at these supposed birthrights being threatened were the female students who had arrived *en masse* on coeducational college campuses in the early 1930s. Male students fought back against the perceived female encroachment by using rhetorical strategies to protect their shaky, but still dominant status on campus. Young men wrote articles and editorials that attacked their female peers on three fronts. The first line of attack was questioning the intellectual ability of co-eds and raising questions about how they managed to get good grades. The second means of resistance involved questioning women's rights to hold jobs on campus and in the larger world. Finally, men attempted to protect their dominance at coeducational colleges and universities by trying to bar women from holding offices and positions of power. Young women who wanted to prepare for careers often were shut out of key societies on college campuses, including student government, campus newspapers, honor societies and athletics.[27]

WHY WERE WOMEN THERE?

As jobs became scarcer and the possibilities for getting married dwindled, thousands of young, middle-class white women who might otherwise never have considered higher education enrolled in colleges and universities across the country.[28] At first, the presence of female students was welcomed on coeducational campuses, but as the Depression wore on and women began speaking up in classes and taking positions of power in campus offices the level of gender-based resentment rose incrementally. The anti-female rhetoric that spewed forth in campus publications resembled the discursive backlash that occurred on coeducational college campuses during the 1870s when women were first admitted to land-grant universities.

The passage of the Morrill Land Grant Acts in 1862 and 1890 greatly altered the educational landscape for many young women. A number of private women's colleges founded in the nineteenth century, including Vassar (1865), Smith (1875) and Wellesley (1875), received a lot of attention in the mainstream press, yet only a small percentage of female college students attended all-women's schools.[29] In the 1870s, large universities including Cornell, the University of Michigan, Boston University and the University of Wisconsin began accepting female students.[30] The Morrill Land Grant Acts stipulated that the University of Michigan had to admit "all persons of the state," but women were not understood as "persons." Taxpaying parents in the state of Michigan argued that according to the Morrill Act the state was obligated to educate both young women and men. Regents at the University of Michigan voted to admit female students to the school in 1870. Having a coeducational institution was much less expensive than supporting a separate female-only institute of higher education .[31]

Young women attending co-educational schools in the 1930s were "thrown into daily contact with men," therefore, one expert author explained, they needed to learn how to "compete against them and for them."[32] Men at the University of Michigan had dual reactions to so many females enrolling in college. On the one hand, they were excited to have the gender ratio balanced a bit, on the other hand, they admitted to being annoyed by women's presence in the classroom. The male undergraduate students, who welcomed the arrival of women, argued that the presence of more females improved the social life for men on campus.[33] One student explained that during the previous year there were 2.12 men on hand for each woman—in 1934 enrollment figures demonstrated the gender ratios had shifted to a point where there were only 1.92 men for each woman. Many men made it clear that they valued the young women for purely decorative purposes, stating that females were "not necessary during our four-year sojourn here, but they are very nice ornaments to have around."[34] Female students who were perceived as docile and lacking career ambitions were more acceptable to most male students than intellectually-driven young women who competed with men in the classroom.[35] Many female students at coeducational universities who wished to garner approval from their male, and often female, peers let it be known that they were attending school not to pursue serious academic goals. These young women who valued being socially accepted by their peer groups clearly stated that they would be using their college years to prepare to become "wives, mothers and gracious hostesses."[36]

When women moved beyond their ornamental status and began speaking up in classes, taking jobs on campus and getting involved in student activities numerous scathing articles portraying women as interlopers filled the pages of student newspapers. The female sector of the student body was collectively treated like intruders who should "know their place" and keep quiet in intellectual matters. White males who were invested in maintaining gender boundaries and male privilege used discursive means to accomplish these goals. Female students were ridiculed in cartoons, campus newspaper columns and other public forums including debates. Males also erected policies of exclusion that kept female students out of eating halls, clubs, honor societies and almost all activities that were associated with campus prestige.[37]

Historically, male students dominated the classrooms, political offices and social life of coeducational campuses because of their greater numbers and a longer history of attendance.[38] These students operated defensively and attempted to maintain the status quo by contending that the social relations on campus, which were largely based on gender, were as they should be.[39] Female undergraduates who challenged the "unproblematic, taken-for-granted world of the dominant group" had much to gain by their actions, including opportunities to make their voices heard, to enact change, to overthrow outmoded traditions and to replace them with new practices that better suited their interests. The hostility that many young male writers expressed toward females echoed the larger cultural discourse about the roles of women in the home and in the work place. The struggle was rooted in the desire to maintain a sense of stability, order and status in a time when previously-established hierarchies were toppling. When male students, members of the faculty or administrators felt vulnerable about a new situation they almost invariably turned to the vital importance of keeping old traditions intact. Not coincidentally, many of the campus rituals, mores and practices that males valued most were the very customs that helped males retain their power and access to privilege.

As the numbers of female students on coeducational campuses rose, male students voiced resistance and hearkened back to the days when all-males spaces were held sacred on campus. For students at the predominantly white coeducational campuses, themes of invasion and violation resonated throughout articles about females who dared to tread on previously male-dominated territories. The places that were invaded were both material and symbolic. Female students demanded attention in the classrooms, entered buildings from which they had previously been banned, attained positions of power on campus and sought employment for jobs on campus and beyond that used to be reserved for males.

A profusion of stories detailing female students invading male territories were published in 1932. The University of Michigan Student Union's sanctity was "violated by feminine swarms" who were allowed to walk through the building without male escorts for one evening. Up until that point woman, even full-time tuition-paying female students, were only allowed access to certain parts of the student union and had to use the back door to enter the building.[40] Even though the usual restrictions placed on women were lifted for just one night, many male students feared that it was a harbinger of things to come.[41] They were correct. Just two weeks later, Athena, the newly-named women's forensic society, took issue with the tradition banning women from using the front door of the Union. This policy represented a "thorn in the side" of female students who had to use the back entrance even when they were attending student-sponsored dances. Male students fought hard to keep the tradition fully intact. One writer opened his exasperated editorial on the issue with the lines: "You can't tell a woman anything. You can point to tradition and remark that it just isn't done, or you can trot out rules, regulations and by-laws by the dozen, but it won't do you any good."[42] Although this editorial was written in a lighthearted tone, many male students feared that their once-sacred gender-demarcated territories were being invaded and destroyed by women. These tensions were likely escalated in a time when the economy, the job market and society as a whole were moving in unpredictable directions.

Just a few weeks earlier female students at McGill University in Montreal, Quebec had "carelessly shattered" the long-standing tradition of women not being allowed to enter the student Union dining room. The formerly all-male sanctuary was "invaded by the unfair sex" who dared to wander into the room where no women had ever set foot.[43] Two female undergraduates nonchalantly entered the dining room, collected their food and sat down, looking like "two roses among countless astonished thorns."[44] Angry employees attempted to escort the women out of the all-male enclave, but the female students refused to back down. Moments later an "imposing procession" of young women proceeded through the doors of the dining hall and permanently altered campus policies about where they were allowed to enter. This victory for female students was perceived as a huge defeat for male undergraduates who sought some force to repel the heinous encroachment on their domain.[45] In times of stress, when resources are scarce, if one group begins to accrue any type of advantage, it can be perceived as a loss by the another group, regardless of whether the second group had to give up or forego anything as a result.[46]

Although female students consistently received higher grades than their male counterparts at all of the coeducational campuses described in this book, male undergraduates insisted on going to great lengths to prove that men were inherently more intelligent than women.[47] One student at Howard University explained that more women than men had straight A averages because female students consistently took easier courses in less complicated fields and had more time to study than their male classmates.[48] He believed that if men were given a fair chance they would be able to get equal or higher grades than women, because males had more "native ability" than females.[49] Many of the men at Howard—up to 85 percent according to the author—worked for wages to make their way through school. These men lacked time to study, while women on campus often had their tuition, fees and other expenses paid in full by their parents.[50] Women at Howard, according to this student's editorial, had nothing better to do than study and make good grades and therefore held the advantage in attaining straight A averages. While this student's points about men having to work while attending school resonate as plausible, the rationalizations conjured up by males at other schools prove less convincing.

Members of the Alpha Nu male debating society at the University of Michigan faced off against the women of the Zeta Phi Eta society to figure out why women got better grades than men. The males opened the proceedings by stating that women on campus "prostituted intellectual activity" and received good grades only by using their feminine wiles to charm their male professors.[51] They compared the young women to Hester Prynne from *The Scarlet Letter* because, according to the members of Alpha Nu, both kinds of women earned their A's through similar means.[52] The men of Alpha Nu continued on, making comments about "Cleopatra making her Mark" and producing a poster of a couple embracing to show how female undergraduates received good grades. The debate closed with males citing statistics to prove that the brains of women weighed less than men's, supposedly proving beyond a shadow of a doubt that males were intellectually superior. Symbolic attacks like these became more frequent as the Depression wore on. This form of symbolic verbal violence worked as a process "by which the social structure is constructed and reified by the dominating over the dominated."[53] Bourdieu points out that insults, a form of symbolic violence, often work as magical attempts at categorization.[54] The word category is derived from kathegorein, which means "to accuse publicly"; rumors, gossip and slander all fit into the category of insults.[55] I would add that jokes made at the expense of groups and classes of people also fit into the realm of insults intended to magically categorize individuals.

During the years of 1933 and 1934 many disparaging quips about co-eds appeared in the pages of *The University of Michigan Daily* and *The George Washington University Hatchet.* Most of the jokes played on stereotypes about women, that they were gold-diggers, fickle and dumb.[56] A poem entitled "Co-Eds—Blah," demonstrates the types of jokes that ran in student newspapers and how the stabs at humor naturalized categorical beliefs about women. It should be noted that the final lines of the poem make it clear that even though the male author found the female students repugnant on many levels, he still showed interest in dating them.

> Co-Eds—Blah
> There is one thing a college man can't go and that's a co-ed—
> She's the finest living example of a flop, a dub, a dough-head
> She's a bit of fluff, a smear of lipstick, a couple eyes, a hat
> She has no conception at any time exactly what the score is
> She has the bad taste to refer to a man's fraternity as a frat
> She makes one realize in full what a complete untiring bore is
> Her vocabulary includes a few words other than smoking, drinking, dating
> To be thrown in daily contact with her is most degenerating
> She thinks a man becomes her slave by one long side-way glance
> She does nothing really well, can't walk or play or dance
> Dance! Say! I meant to take in that brawl tonite and its sort of late
> I wonder what co-ed on this campus doesn't have a date.[57]

While this poem was definitely written in a humorous tone, where the man pokes fun at himself at the end, insulting gibes like this appeared on a regular basis on the editorial pages of student newspapers and contributed to a hostile discourse about the presence of women on coeducational college campuses. These attempts at humor related to the "battle of the sexes" fed into a larger discourse where women's opinions were discounted in the classroom and female students were barred from entering campus buildings and holding campus offices.

The consensus between male experts and students appeared to be that women were innately biologically inferior to men, and therefore less suited for intellectual activities. Oppressive practices and beliefs often become naturalized when a discourse is created that argues that nature and biology are responsible for the unequal power relations instead of social practice.[58] Through practice the social order is naturalized, internalized and reproduced. Psychologists, including a professor from Wichita University put forth the notion, based on an "actual" psychological experiment, which determined that female student's academic success depended "85 percent upon personality and 15 percent on brains."[59] The male professor deduced that young women who were succeeding in college and earning high grades were attaining academic accolades because they possessed personality traits including courtesy, cooperation, dependability, friendliness and charm.[60] The professor defined a set of palatable skills that young women naturally possessed, which made females capable of attending college, yet barred them from attaining lucrative work after college. Friendliness and charm could be used to captivate a potential husband, but the rough and tumble world of corporate business needed men who had skills including innate intelligence and tough-mindedness.

Studies showed that, for the most part, undergraduate men preferred "rather shallow" types of women, so academically-adept coeds faced a different set of criticisms than their less scholastically-driven female peers.[61] Highly intelligent females often found that they were considered too intellectual for men who were in search of recreation in their contacts with women.[62] These serious female students, also known as "grinds," were often from more modest socioeconomic backgrounds than their peers. Grinds took their studies seriously and used their time in college to prepare for future careers.[63] Female students who wished to be encouraged about their academic pursuits could attend schools like Mount Holyoke where students were openly supportive of academic rigor, fiercely competitive for good grades and extremely devoted to achievement in the classroom and beyond. This dedication was often ridiculed by outsiders, but in the insular community of Mount Holyoke women were encouraged to be powerful, strong and driven to succeed.

Although women from Mount Holyoke were safe from mockery on their own campus, this did not spare them from being lampooned in the national discourse. The magazine *College Humor* ran an article stating that women's colleges were "a holy terror" that destroyed the lives of their female students.[64] The article explained that women were naturally incapable of herding together the way men did, meaning that the campuses of all-female colleges were "simply crawling" with young girls who "aped the independence of men without achieving the solidarity of men."[65] In closing, the author prescribed that Americans "keep college for the grinds" while letting their marriageable daughters "strut their stuff at home" because most young women would learn nothing of value during their four years at "Wreck'em College."[66]

Even though undergraduates at Mount Holyoke were often perceived as Others, they expressed similar anxieties as their male peers about the job market, future roles and fears about the ongoing Depression. Most Mount Holyoke students also realized that they occupied a privileged position in that they did not have to struggle with the immediate burdens presented by the economic depression. Thoughtful students recognized the contingency of their privileged location and worried what the future might hold in terms of power, prestige and position.[67] Many Mount Holyoke women seemed more concerned with working-class women's opinions of them, rather than the impressions published in the popular press. In a March 1932 editorial entitled "Our Rating" a Mount Holyoke student stated that she had spoken with factory girls at the recent Student-Industrial Conference and that many young female factory workers found it easier to talk with college girls than with the secretaries and stenographers who worked at the factories. When she asked why, one of the workers explained that students recognized workers' problems and showed interest in making changes while stenographers merely looked down upon them. The student writer was troubled by the fact that many of those same secretaries and stenographers were recent college graduates. The student wondered whether life in the outside world caused graduates to lose their idealism or that maybe others were not "bitten so badly by the idealistic bug" as students who had studied through Depression. Finally, she raised the question of whether it was possible to keep the confidence and precious trust of the workers throughout college and beyond.[68]

African-American students attending college during the Depression era faced a whole different set of issues than the white women who were enrolled in coeducational and all-women's colleges in the 1930s. Several excellent African-American colleges were established in the nineteenth century, including Fisk University (1865), Morehouse College (1867) and Howard University (1868). The Morrill Land Grant Acts provided federal support to African-American colleges that offered courses in agriculture, engineering, home economics and industrial or vocational arts.[69] African-American men and women eagerly took advantage of their increased access to higher education. In 1890, there were 17 African-American colleges in the United States; by 1899 there were a total of 81, with 75 existing in the South.[70] From 1890 to 1929, the number of African-Americans holding college degrees climbed from 3,700 to nearly 25,000.[71] These changes in access to education provoked fear in many middle-class white males who were concerned about protecting their privilege in a time of economic crisis. Many whites were apprehensive about providing access to education to African-American youths, because they feared that it would affect white access to middle-class white-collar jobs.[72]

Government officials tried to promote the notion that providing education for racial and ethnic Others would prove beneficial for the entire nation because it would have a culturally homogenizing effect that would speed the process of assimilating immigrants and African-Americans into the normative whole. The NAACP youth movement, which was strongly supported by Mary McLeod Bethune and Eleanor Roosevelt, campaigned for educational equality for African-American youths. In the early 1930s the NAACP legal department launched an intensive campaign to compel southern school systems, colleges and universities to provide equal facilities and access to education for African Americans.[73] In 1934 Roosevelt addressed the National Conference on Fundamental Problems in the Education of Negroes about the issues. Roosevelt commented on how certain state's per capita spending for the education of African-American children and white children differed greatly, and how this undermined the strength of the democracy because every child should receive the best education possible in order to assimilate.[74] In his report to the American Youth Commission and the American Council on Education, Homer P. Rainey touted the homogenizing benefits of education. Young "foreign types" who received education would be more likely to rid themselves of the cultural traits that characterized them as immigrants; education would help to absorb these foreign types into the masses of "adjusted children."[75]

Roosevelt framed her arguments to appeal to white middle-class people's economic self-interest, by stating that equal access to education "should be done for the preservation of the best that is in the ideals of this country," because the country would suffer economically if a large part of its population continued to be beaten down and underprivileged. Maintaining unequal access to education lowered the standard of living for the entire country, because wherever the standard of education was low, the standard of living was low, so for their "own preservation in order that our whole country may live up to the ideals and to the intentions which brought our forefathers to this country, that we are interested today in seeing that education is really universal throughout the country."[76] She addressed the issue of people concentrating wealth in order to protect their privilege in a time of crisis, by pointing out that people had to learn to be a little less selfish about sharing their resources in order to realize that it would prove profitable to all of them in the long run.[77] While the Federal Government was attempting to help in every way that it could during the economic crisis, Roosevelt contended that even before the Great Depression, most Americans did not understand that depriving children of education because of their race worked as a menace to society, and that, conversely, having a uniformly-educated population would benefit the nation as a whole.[78] She closed with the warning that people who were denied the opportunity to access as much education as they desired would grow resentful toward those who denied them the opportunity for self-expression and intellectual growth.[79]

COLLEGE STUDENTS QUESTION WHY THEY WERE THERE

Even students who had access to college educations still questioned why they were bothering to get degrees during a time of economic crisis; many collegians wondered aloud whether attaining a college degree was worth all of the time, effort and struggle. Mary R. Beard, co-author of *The Rise of American Civilization* famously stated that the "most helpless people in the world are the formally educated and there is a great deal of evidence that college education is not only negative but is a liability in the business world."[80] This notion struck a chord with many students, prompting them to question the wisdom of pursuing a college degree that may or may not lead to future employment. Other undergraduates expressed guilt about spending several years pursuing a degree when they could ostensibly be participating in the work force earning money for their families. This sense of guilt was tempered by the realization that attempting to find a full-time work would be a risky enterprise as well. The process of attaining a college degree involved a long production cycle that was based on "acceptance of the risk inherent in cultural investments."[81] College students had few markets for their skills in the present, so their participation in an "entirely future-oriented production" seemed like a high-risk investment.[82] Even so, youths of the early 1930s held fast to the notion that education represented the magic element that would "open the gates to the Promised Land."[83]

Some experts advised that young people conceptualize the cost of their education as a part of their "personal capital" that had to be "invested as to produce increased capacity for service" and personal satisfaction.[84] During the first few years of the Depression experts and youths spent much time appraising the costs and benefits of earning a college degree in terms of dollars and cents while also taking into account the expenditure of mental and emotional energy for an uncertain outcome. Students who concluded that college was a worthwhile endeavor mentally, emotionally and financially, still faced considerable college expenses that put higher education out of reach for many Depression-era families.

Student's cost-benefit analyses usually focused on the psychological aspects of struggling for a degree, but in the 1930s college costs could prove staggering. A study released in April 1930 in the journal *Schools and Society* reported that four years of collegiate study cost about $9,200 per student. This figure takes into account college fees, contributions from the state and federal government, and the wage losses that each student would incur by not earning a salary during their four years of schooling .[85] *The Mount Holyoke News* reported in 1933 that the average Mount Holyoke student spent about $1650 to $1700 a year to cover her school-related fees. Tuition, room and board cost $900—$1000 for nine months.[86] When one added laboratory fees, books, dances, weekend trips and movies the grand total reached almost $2,000 a year.[87] *The George Washington University Hatchet* revealed in 1934 that 75% of female students attending the university lived at home with their parents to save money, while 38% of male students did the same.[88] Male students who lived on the George Washington University campus paid about $48 a month for room and board, while female students paid $46 a month.[89] Students at the University of Michigan paid only $100 a year for tuition, with $60 due in September and $40 due in January.[90] While the tuition fees at the University of Michigan were relatively modest, the additional expenses of room, board, books and miscellaneous expenses put college out of reach for many young people.[91]

The combination of the expense of attending college coupled with the lack of pecuniary protection provided by a degree made students doubt whether the benefits of having a bachelor's degree balanced the cost.[92] Many undergraduates wrote articles debating the value of having a college degree. Young writers of these pieces used similar rhetorical strategies to convince youths that college was worth the effort and cost even if the degree failed to guarantee fame and riches. Most of these articles began with a series of questions that probed their peer's minds about their purposes for obtaining a degree. The writers then chided their readers for having a shallow outlook about the meaning of the degree and explaining that the purpose of a college education was for enrichment, enlightenment and expanding boundaries. If students only viewed their college diploma as a passport to a well-paying profession, then they ultimately lost the most important lesson of all. This somewhat trite rendering appeared in each and every one of the student newspapers during the early 1930s.

A farewell letter to graduating seniors that appeared in a May 1933 edition of *The George Washington Hatchet* fit the aforementioned format to a tee. The author opened the letter by posing difficult questions about whether the college experience had been worth the cost, whether an education made opportunities more accessible, whether the degree would provide any leverage in the tight job market and whether youths felt that they held the keys to success. After raising these challenging queries, the student reminded graduating seniors that they should not let financial hardships get in their way of happiness since "material success wasn't the chief objective of your years of college training."[93] The writer attempted to persuade graduating seniors that college prepared them to seek out "the only real form of success—happiness."[94] Getting a university degree meant broadening their cultural backgrounds, expanding their horizons and learning to estimate the worth of other people.

While students were counseled not to think of their degree purely as a means to attain more earning power, they were often still advised to consider the market value of their education. Economists helped them out by spending some time calculating the exact cash value of an education. Dean E.W. Lord of the Boston University College of Business Administration explained that every hour students spent in high school translated into at least $5.00 in later life, and every hour spent in college earned at least $10.00 after students graduated.[95] Statistician William Atherton Du Puy estimated that the monetary value of a college education amounted to about $65,000. A male who had a high school diploma was likely to earn about $110,000 in his lifetime, while a male with a bachelor's degree would earn $175,000.[96]

Most studies about the economic capital one could accrue by having the symbolic capital of a college degree focused only on white males. Many young women at Mount Holyoke, who had once felt safe embracing the notion that a B.A. represented the key to any job, feared that they would need to have a graduate degree or some type of specialized training if they wished to find any kind of employment.[97] One editorial writer criticized her classmates for focusing on "trade value" of their degrees and reminded them that they were welcome to attend secretarial schools, normal schools or technical institutions if their sole aim in life was finding a paying job.[98] Comments like these are laced with class privilege and assumptions that all students attending Mount Holyoke were from families that would support them financially after graduation.

Mount Holyoke women who were attending college to prepare for future careers and who wanted or needed to get jobs after graduation had good reasons to be concerned about the so-called trade value of their undergraduate degrees. A study by The American Women's Association told of "serious income reduction" for college-educated women employed in traditionally female-dominated fields like teaching, social work and library work; many women had their wages reduced by 20% to 30% during the worst years of the Depression.[99] College educated females who held jobs in male-dominated fields like design and sales analysis fared even worse; they were "likely to be thrown out of work or to have their income greatly reduced."[100] Even though young women had "lost big in the Depression" experts advised them to stay in school to earn their degrees, since having a degree might still provide them with some type of leverage in the tight job market.[101] In the years before the Depression, many women had the fall-back option of getting married rather than finding a paying job, but the job market in the early 1930s was so bleak that marriage often was not possible either.[102] Employers, for the most part, valued female employees because they were willing to accept low wages, were perceived as docile, agile, willing to perform routine work and lacking in career ambitions.[103] Women from Mount Holyoke did not fit this stereotype, but many planned on taking secretarial courses after graduation so that they could find positions as stenographers, typists and secretaries.

THE JOB MARKET AFTER COLLEGE

White female students seemed most concerned about being able to find interesting work after graduation. They feared that they might be shut out of the job market because of the Depression. Student newspapers addressed these fears by running multiple stories about the interesting occupations that were open to women, even though most of the articles proclaimed that young females did not need a college degree in order to pursue these intriguing avocations.[104] Young female students were informed that they could be aviators, architects, artists, designers, salespeople and managers. Female graduates who were wary of branching out into new fields could choose to play it safe and take on the traditional careers of teaching and social work.

With all of these doors to fascinating careers apparently open to young college educated women, teaching still represented the favored profession for most female graduates in the early 1930s. Even the so-called "safe" field of teaching was not that safe in 1933–1934. An official from the University of Michigan explained that a seven percent increase in the number of students in Michigan high schools was accompanied by a three percent decrease in the number of teachers."[105] The increasing work loads were paired with salary cuts of 10% to 40% which put an "unparalleled burden on teachers and school systems to keep state educational standards up to normal."[106] Historian Robert McElvaine demonstrates that married female teachers were targeted for harassment and that "campaigns against firing women were common in the 1930s." He shows that 77% of school districts refused to hire married women as teachers and 50% would fire women who chose to marry.[107]

In October and November of 1932 *The University of Michigan Daily* published statistics about jobs for men and women after graduation. The figures elucidate the occupational and pay discrepancies between the genders. The Federal Office of Education compiled statistics based on a survey conducted of 6,665 women graduates of land-grant colleges in the United States. The survey showed that after graduation college-educated women earned about $1,655 per year.[108] The statistics that delineate men's wages were based on a three-year research project conducted by a professor at Columbia University.[109] The major professions open to white female college graduates included teaching, which paid about $1,640 a year; executive positions $2,078 a year; fine arts work at $1,746 a year; professional work $1,690; and business positions that had salaries of about $1,533 a year. The major professions for white men paid much higher salaries and many required several years of schooling beyond college. These professions included medicine and law, which both paid about $5,250 a year; engineering at a salary of $5,000 a year; dentistry $4,725; college teaching $3,250; social work $2,517; library work and journalism, both of which paid about $2,250 a year. The worst paying male professions still exceeded the top pay that women could expect for performing similar jobs. The job market was segregated by race as well as by gender. White women dominated the professions of sales, communications and secretarial work, while African-American women had almost no access to these fields.[110] Many college-educated African-American women became dentists, doctors, lawyers and nurses who worked within the African-American community.[111] Often African-American professional women subsisted on the small fees that could be paid by members of their race who were underpaid themselves. When African-American women sought jobs in professions like teaching they often received the jobs, but at lower wages than white women earned.[112]

JOB OPPORTUNITIES AFTER COLLEGE

Even the advantage of having a college degree could do little to protect young women from the discriminatory hiring practices and psychological pressures that women faced in the work world. Most women who worked for wages outside of the home faced antagonism from their male co-workers and their wives who believed that women were taking jobs from men.[113] It was true that during the early years of the Great Depression women had lost proportionately fewer jobs than men, but this was often because male and female types of employment were not considered interchangeable. Women often held jobs as school teachers and low-status office employees, jobs that most men would not want to take, or would not be offered, under any circumstances.

Students from Howard University expressed concern that if white students worried about their futures and often failed to reach their goals, "what are we supposed to expect as Negroes in white America graduating from an institution less recognized than Harvard, Yale, Princeton . . . and the rest?"[114] Howard students expected to face racial discrimination in the constricted job market, especially since by 1932 the unemployment rate for African-American workers reached almost 50% nationwide.[115] While the notion of what constituted "women's work" and traditional female occupations held fairly steady during the 1930s, the concept of "Negro occupations" shifted as white people began to get pink slips. In the 1920s

African-Americans who lived in urban communities in the Northern United States often held positions as bellhops, elevator operators, waiters, trash collectors and street cleaners. As the Depression wore on, these previously "undesirable" positions became much more appealing to unemployed whites.[116] African-American employees were usually the last hired and first fired in most industries and often they were displaced by white workers in fields that had once promised dependable jobs.

According to economic historian Arthur Ross, the labor contracts for the "Negro jobs" of waiters, domestic servants and other service positions often had casual contracts, which gave employers the freedom to hire and fire employees at whim. Also, the service nature of many jobs delegated to African-Americans required close contact between employees and customers; public sentiments about the importance of hiring white men often prevailed in the tense climate of the 1930s.[117] In addition, many of the labor policies created during the New Deal years had an adverse effect on available employment for less-skilled, less-educated workers, including African-Americans. Even educated African-Americans had strong fears about being able to find jobs. The minimum wage codes instated as part of the National Recovery Act (NRA) often prompted employers to replace black employees with white ones, who prior to the code "would have been unwilling to accept the market-clearing wage."[118]This phenomenon was so pervasive that many African-American social critics referred to the NRA as the "Negro Removal Act."[119]

One Howard student pointed out that out of five million unemployed youths more than 15 percent of them were African-American. Howard students had come face to face "with a blank wall of economic insecurity" and the positions for which they qualified were "completely non-existent."[120] Instead of using their college training to find jobs in their respective fields, they were forced to compete for unskilled jobs that barely paid subsistence wages.[121] Male graduates from Howard could look forward to finding positions as porters and elevator operators, while female graduates could set their sights on working in tea rooms and restaurant kitchens. Howard students who worked part-time while attending college faced drastic deductions in their pay. The annual figure of total student earnings at Howard dropped from $40,000 a year to $2,500 during the early years of the Depression.[122]

Intelligent experts recognized that African-American youths faced several unjust handicaps, including "economic under privilege, inferior educational opportunities, disproportionate health hazards and the manifold disadvantages and discouragements that grow out of persistent prejudices."[123] Even so, a report prepared by Homer P. Rainey, the Director of the American Youth Commission of the American Council on Education, perpetuated racist ideologies by stating that aside from questions about racial equality on intellectual and social planes, "all will agree that Negroes possess natural endowments which supply a dash of variety in a predominantly Anglo-Saxon society."[124] Rainey described African-American people as having a capacity for a tolerant good-nature, a penchant for mirth, a love of rhythm, music and dance that all helped to counterbalance the grim acquisitive nature of American capitalist society.[125] Eleanor Roosevelt contributed to this discourse by stating that she believed that African-Americans, as a race, had tremendous gifts to share with the country, including a natural "appreciation of art and of music and of rhythm, which we really have to gain very often through education."[126] Roosevelt argued that these gifts that came naturally to the African-American race could be utilized for the good of the nation and that people should be encouraged to make their greatest contributions "along the lines that you want and that give you joy."[127] Comments like these naturalized racial hierarchies by casting African-Americans in the role of minstrels who could entertain whites during the Depression-era crisis. These ideologies undermined the potential for African-Americans college graduates to gain employment during the Depression era. Students from Howard University concluded that African-Americans would need to have a college degree if they wanted access to even the most menial jobs. Howard students writing for the *Hilltop* in the 1930s advised their peers to choose their fields of study carefully, work hard, get good grades and prepare themselves as best they could for the world after college.[128]

SELF-COMMODIFICATION & MARKETING COLLEGE LIFE

Even the students who worked hard, studied and got good grades to prepare themselves for the world after graduation still knew that they would have to shape themselves into desirable commodities if they wanted to succeed in the Depression-era job market. Karl Marx defines a commodity as an object produced for exchange, which has use value or properties that satisfy some human wants or needs.[129] Although most middle-class students probably would not have considered themselves Marxists by any stretch of the imagination, they appeared to have tapped into veins of Marxist thought in their own thinking about self-commodification. Youths surveyed what qualities employers desired and then labored mentally to make themselves valuable in the marketplace.

In theory, the commodification process would function as an equalizing force where all commodified entities would be rendered interchangeable and exchangeable, meaning that students who graduated from the same programs at four-year colleges or universities—regardless of their race or gender—would have equal exchange value because they would have equal levels of mental labor embodied in them. In practice, social forces, including historically-produced racial and gender hierarchies, intervened to determine which commodities would be more valued in the job marketplace.

In the 1920s a white-collar corporate job offered the promise of constant promotion up the corporate ladder.[130] By the early 1930s, young people who wished to have white-collar positions learned that they needed to engage in constant *self-promotion* to get into the entry level of big businesses. Depression-era students drew on 1920s ideals of personal advertising to make themselves viable in the competitive job marketplace. Students seemed to presuppose C. Wright Mill's notion that people who wanted white collar jobs had to sell "not only their time and energy but their personalities as well."[131] Individual students utilized the psychology of advertising, concentrated intently on creating an aura, while embracing an "open and unabashed focus on self-presentation."[132] Personal advertising was touted by many in the late 1920s and first couple of years of the 1930s as the "sure road to fame and fortune."[133] Some contended that personal advertising worked because Americans were raised on a steady mental diet of catchwords, propaganda and advertising campaigns.[134] By 1932 some students were advising their peers that they should revise their ideas about the value of self promotion and focus instead on becoming outstanding laborers if they wanted to get jobs, because "Work, study and skill must replace ballyhoo, hero worship and personal publicity. That is the sign of the times."[135]

Many Depression-era college students still clung to the notion that a good advertising campaign would make or break their chances for finding employment after graduation. Students had assumed that they would be required to market themselves as individual units when they ventured out to find employment. Students went beyond selling themselves as individual commodified entities and began advertising particular images of college life to gain a foothold in the post-graduation marketplace. They implicitly understood the notion that a class is "defined as much by its being perceived as by its being" and filled editorial pages with debates about how best to create and sell an image of college life to the public and future employers.[136] Depression-era youths recognized that the popular portrayal of collegians and college life in the press could prove profitable or punitive when they went out to find work. Undergraduates hoped that having a degree might give them an edge in the job search, but believed their chances would be improved if they projected a positive mystique about college life.[137]

Students held wildly opposing views of what images of college life to promote to the public. During the prosperous 1920s, life on college campuses captured the public imagination and was seen as a four year bout of parties, dates and football games. Hollywood films added to the mystique of college life, leaving the impression that all students were "athletes, smoothies and beautiful girls," who spent a good portion of their time on campus drinking, dancing and pulling pranks.[138] Even though Hollywood stopped making films about college in the 1930s, the public still longed to hold on to the fantasy that life on college campuses had not changed since the onset of the Depression. In 1931 *The Detroit Free Press* described the ongoing public interest in campus life in a lengthy feature entitled "We Have All Gone Collegiate." Members of the public who felt pummeled by the impact of the Depression would escape their daily lives by journeying to college campuses to attend football games, browse in local shops and visit student hang outs. Many of the people mentioned in the *Free Press* article would travel to the University of Michigan even thought they had no formal connection to the school. The public's fascination with college trends, student fashions and the university lifestyle that began in the 1920s carried over into the 1930s, provoking mixed reactions from Depression-era students.[139]

Many undergraduates greatly resented that the public still envisioned life on Depression-era college campuses as "halcyon weeks and months given over to recreation and class dodging."[140] Student writings attempted to demystify the college mystique by explaining the lives of undergraduates did not involve endless round of "fraternity parties, football games, bull sessions and formal dances."[141] Undergraduates argued that the wild, hard-drinking, noisy college boys who had populated films, novels and real-life campuses in the 1920s faded into oblivion during the first few years of the Depression.[142] The majority of Depression-era undergraduates were hard working, competitive, serious and interested in practical knowledge and liberal ideas.[143] Serious students wanted people from the outside world to see their dignified demeanor, earnest attitude and serious scholastic striving.[144]

Other collegians believed that students should preserve the illusion that life on campus in the 1930s was still a rollicking good time, arguing that if the public "got a kick" out of imagining college life as a lark, undergraduates should let them enjoy the fantasy.[145] The proponents of preserving the illusion explained that retaining the "approval of the masses," even if it was based on inaccurate images, could improve their job prospects in the future.[146] Some student writers advised their fellow undergraduates to refrain from complaining about the highly-fictionalized images in the public's imagination, because the lackluster reality of campus life, with its conservative young men and women seriously pursuing education goals would bore the public and destroy the college mystique. The campus ideal types of sweet Betty Coed and fun-loving Freddie Fraternity might be purely fictional, but "Betty and Freddie will always be a little more colorful and popular" than real-life college students.[147] Some youths argued that they could potentially cash in on this popularity, so they should take care not to ruin the public perception of college life as a free-wheeling, fun-loving, four-year frolic with the boring truth.

In an excellent example of cross-campus discourse, a student from the University of Indiana wrote a response to the "Preserve the Illusion" editorial which was reprinted in both the Northwestern and University of Michigan newspapers proclaiming that depicting college students as glamorous and fun-loving would be fine if youths were only seeking to win popularity contests with the public.[148] The image of collegians as happy-go-lucky types could ultimately damage an undergraduate's chances on the job market. If a newly-graduated student applied for a job and the potential employer only had the image of collegiate youths as "crooning whoopee boys" the graduate might fail to get the position. Back in the 1920s, when the economy was strong, it was okay for colleges to represent a "realm of forbidden naughtiness" but when that reputation became strong enough to jeopardize graduates' chances for finding jobs, it was "time to call a halt."[149]

African-American students had an even more onerous task than selling their school to potential employers; as James Weldon Johnson emphasized in his "Negro Americans, What Now?" throughout the 1930s every African-American had to conceptualize himself as "a salesman of his race."[150] Howard students concurred with the sentiment that students should project an image of earnestly preparing for the world beyond campus. One student stated that African-Americans students had to project themselves and their schools as serious because the world would not accept "shallowness, frivolity, false sophistication and collegiate airs."[151] Although students failed to reach a consensus about how to portray college life to the public, they agreed that their standing in the public imagination could shape their futures.

Savvy students had figured out how to commodify, advertise and market themselves, yet another lingering fear remained; students worried that there would be an overproduction of college graduates. Enrollment numbers continued to swell throughout the 1930s, especially at state universities and land-grant colleges, where student populations could be unlimited in number.[152] Some students suggested raising tuition fees to stem the tides of enrollment, arguing that recent history had demonstrated that only a limited number of white-collar jobs were available, so educating the masses would only breed discontent.[153] Even though raising tuition fees would mean that many students would have to drop out of school people had to realize "after all, not everyone can go to college."[154] An article published in *The New York Times* in November 1934 showed that some experts concurred with the sentiment that not everyone was suited for college. Dixon Fox, the president of Union College stated that opportunities for higher education should be reserved for only "first-rate minds" that were fit for leadership. Fox contended that, "Obsessed with the idea that everybody was fit for college, we have tended to make college fit for anybody."[155] A reporter for *The Mount Holyoke News* noted that Fox's statements were in striking contrast to the many extension-of-learning ideals that thrived during the more prosperous 1920s.

Depression-era young people who wanted to attend college, or stay in college if they were already enrolled, had access to some of the federally-funded New Deal programs that were designed to provide relief for youths. The Federal Emergency Relief Administration's college aid program, created in 1934, developed work-study positions for college students so they could remain in school.[156] Some elite colleges and universities, including Yale, Harvard and Williams declined accepting FERA's government aid for students.[157] The Director of FERA, Harry L. Hopkins, criticized "overly-endowed aristocratic" institutions that failed to support the FERA program. Hopkins accused the schools of upholding the notion that college was for "a privileged few" and stated, "Well, let them hang on to it up there in New England as long as they want."[158]

JOBS ON CAMPUS

Many students who felt a sense of dread and foreboding about future job prospects faced more pressing concerns about finding ways to fund themselves through college. During the Depression era increasing numbers of undergraduates took part-time jobs to help pay their way through school. By 1932 young women began "muscling in" on jobs that men used to monopolize.[159] The University of Michigan Union would only hire male workers, so females suggested that the Michigan League should follow suit and only hire women to serve the public.[160] The League adopted a new policy where all jobs that could possibly be filled by women were given to women, which resulted in 33 women earning a living by performing tasks that males formerly did. Twenty of the new female employees worked in exchange for their board only, while the other thirteen took up residence in the building and had both room and board covered as part of their earnings.

The number of female students who were earning all or part of their way through the University of Michigan was larger than ever by 1933. One article revealed that over 140 female students had been placed in private homes to earn their room and board. Another 100 or so women students were waiting on tables at the League, in dormitories and in tea rooms to earn boarding. Other female students held part-time positions as cashiers in restaurants, cafes and theaters.[161] The female student workers at the University of Michigan earned a sum total of $77,000 in 1932.[162]

In the early-to-mid 1930s students at the George Washington University were holding down jobs in record numbers. An economics student from the University who worked for the Department of Commerce performed a survey that found that 38% of the male students and 21% of the female students were employed full time. An additional 16% of men and 12% of women students from George Washington University held part time jobs.[163] Positions that had previously been identified as "women's work" including "domestic service, primary education and many clerical and social service jobs" were being filled by white male college students.[164] In the desperate early years of the Depression, some of the gender distinctions about work that existed before the stock market crash of 1929 were cast aside and male University students took on the previously undesirable domestic work that had once been the sole domain of women.[165] In many cases young women working for wages during the Great Depression earned more money than their male counterparts. The study of George Washington University students revealed that men who worked full time earned monthly salaries of about $110 while female full time employees brought home $115 a month. The same pattern held true for part time workers, with men earning $32 a month and women taking in $43. The student who conducted the study noted that "the fact that women workers earn more than the men is perhaps surprising and unflattering to the vanity of the campus males. The explanation is that most of the women hold stenographic positions, which pay more than the minor jobs the men are willing to accept while working their way through college.[166]

Suddenly, in the face of all of the female financial success in the part-time and full-time job markets, there was a great outcry on college campuses about working being injurious to female students. Female undergraduates who spent their semesters studying and working for room and board, according to one study at the University of Michigan, were prone to have physical breakdowns.[167] The article proposed that coeds should be banned from working on campus.[168] This protectionist argument for women being restricted from earning wages reiterated similar debates about women's work that had played across the pages of national publications for several years prior. Labor organizers, who fought for equal rights for women industrial workers, stated that benefits should be decided based on a worker's merit rather than gender. Female labor organizers explained that protectionist policies often proved detrimental to female workers since they had the potential to "protect" women out of desirable positions. "Protection is not protection when applied to women alone."[169] Even though labor unionists were fighting to end protectionist policies, campus administrators upheld the gendered status quo when they began questioning young women's ability to work and attend classes. *The Mount Holyoke News* ran an item about "college fatigue" puzzling over the increased weariness in female college students. The article posited that perhaps the pecuniary worries generated by the Depression and the "increase in the number of girls earning part of their way through college" could be blamed for the fatigue.[170]

CLUB POLITICS

Male undergraduates who recoiled when female students exhibited the audacity to invade the sacred all-male spaces for dining, leisure, work and recreation reacted even more vociferously to co-eds attempting to take positions of power that were previously held by men only. An article that ran in *The University of Michigan Daily,* reprinted from the *California Daily Bruin,* described how two first year female students from University of California at Los Angeles (UCLA) demanded and received petitions to run for class treasurer. The UCLA male student wrote that "Nothing, apparently, in the masculine realm is held sacred by the emancipated women" of the 1930s.[171] Traditionally, male students were elected to the offices of president and treasurer and female were allowed to run for vice-presidents and secretaries for each class.[172] This "real, sterling, untarnishable tradition" had existed for as long as anyone on campus could remember, and the male students did not want it to change. This traditional set up insured that male students—the rightful class presidents and treasurers—held the most authority by handling large decisions and the money. Female students were expected to play the auxiliary roles of helpmates, as vice presidents, or as support staff as class secretaries. The mere thought of "the weaker sex trying to dissolve masculine prerogatives" made the male UCLA student livid; he believed that this outrage should force "every true tradition lover on his feet ready to fight in a minute." The article closed with the warning that male students had better take swift action against this assault on masculinity, lest they face being "driven out of everything on campus" and having the University taken over by women.[173]

When confronted with a similar situation, The Johns Hopkins University Undergraduate Council took immediate action and created a policy barring women from participating in extracurricular activities. This decision was made in reaction to the fact that a female student had been chosen to be the editor-in-chief of the campus magazine. The students, alumni and heads of other activities were outraged, objected to having a female hold office and demanded the immediate change in policy to keep atrocities like this from happening again.[174]

The pervasive fear about women taking up space, making their voices heard and holding positions of power raised fears that educated women were in the process of creating an American matriarchy. All the evidence was there: President Roosevelt appointed females to important posts in his administration,[175] women controlled about half of the nation's wealth[176] and men were doing little to protect themselves from these cultural shifts. Paul Popenoe, a sociologist and popular author in the 1930s, argued that a matriarchy would emerge if men failed to protect themselves against the forces of female power. Some experts believed that the matriarchy already existed and that women controlled everything, including the fields of education, publishing, religion and the arts.[177] The article in *The University of Michigan Daily* was based on an article that Columbia University Professor Albert Jay Nock wrote for *Atlantic Monthly.* Nock's definition of "control" proves very interesting because it hearkened back to Victorian era beliefs about women exercising moral suasion as a means to control men. He stated that in the United States the "musical director, preacher, publisher, lecturer, editor, playwright, schoolmaster always instinctively addresses himself to the quality and character of interest peculiar to the female portion of his constituency."Even in this rendering it is obvious that men controlled the fields of production, but aimed their messages at a female audience. So it seems that the fears about a matriarchy developing in the United States were based more on anxieties about females manipulating men's emotions to sway them to produce what women desired. This is very different from women taking control of the fields themselves and producing publications, lectures, works of art and musical pieces. This demonstrates that the angst about women accessing any forms of power, personal or political, was perceived as a large threat in the early years of the Depression.

Popenoe appropriated Freudian theories to explain the inherent inadequacies of women, describing a phenomenon that he called the "masculine protest." Women who attempted to achieve educational goals beyond their supposedly inborn innate capacity disrupted and distorted traditional societal and biological patterns. These attempts to repudiate "natural patterns" ultimately failed because women were unable to "repudiate the biological differences that underlie" these patterns.[178] Abnormal women who failed to adjust to their proper station in life were seen as exhibiting traits of the "masculine protest." These deviant females avoided marriage or became frigid wives. They often exhibited stereotypically masculine behavior, and were especially prone to aggressiveness. Popenoe argued that this "dangerous form of female initiative" was spreading to the masses and destroying traditional ideals of masculinity. This, in Popenoe's estimation, was a serious threat, because American men were being "guided, cajoled and controlled by females."[179] To assuage masculine fears about this impending menace, Popenoe assured young male readers that masculine women were universally hated: "Behind her back she is either laughed at, despised, or a little of each."[180]

Undergraduates from around the country created distinctive discourses in their student newspapers that focused on self-commodification, marketing and advertising as the means to accrue symbolic capital and gain access to jobs and a middle-class lifestyle. The economic reversals and social dislocations that struck many members of the middle class during the early 1930s challenged the systems of gender-based domination that had been naturalized during earlier decades. Agents, many of whom were white, middle-class, college-aged males, wished to accrue the symbolic capital of a college degree in order to access middle-class privileges in the future. These male middle-class youths, with the assistance of expert authors, successfully constructed ideological and discursive barriers to protect their privilege and exclude Others, as much as possible, from obtaining the spoils of middle-class life.

Chapter Three

Selling Out or Buying In: Ritual, Tradition and Standardization, 1931–1935

> Another campus tradition flickered faintly . . . then pulled a shroud over its head and settled down on its shelf for what will probably be an all-time rest[1]
>
> -*The University of Michigan Daily*, October 29, 1932.

> That such respect be shown is only right as these traditions are the heritage of the college, an integral part of . . . life to be preserved and passed on to successive generations.[2]
>
> -*The Amherst Student*, September 29, 1932.

In 1932 students from colleges and universities around the nation ardently argued either for preserving time-honored rituals including freshman rules, freshman hazing and hell week or, conversely, for ridding campuses of these hazing traditions that had shaped collegiate social life during the previous decades. The students and experts who wanted to keep the rituals intact contended that the traditions represented the glue that held campus life together. They believed that if these customs were left by the wayside the collective campus social structure would suffer. Those who wished to rid the college campuses of hazing countered that the practices were remnants of adolescent folly that had no place on campuses populated by the serious, dedicated and intellectually-driven students of the Depression era. Most of the arguments, which appeared as letters to the editor, columns and articles during the years of 1931–1935 focused on either the importance of maintaining traditions during a time of national social, political and economic crisis or, on the other hand, the necessity of vanquishing childish rituals from college campuses when the rest of the country was facing huge economic and social disruptions.

During the more financially stable 1920s class distinctions—both social-economic class and class as in freshman, sophomore, junior and senior—were demarcated using clear criteria. By the early 1930s traditional campus systems of distinction, prestige distribution and class formation were being called into question, mainly because fears about jobs, salaries and financial security that used to be relegated to post-graduate years cast a pall over old uproarious campus traditions including freshman rules, the hazing of first-year students, hell week and pledging to fraternities or sororities. There was much anxiety on college campuses about how class formation would occur if the traditional rituals were phased out of existence. Students of the 1930s were, for the most part, from fairly similar socioeconomic backgrounds; they struggled to define how to distance themselves from those below them, bond with their own and attempt to approach those above them.[3] Depression-era students used college-class status and interclass rivalries to make sense out of looming socioeconomic class issues in the larger society. Debates about tradition, ritual and heritage masked nagging concerns about conservative forces clashing with up-and-coming parties who were brandishing new ideals. The exchanges in student newspapers exhibit deep concerns about campus power dynamics, social hierarchies, prestige distribution and symbolic capital on college and university campuses of the 1930s.

This chapter explores the discourse created by collegiate youths and experts surrounding the ideas of identity, group membership, maintaining discrete hierarchies and the continuation of traditions and rituals in a time of crisis. It elucidates how individuals and groups on college campuses of the 1930s invested in classificatory systems that helped them to define the parameters between "us" as opposed to "them" by enacting rituals that functionally excluded Others.[4] It illustrates how middle-class students organized around their shared middle-class status while creating hierarchies within hierarchies.

A study published in *Fortune* magazine pinpointed the year 1932 as a key historical moment when campus dynamics shifted dramatically and previously-embraced social hierarchies crumbled. *Fortune's* intensive study of twenty-five college campuses found that the conventional campus heroes from the 1920s—star football players, captains of sports teams, smooth-talkers and prom leaders—were being surpassed for big man on campus status by intellectuals who once would have been considered "queer" or "wet."[5] Part of this, *Fortune* writers posited, stemmed from the economic reality that academically-oriented, focused, single-minded students might be more likely to land jobs in the competitive Depression-era marketplace. While it is doubtful that awkward intellectuals effortlessly ascended social hierarchies to claim the titles of Big Men on Campus or campus belles, it proves intriguing that students at the five college campuses in this book in conjunction with the 25 campuses *Fortune* studied, all experienced shifting attitudes about what rituals, traditions and collegiate heroes should be honored. The effects of the Great Depression, which struck the poorest people first, filtered up into the lives of members of the middle class by 1932, causing students to reevaluate the ways in which they conceptualized prestige.

Students who had once been relegated to the bottom rungs of campus hierarchies recognized the "space of possibilities" that opened up because of the Great Depression. They had the opportunity to challenge the status quo and the taken-for-granted reality created by dominant groups by questioning the relevance of the pre-established campus hierarchies.[6] The people who had once held esteemed positions—members of fraternities, sororities and sports teams—had a definite interest in perpetuating ideals of the 1920s and upholding the basic principles on which their dominance was based. Pierre Bourdieu notes that once the *doxa*—or dominant way of seeing—is brought to light, discussed or challenged, the previously undisputed ways of perceiving reality enter into the realm of discourse. This enables members of society who are affected by the ways of seeing to engage in verbal debates over its legitimacy. This discursive process creates new rules and understandings concerning the previously unquestioned ideals.

A large part of the college experience for the middle-class youths of the 1930s involved the process of identity formation through course work, extracurricular activities, friendships, dating and other social activities. In times of crisis, when class boundaries are "vague, changing and precarious," maintaining small differences in social status takes on paramount importance.[7] The freshmen hazing practices, along with the whole Greek fraternity and sorority system, worked to mark differences between undifferentiated agents.[8] Undergraduates of the early 1930s recognized that their social status was predicated upon making themselves different from others, but were unsure about how to establish socially-profitable identities during the Depression era.[9] Many cultural historians note that membership in a class strata is largely a matter of perception and a state of mind.[10] Students of the 1930s appeared to be particularly invested in constructing and maintaining distinct boundaries between class strata. The process of identity formation was inexorably linked with daily social practices. [11] Identities—including, race identity, gender identity, identity as a fraternity or sorority member, a non-pledged "Barbarian," a "gold-digger," "greasy grind," "College Joe," were all negotiated and renegotiated as part of the practice of everyday life on college campuses. Bourdieu explains that the "reality" of the social world is made up from schemes of perception, thought and action. Habitus is a system of both the production of practices and the perception of practices, but these practices and representations can only be perceived by agents who possess the code necessary to understand the practices' social meanings.[12]

Even before the Great Depression and the fateful year of 1932, the values that students embraced and upheld often depended on the campus environment, peer culture and ideals that had popular currency with students. A study conducted at Bennington College in the 1930s showed that students received social and material rewards for conforming to liberal, rather than conservative, peer expectations during their college years.[13] Many Bennington students recognized that the most popular undergraduates embraced liberal ideologies; first-year students adopted the liberal beliefs of the older students because they had prestige value and the social rewards of popularity for conforming were better than being socially isolated.[14] The colleges and universities discussed in this chapter had students who tended to favor conforming to middle-class, middle-of-the-road gender and political norms more than the liberal ideals embraced by students at Bennington. The winds of change brought about by the economic reversals of the 1930s inspired more liberal thought and action from students at George Washington University, Amherst and the University of Michigan.

RIBBONS, POTS, PEA GREENS & SPOTS

All of the schools included in this book had some form of "hell week" rituals where members of the upper classes hazed first-year students. Hazing traditions are inherently designed to maintain differences in status by setting individuals or groups, in this case freshmen, apart from the rest of the social body. The hazing traditions varied from campus to campus, but all of them created a sense of separation by having the new arrivals wear a visual marker of their status, almost always an item colored green. "Green" freshmen were required to wear green ribbons, hats, buttons or sweaters that segregated them from upper-class students.

In the early 1930s, first-year students at Mount Holyoke paraded around campus with green ribbons tied in their hair during the initial weeks of the fall semester. Howard students donned "freshman caps" for their entire first semester; Amherst men wore "pea greens," and University of Michigan students grudgingly wore "pots," small green caps, during September and October of their first year. Freshmen at George Washington University were required to wear green buttons called "spots" to identify themselves as new arrivals on campus. At Amherst, the University of

Michigan and the George Washington University, upper-class students were allowed to harass, hit, bully and degrade first-year students who were wearing their green regalia.

One Amherst student fondly recalled a hazing incident that occurred during his freshman year in 1933 when a group of upper-class students came to his dorm room at the stroke of midnight, blindfolded several first-year men, and took them into the woods for some hazing. The hazing mostly involved, "compelling the victims to walk about according to orders issued in assumed bass voices, and hugely enjoying their consternation when tree trunks rudely bumped into them."[15] The elder students also tormented the blindfolded first-year men by applying paddles loudly to the soles of their own shoes and watching "their faces twitching in anticipation." The hazing was cut short when a police officer arrived on the scene; the older students told the freshmen not to budge and then took flight.[16] An article in the *University of Michigan Daily* mockingly described how the first Monday of the school year "invariably sees the inevitable outbreak of the alleged school spirit in the form of freshman hazing."[17] Usually, twenty-five or thirty sophomores would decide to "appoint themselves to initiate the freshmen into the mysteries of the campus, provide a little of what they think constitutes amusement for bystanders, and in general make the freshmen understand that one year on the campus has given the former such a superior outlook on life that they may indulge in this sort of activity."[18]

The traditions on the all-women campus of Mount Holyoke usually focused on embarrassing the first-year students and making them perform songs, dances or other slightly humiliating tasks in a public forum. In 1932, first-year students at Mount Holyoke had to endure one day of hazing, which entailed wearing a placard with each girl's name and weight on it, adorning their hair with ribbons and wearing too much rogue.[19] Frosh students had to carry umbrellas all day, tote their books to classes in pillow cases, only use certain doors on campus and visit seniors at night to tell them bedtime stories.[20] In earlier years, Mount Holyoke seniors had forced first-year students scrub the steps of the library, while other times freshmen women only had to suffer through moralizing lectures about manners or skits about good freshmen and bad freshmen.[21] The entering class of 1933 was required, for one day, to wear green tunics, placards with their names on them and lampshades on their heads. First-year women were compelled to cavort at the will of any senior and to walk around campus with one step backward for every five they took forward.[22] After one day of this "servitude to her majesty, the senior," the freshmen were allowed to "resume their studies undisturbed."[23]

Upper-class students explained that the rules regarding wearing caps, ribbons or buttons were designed to help new students get acquainted with their peers, with Amherst writers arguing that hazing the green freshman welded the class into a group as quickly as possible.[24] Writers for the Mount Holyoke paper contended that hazing helped the young women develop good will and friendships.[25] University of Michigan journalists defended the wearing of the pots tradition as one that created feelings of school spirit and class unity, thereby engendering *esprit de corps*.[26]

Along with wearing green regalia, first-year students at Amherst College, Howard University and George Washington University had to obey freshman rules, which introduced students to campus traditions, produced a sense of class and school spirit and helped the returning student get acquainted with the freshmen. Freshmen were required to show deference and respect to upper-class students by greeting them with a customary hello, avoid walking in certain areas on campus, attend sporting events and learn the history of the school. The rules at George Washington University mandated that freshmen attend all in-town major sports events and know all of the university yells and songs.[27] All first-year students at Howard University were required to memorize the Alma Mater and school yells during the first week of classes.[28] Members of the upper classes explained that the freshman rules were not "merely a series of annoyances concocted by a group of fun-loving upperclassmen for the purpose of baiting a freshman," but that they were designed to bring students into the collegiate fold as quickly as possible.[29]

People often turn to rituals in times of stress and danger because they provide humans with feeling of community, continuity, normalcy and heritage.[30] The class-based hazing processes functioned as social performances and provided a shared symbolic language where students could hearken back to traditions, rituals and known hierarchies to foster a sense of stability. For the die-hard fans of preserving the rituals, reenacting old traditions represented a shared wish to return to the imagined past with stable norms and identities.[31] An article published in *The Amherst Student* in the fall of 1932 entitled "Amherst Traditions and the Freshmen" expressed the belief that undergraduates of the 1930s owed a debt of gratitude to the generations that preceded them, and that campus traditions should be preserved.[32] One year later, an article bearing a strikingly similar title of "Freshmen and Amherst Traditions," contended that the customs and traditions of the college represented the ties between students of the past and present that lent "color and vitality" to the institution.[33]

Some first-year students at George Washington University were adamant about keeping traditional freshmen rules. When the faculty at George Washington University proposed banning them altogether, several freshmen stepped up and rallied to maintain the traditions. One student performed surveys of 50 undergraduates from surrounding campuses including Catholic University, Georgetown, American University and the University of Maryland and found that "freshmen everywhere" favored keeping the traditional rules and rituals.[34] Students who wanted to keep the freshman rules may have been subscribing to the ethic of delayed gratification; if they submitted to the discipline meted out by upperclassmen they would be entitled to treat the next batch of freshman as poorly as they had been treated. Other students who craved belonging to a group over all else often condoned "attitudes, behaviors and group mores they would ordinarily find objectionable" including class-based hazing rituals.[35] While some freshman favored keeping the old practices intact, first-year students at several campuses resisted blindly following the customs initiated by their forbearers.[36]

In the early 1930s members of the freshman class at the University of Michigan took cues from the labor movement and organized formal resistance efforts against campus hazing and the tradition of wearing of pots. The young organizers asserted that it was unfair to make students who "have had but little opportunity to learn the value" of certain traditions be forced into obeying them, especially when they "appeared to be worthless."[37] They posited that the Student Council should make efforts to educate the freshman about the value of the practices rather than "endeavoring to force the freshmen to do something they are firmly resolved not to do."[38] First-year students united to petition against the pot tradition, arguing that it was archaic and needed to be vanquished.[39]

Howard University first-year students' resistance to freshman rules and hazing traditions became so apparent that one upperclassman argued they should instate the HRA—The Howard Recovery Act—to reinstate Howard campus spirit.[40] While some Howard students believed that the phasing out of hazing traditions heralded the end of the celebration of school spirit, many countered that they were mistaken.[41] Students who were against hazing believed that school spirit could be manifested in other ways and that the movement away from hazing demonstrated that college students had outgrown the "childish rah-rah" traditions of previous decades.[42]

On other campuses around the country, violent forms of resistance to old traditions occurred. At New York University a large group of male freshmen held a mass meeting and rallied to discard the ties and hats that marked their first-year status. Several sophomores appeared on the scene, a scuffle ensued and the police had to be called in to subdue the group. Minutes after the police departed the first-year students commenced beating up the sophomores and "finished things up by marching across the campus cheering their class and throwing away the hated ties and caps."[43]

SHIFTS IN ENROLLMENT

Much of the jarring shift from the rollicking campus atmosphere of the 1920s to the anti-hazing sentiments of the 1930s can be attributed the shifts in enrollment during the Depression years. Enrollment records show that the average first-year students of the early 1930s were older, and perhaps more sophisticated, than their predecessors of ten or twenty years before.[44] Many students were working their way through school and had neither time nor the interest in participating in the hell week rituals. Some students contended that college campuses had become more liberalized in the preceding couple of years, and the liberalizing influence led to downfall "many decadent institutions."[45] Liberal students declared that the hell week traditions that remained made the participants appear to be "unclassified morons with the mental age of 12."[46] Hell week represented a serious affront to the sensibilities of the more mature collegiate youths.[47] Students at Howard University sought to rid campus rituals of their vengeful spirit and regulate freshman by banning them from privileges rather than beating them up.[48]

Not only were Depression-era students older than the collegiate youths of earlier decades, there were also many more female students present on campus. Undergraduate women acted as outspoken critics of hazing and as proponents for ridding hell week rituals from coeducational college campuses. One young woman from the George Washington University criticized the wearing of spots and the hazing that followed as barbaric practices that functioned to make freshmen targets of aggression from older students. She mocked male undergraduates who wanted to continue the tradition of freshmen wearing "the ancient and dishonorable" green spots, stating that only immature boys who failed to grow up when they entered college would need such arbitrary methods to set freshmen apart from the rest of the student body.[49] She described the antiquated practice of having freshman don the spots as a method for upperclassmen to displace their own feelings of inferiority onto first-year students.[50] Even scholars at conservative Amherst acknowledged that the "time-honored unrestrained horse-play" of freshmen hazing during hell week could be detrimental for incoming students who were trying to acclimate to life on campus.[51] Amherst students who wished to maintain hazing and hell week argued that it could be a "constructive, enjoyable part of the freshman year, *when properly minimized and controlled.*" They believed that cocky freshmen needed some hazing to put them in their proper place on campus; but that the traditions required regulation and time limits in order to maintain their value.[52]

The undergraduates' resistance to the hell week hazing rituals brought traditional practices on many campuses to a halt.[53] By 1934 most colleges and universities phased out the wearing of pots, spots and freshman caps and vanquished class-based hazing and hell week from their campuses. In September 1934 an article appeared in *The University of Michigan Daily* explaining that the pot tradition had ended "abruptly and undeniably by mutually spontaneous consent."[54] The writer ruminated that:

> It will be a long while, if ever, before the pots are again worn on the Michigan campus. They have been relegated to the same waste basket that bustles, pantaloons, and raccoon coats occupy. They are out-dated, out-grown. They pass into the limbo of forgotten things a good deal like the mournful figure of Sir Walter Scott's imagination: "unwept, unhonored and unsung."[55]

Students who wished to participate in the time-honored hazing rituals that had once shaped a large part of campus culture had to join fraternities and sororities, which appeared to be the final bastions of "college foolery" in the 1930s.[56]

GREEK LIFE

Some undergraduates may have been questioning the validity and necessity of many campus traditions, yet even during the 1930s, fraternities and sororities continued to control a significant portion of campus social life, including proms, student plays and elections.[57] On most campuses that had fraternities and sororities, the Greek system helped to establish the ranking orders of prestige, and their collective strength was recognized by the administration, confirmed by undergraduate organizations and endorsed by the campus newspaper.[58] Belonging to a fraternity or sorority could broaden students' social horizons, bestow prestige upon them and give them access to symbolic capital. Fraternity and sorority members had more social opportunities than independent students. One expert described how the Greek system created a privileged minority who lived in luxurious settings and had the campus "served to them on a silver platter, garnished."[59] Only 20%-30% of the student population at any given university belonged to exclusive Greek organizations, but fraternity and sorority members usually held a large share of power on campuses.[60] Greek members had a sense of safety in numbers, could act as powerful voting blocks on the campus political scene; they also had a ready-made set of friends and traditions to fall back upon when times got rough.[61] One expert explained that fraternities and sororities had the power to control the collective "student opinion" because other students lacked the organization and numbers to voice their sentiments to the larger public.[62] A Dean from the University of Michigan explained that it was more difficult for non-pledged students to take leadership roles in extracurricular activities because the pledged students had their "organizations behind them, pushing them into activities," while independent students had only their individual initiative to spur them onward.[63]

Greek-letter fraternities and sororities established well-recognized ranking orders on college campuses across the United States.[64] The Greek system performed the cultural work of class formation by excluding people who failed to fit the mold and including their own kind.[65] The process of campus domination by the Greeks worked by legitimizing their practices as "naturally superior" to outsiders, so even those who did not participate were led "through a negative process of inculcation" to see their own practices as naturally inferior.[66] *Baird's Manual of American College Fraternities* describes social fraternities on college campuses as groups that are "mutually exclusive and self perpetuating that select their members from the undergraduate student body through a series of rushing processes that narrow down the field of potential candidates."[67]

Campus Greek houses wanted to attract good-looking, wealthy and popular students to join their ranks; they wanted to find students who were from comparably privileged backgrounds so they could form friendships and date people from similar social strata. First-year students competed for membership in Greek houses by attending a series of social events during the campus rushing period. Greek life promised students social mobility if they accepted group norms, blended in with the crowd and followed previously-established traditions. This training offered not only success in campus hierarchies, but also provided invaluable training for the corporate life for men and created many opportunities for heterosexual mixing so young women and men could find potential husbands and wives who had equally-privileged upbringings.

Fraternity and sorority members usually came from wealthier families than independent students and spent twice as much money on clothing, refreshments and entertainment than non-pledged students.[68] Elizabeth Eldridge, an expert author, former sorority member and national president of her sorority chapter described Greek-letter houses as being akin to country clubs, because the members were selected by invitation, paid dues to belong and had the advantage of having places to hold lavish parties.[69] The expenses for fraternity-sponsored formal dances could run up to $1,000, while dances held outside of chapter houses usually cost about $365. In the early 1930s the president's council at Ohio State University conducted a survey of formal dances on campus and found that out of 647 dances given that year 476 of them were held by fraternities or sororities.[70] Compared to their non-pledged peers, fraternity and sorority members drank more, dated more and were more likely to state that they were having a very good time in college.[71]

Becoming a member of these elite organizations was an important part of college life for many undergraduates. Students who were denied membership to their house of choice often stated that they wanted to drop out of school. Others felt too ashamed to return home for the holidays because they did not want their families and friends to find out that they failed to make the cut.[72] Robert Cooley Angell's sociological study of college students at the University of Michigan entitled *A Study in Undergraduate Adjustment,* published in 1930, details how important membership to Greek houses was for many undergraduates. The data, generated through interviews with 216 sophomores (133 males and 83 females), suggested that being part of the Greek system was commonly viewed as the key to social success for young people. Angell states that of the 123 "independents" interviewed for the study, approximately half desired to be part of the Greek system. Most often financial reasons held students back from rushing; Angell noted that some students who lacked the economic resources to pledge to a fraternity or sorority became self-selected groups who proudly celebrated their "independent" status. Other students who lacked funds to join the Greeks felt like social failures. Some undergraduates who rushed and failed to rate a bid felt a diminished sense of self-esteem in the face of the rejection. Angell contended that the "terrible discouragement which often ensues upon failure to be bid to a fraternity or sorority is pathetic in the extreme."[73]

Writings from student newspapers bear out the fact that in 1932, even with the Great Depression in full swing, students still focused a great deal of attention and energy toward pledging to Greek houses. An article in *The George Washington University Hatchet* explained that in the wake of pledging results being announced, many would-be sorority sisters and fraternity brothers felt "weary and ashamed" and loudly lamented that their names were not on the final list.[74] The author explained that this behavior was absurd and that the failure to gain acceptance to a fraternity or sorority signified very little in about the students' potential possibilities to be successful on campus. The article closed with the admonition, "FRESHMEN, DON'T LET IT GET TO YOU!"[75] A similar article appeared during the same week in *The University of Michigan Daily.* It opened with the lines,

"Buck up, rushees. Don't be glum and sour just because you didn't make a Greek lodge."[76] The article stated that Greek houses chose their members based on clothing, money and social standing but that these things had little to do with individual character. The articles ended with the rousing statements, "So, don't give up yet. The game lasts four years. It's your battle. Get in and fight!"[77]

One expert consoled the young women who failed to rate a bid to a sorority by explaining that many forms of popularity were available "on the present social market" and that self-management in the "business of living" was the key to accessing better ratings.[78] Using rampant marketplace language, she rationalized that some types of popularity required "less of a down payment" but ended up being "ruinously expensive in the end" while others required heavy investment but paid "larger and choicer dividends as friendships grow."[79] Another expert dedicated an entire chapter of her book to consoling young women who fumbled during sorority rush and failed to make the final cut.[80] She admonished dejected female readers not to leave school just because they did not get a bid and explained to disheartened coeds that they would still have a chance to meet men in classes and in other campus activities. Still, throughout the rest of the text, she refers to non-sorority and non-fraternity member as "independents," "non-pledges," and "barbarians."[81]

CONNECTIONS & POWER

For collegiate youths, the Greek system functioned as a place for making valuable connections that could lead to opportunities during their time on campus and after they graduated. In the competitive job market of the Great Depression, American businesses favored people who possessed both capital and connections.[82] An article published in *The Amherst Student* in 1933 explained that most Amherst men wisely valued their extracurricular activities over academic pursuits; because most of the world did not consist of scholars, therefore, having social training and connections would ultimately prove more profitable than possessing a strong academic record.[83]

The Greek system of fraternities and sororities operated as fields of restricted production that structurally excluded Others on college campuses in the 1930s.[84] Fraternities and sororities functioned as a distinct market, and the Greek system generated specifically cultural types of scarcity. [85] The value that fraternities and sororities created was not reducible to economic scarcity or the value of the goods in question.[86] The Greek system produced fraternity brothers and sorority sisters, generated a sense of scarcity by letting only a select few join and created symbolic capital that members could cash in on during their college years and beyond. The producers, in this case the members themselves, were endowed with marks of distinction that were recognized within the historically available cultural taxonomies of the 1930s.[87]

Amherst had a strong history of having fraternities on campus. Many fraternal organizations that were started at schools in the nineteenth century were originally created to nurture a sense of familial bonds, brotherhood and stability for young men who were living away from home for the first time.[88] Although fraternity brothers shared living quarters, meals, recreational time and conversations together, life in a fraternity house still contained elements of competition, rough play, violence and hedonistic behavior.[89]

Although fraternities existed at elite universities since the early nineteenth century, they began to crop up in profusion at large land-grant Midwestern campuses, like the University of Michigan, toward the end of the nineteenth century.[90]. Cultural historian Michael Kimmel posits that part of the growth of college fraternities can be attributed to an effort to retain a homosocial white world in a rapidly-diversifying collegiate environment.[91] Fraternities helped to shield "traditional" white, middle-class and upper-middle class, Protestant students from female, African-American and Jewish students who sought admission. Because land-grant universities were forced to admit all state residents, they proved to be fertile ground for fraternal organizations.[92]

Male students who made the cut, rated a bid and pledged to Greek houses invariably signed on to endure the rigors of the Greek version of "hell week" which could include being forced to stay awake for several days in a row, being beaten by one's fraternity brothers, being forced to count railroad ties on a 10-mile hike between two towns, standing outside in the cold counting all the windows of the university hospital.[93] Fraternities promised social mobility to the young men who successfully endured the hazing rituals.[94] University of Michigan officials revisited a letter that had been sent to them in 1927 about harsh hazing practices. In January 1930 the practices still continued unabated. The letter explained that:

> While a certain amount of discipline may be wholesome for the initiate, and while a reasonable degree of spontaneous fun may add an element of brightness amidst the soberer pursuits of academic life, hazing, in its cruder and crueler forms, leads to resentment and, on occasion, to serious suffering on the part of the victim; moreover, the effect is detrimental to the finer instincts of those who presume to inflict it.

The writer of the letter spoke out against personal abuse and humiliation, stating that mauling and insulting someone whom you expect to live with as a "brother" fails to build character. He also thought that hell week interfered with students' studies and often created bad publicity for the Greek system as a whole. At the University of Michigan, Ann Arbor residents complained about yelling, gun fire and other disturbances of the peace. One woman endured a fake robbery that was part of a hazing prank. In 1930 the deans proclaimed that hazing rituals had to take place in the house, pledges could not be physically abused and vulgar practices had to be abandoned.

College attendance and fraternity life prepared men for the competitive world of capitalism. Fraternal organizations provided a space for young men who were bound for middle-class professional life to rid themselves of crude habits and acquire manners and social graces.[95] Middle-class men who aspired to succeed in the world of business attended college not only to learn skills but also to acquire manners, contacts and style in order to function in the business realm.[96] In the modern corporate era, standing out became a matter of fitting in and fraternities taught young men how to conform to group norms and shape themselves into desirable commodities.[97] Bourdieu explains that the process of "doing one's duty" as a man involves conforming to the social order, respecting the dominate rhythms, keeping pace with the pack and not falling out of line.[98] This training, in some part, prepared young men with tools to cope in the rough-and-tumble business world that many of them would join after graduating from college.

SORORITY LIFE

Sororities offered women a place to build friendships, to find "sisterhood," and to meet young men to date and potentially marry. The meanings of sisterhood shifted in the early decades of the twentieth century. For middle-class women of the mid-to-late nineteenth century, the "female world of love and ritual" prevailed, and the ideal of sisterhood was built upon emotional and affectionate bonds.[99] By the 1920s and 1930s, the widely-held conception of what sisterhood entailed began to alter. Historian Linda Rosenzweig contends that societal shifts, including an increased reliance on expert advice, cautious management of one's emotions and a focus on consumerism promoted a new type of sisterhood where young women looked out for their own interests, were cautious of confiding in friends and used female friendships as a means to access and discuss heterosexual pursuits.[100] This new form of feminine bonding was apparent in the social life of sorority houses of the 1930s. Young women functioned as both allies and adversaries to one another in the realm of heterosexual pursuits; they assisted one another by arranging dates and discussing boys, but also kept each other in line by comparing notes about appropriate sexual behavior.

In this new realm of sisterhood young men played a big role, becoming the focus of conversation, the locus of competition and the basis for female friendships to develop.

Being affiliated with a sorority brought female students prestige and the opportunity to form strong friendships, as long as they were willing to adhere to stringent social conventions defined by their peer group.[101] Sororities provided a space where female roles were delineated and monitored by their "sisters" who were usually only a year or two older than the pledges. Most sorority houses promoted conservative gender norms as the ideal to which members were expected to conform. Young women who beat out the competition to gain acceptance to their house of choice had to adapt to peer expectations and aid their sisters in heterosexual pursuits, but also were expected to maintain a constant sense of self-interest. One expert on sorority life, described female competition in the following fashion:

> The girl who shows that she has no time for other girls is at least honest. She turns her charm on and off like a faucet. She bubbles and scintillates when men are around, and she is always thoroughly disliked for it by her 'best friends.' But girls must learn to be popular with other girls as well as with men if they are going to live happily in college.[102]

Sororities, even more so than fraternities, often had highly-calibrated campus-wide pecking orders that were understood by the student body as a whole. A study at the University of Minnesota found that when they asked female students to rank twenty sororities according to their level of prestige on campus, the women students all ordered the groups identically, even if they were members of sororities that ranked lower on the list.[103] Sorority members of the 1930s understood that men from the top fraternities only wanted to date women from the highest-ranking sororities, therefore sorority sisters had to be careful to choose new members who would conform to the norms created and upheld by their sisters.[104] Young women who were accepted to the "right" sorority had numerous opportunities to meet suitable young men who were from similar socioeconomic and cultural backgrounds as the young women.[105]

Sorority houses that rated the highest level of prestige on college campuses usually boasted the wealthiest women as members, so a young coed who wanted to belong to a high-ranking sorority house had a distinct advantage if she was from a well-off background.[106] An expert warned young women who wanted to join the Greek system that often sorority sisters would only value prospective pledges by what material possessions they could contribute to the house. She stated that college sororities often operated "wholly on the profit motive" and valued young women for what they added up to in terms of the size and style of automobile that the girl would make available for their use, the "supply, quality and smartness of wardrobe," and the size of the young woman's monthly allowance.[107]

Many undergraduates of the 1930s criticized fraternities, sororities and their members for being irrelevant in a time when Americans were facing incredible economic hardships. They blasted the Greek system for promoting socioeconomic snobbery and "financial aristocracy" in a time of national crisis.[108] One expert felt compelled to defend the sororities by listing their positive attributes and stating that in spite of its flaws, the Greek system "did accomplish good. They took ill-at-ease youngsters without poise and they taught the social graces. . . . The system had glamour"[109] The glamour associated with the Greek system, and the social graces one could potentially learn in the presence of its members, made the idea of sorority membership highly appealing to many young women.

STANDARDIZATION

Some critics of the Greek system—expert authors and undergraduates alike—stated that the sorority system contributed to the standardization of women, arguing that sororities did not just teach young women social graces, but that they actually completely altered members' personalities, stripping away all of their unique qualities until they were indistinguishable from one another. One student pointed out that young women in their first semester of college pledged their loyalty not only to the older members of a sorority whom they had met several times at social events, but also to the other new pledges whom they may have never even met.[110] An expert author supported this argument, adding that young women who joined sororities became "sisters" and were immediately thrust into a standardization process, made up of night sessions, meetings, criticism, discipline and analysis that continued until all vestiges of the girls former selves were washed away.[111] She described sorority life as a tragedy that occurred in the American educational system because parents willingly turned their daughters over to be molded by girls who were only a couple years older and hardly wiser.[112] A student at the University of Michigan commented that life on campus would be much more pleasant if sororities did not exist because "astounding proportion" of young women living in sorority houses were "downright unhappy in their groups."[113] Critics of the sorority system stated that new students were not stereotypes when they first moved into the houses, but the intensity of living within a system that condoned cliques and shared behavioral norms churned out Greek products that were convinced that their way of life was way God had designed life for everyone.[114] One fraternity brother who had recently graduated from an East Coast school wrote that many men preferred girls who had never lived in sorority houses because sorority life represented "a mode of living as communistic as the Union of Soviet Socialist Republics" which shaped young women into "common types."[115] Many articles in student newspapers and portions of books portrayed female undergraduates as complete dupes who arrived on college campuses in a state of bewilderment, were descended upon by sorority members and pulled into situations that were completely out of their control.

Similar criticisms were not leveled at fraternities. One article stated that a "fraternity may harm a talented boy by standardizing him," but no articles described bewildered young men wandering around campus like so many lost sheep looking for a home.[116] Young men were warned to be skeptical of fraternity member claims about their houses, to ask questions about the house financial situation, academic standing and policies regarding expansion and to weigh all information carefully because "after all, it is your life you are contracting to spend in their company."[117]

Student and expert concerns about the dehumanizing effects of standardization processes echoed larger cultural debates about standardization that played out throughout the 1930s. While students craved systemic means to define their place in campus social fields, they expressed fears about becoming standardized products created by faceless institutions. Some undergraduates worried that belonging to the Greek system could contribute to their own standardization by smoothing out the "rough cut products of the secondary schools" and turning them into drones.[118] Many undergraduates described college as a "large scale production of culture"[119] where youths emerged as mirror-images of their classmates, resulting in a complete loss of individuality.[120] Throughout the Depression era, several economists blamed standardization, mechanization, assembly-line techniques and the overproduction of cheap goods as key factors that created the economic depression. The processes of mechanization and standardization were understood by many to be rigid repressive threats to individuals who sought autonomy and independence.[121] Undergraduates of the 1930s did not want to become standardized items that rolled off of the university system conveyer belt and joined the ranks of the unemployed or underemployed. Herbert Hoover so feared turning American society into something regimented, subsidized and regulated that he resisted taking government action when the Depression first struck.[122] Hoover believed that standardizing business practices served to "dehumanize man" and to create a narrow and bureaucratic ruling class.[123]

Experts and youths alike accused members of Greek organizations of being snobs, promoters of racial hierarchies and proponents of "complete class unconsciousness."[124] The president of Vassar College, Dr. Henry Noble MacCracken, when speaking at Amherst challenged its fraternities to face the realities of the twentieth century, "come down to earth" from their attitudes of social superiority and to begin to value intellectual achievement and manners if they wished to survive the Depression.[125] MacCracken warned that intelligent people who had been touched by the "sum total of the new forces" of the Depression embraced a "more discriminating sense of values" and fraternity members were encouraged to follow suit lest they get left by the wayside.[126]

Discriminating values in the Greek system were very apparent at Howard University. Some students raised the question of whether fraternities and sororities created systems of color segregation at Howard.[127] One undergraduate noted that when students first arrived from all over the country they tended to gel as a class, but after a few months, people with light complexions seemed to organize into an exclusive grouping.[128] Brown-skinned students were said to follow suit by forming their own groups, while students with dark skin were "thrown upon their own resources."[129] Fraternities and sororities overwhelmingly asked only students from the fair-skinned and brown-skinned groups to join their ranks, while darker skinned students were "forced to go through their college careers without being a fraternal man or sorority woman."[130] The color standard of the fraternities and sororities replicated the racist underpinnings of American society by conflating a person's level of skin pigmentation with one's intellectual ability, character and potential. The student accused Greek house members of attempting to "avoid colored association, in order to protect the barriers of recognition and standards."[131] This type of segregation proved detrimental to class cohesion at Howard and caused critical-thinking students to question whether joining a fraternity or sorority would make them complicit in the creation of color-based hierarchies on campus.

Students who believed that socioeconomic and racial hierarchies had no place on campus argued that the Greek system should be ousted, contending that schools like Yale and Swarthmore got rid of Greek letter houses due to the dual pressures of "student indifference and hostility."[132] The youths who wished to rid the campus of fraternities and sororities often held the misconception that if the houses were removed from campus the economically-based hierarchies would be vanquished as well. Students connected their desire to move away from Greek-dominated campus hierarchies with larger cultural shifts, where Americans were embracing equality and intellect over "smugness and reaction."[133] Many college students of the 1930s contended that their families were making large sacrifices for them to attend school; they decided to focus on the problems of the day and to investigate society in which they lived, rather than live in the Greek system where friendships were based on inherited socioeconomic privilege and adolescent rituals.[134] Some Depression-era undergraduates voiced practical concerns about joining the Greek system, questioning whether paying several hundred dollars to join a fraternity or sorority represented a "sound social investment."[135] Being pledged to a Greek house put members in contact with people who could further their careers in the future, but pledges needed to have access to money in the present, with room fees running from about $100-$400 a year.[136]

RESISTANCE & INDEPENDENT ORGANIZING

Greeks had dominated campus activities for many years at George Washington University, but by 1935, many undergraduates were unable or unwilling to affiliate with a fraternity because they were expensive, time consuming and might involve compromises that individuals were not willing to make.[137] In earlier years, students who chose not to pledge stated that they felt disenfranchised from campus politics and student council because they were not organized as a group to voice their opinions. Students who may have formerly felt bereft in the world of campus politics and social life banded together to form a Non-Fraternity group that offered "a means of expression to the overwhelming majority of the student body."[138]

Undergraduates of the 1930s recognized that organizing around a shared identity empowered people. Youths on the campuses of Amherst, George Washington University and the University of Michigan all had groups of undergraduates who self-consciously organized themselves under the "Independent" banner. Students at several colleges purposely chose to remain on the outside of the Greek system. These non-pledged students began using their own initiative to question the orthodoxy of the Greek system, to recognize their shared status and to organize themselves as blocs. The option of remaining proudly independent had always existed, but in 1934 independence took on new dimensions as students began classifying themselves with the "Independent" label. Independent groups demanded to be recognized as distinct entities, allowed sponsors on student council and given privileges for room use that were afforded to other organized groups on campus.

Independent students at Amherst demanded that they be granted a space to meet on campus.[139] Many young men attending Amherst could not afford the costs of belonging to a fraternity, but felt left out of the social life of the college. They contended that having a campus commons for non-pledged men would offer an ideal place for them to gather, but until a commons could be constructed, nonaffiliated students requested that a furnished room be provided on the campus so the non-fraternity group would have a space to meet and hold social events.[140] The group, who dubbed themselves the "Lord Jeff Club," met on a regular basis, and by the fall of 1935 had members representing the club present at events that used to be open to fraternities only. The Lord Jeff Club, according to an article in *The Amherst Student,* had "no desire to undermine the fraternities."[141] Instead, the club was conceptualized as a "support and complement" to the fraternity system, "a temporary stopping place during the first few weeks of college," and an organized group for "others who have no prospect or intention of joining a fraternity."[142]

Even as the newly-formed groups defined themselves as "independents," agents who wished to preserve previous hierarchies referred to them as "non-pledged" students, focusing on what they lacked rather than what they had. Most fraternity brothers and sorority sisters shared a common belief that people were either members of their group or outsiders.[143] One expert explained that most large college campuses had a group of radical thinkers who railed against the fraternity and sorority system because it was undemocratic in that it "glorified money over brains" and preferred "a man whose father was born on the right side of the tracks and who dressed well and danced correctly, to one who hashed his way to Phi Beta Kappa."[144] She accepted these accusations as true, but dismissed the possible threat that the radical thinkers would be able to dismantle the Greek system because "thinkers are in the minority."[145] Furthermore, she stated that if one of the radically-inclined "barbarians" truly demonstrated the potential of becoming a strong campus leader, the fraternities swooped in, co-opted him and offered him a bid which usually resulted in "another rebellion surrendered weak-kneed."[146]

One former sorority member, who became a professional journalist, applauded young women for turning their backs on sorority rushing and refusing to be held up against a "mass yardstick" to determine their worthiness for membership.[147] She recalled that in her days as an undergraduate at Stanford some first-year women were inducted into sororities while others wept bitterly in their dormitory rooms trying to come to terms with being rejected.[148] The author argued that young women will face plenty of discrimination in their lives, so why inflict a "wholly unnecessary injustice" upon them during their first year of college?[149] She was delighted to see students taking the agency to remain independent and put sorority life aside.

Depression-era undergraduates conceptualized themselves as commodified beings with exchange value. Students wanted to control the means of their own production, maximize their symbolic profit and accrue prestige. Students questioned whether the traditional campus branding and commodification processes including freshmen hazing practices, hell week rituals and fraternity and sorority membership would help them further define themselves or whether shaping oneself into an "Independent" entity would give them more prestige. Clearly, students who organized themselves as "Independents" realized that it was important to distinguish themselves as a distinct class. They understood that the fate of groups is often bound up with the words that designate them and that the power to claim recognition depends on the group capacity to mobilize around a name.

NATIONAL RECOVERY ACT & GREEK HOUSES

Life in Greek houses during the early-to-mid-1930s was far from the idyllic oasis that many undergraduates may have imagined. In fact, several fraternities and sororities were struggling to survive the economic hardships of the Depression.[150] The volatile combination of the financial strain of the Depression, poor house management and the fading rah-rah spirit of the 1920s on campuses contributed to the potential demise of the Greek system. In February of 1933 three chapter houses at the University of Michigan had gone out of existence since the beginning of the school year and seven more would not be able to open the next year because of financial difficulties.[151] Sororities were facing difficult financial times and "struggling for existence" too.[152] Articles in *Newsweek* magazine chronicled the demise of several fraternities at Yale and other schools. A joke in New Haven was that the fraternity slogan was, "Join our fraternity and help us pay our mortgage."[153]

The financial floundering of Greek houses created carnivalesque situations where rushees who had once been desperate to be accepted to exclusive fraternities and sororities held newfound power because the houses were in dire need of members. One writer for the *University of Michigan Daily* gleefully described how fraternities were "scared to death" that they would fail to get a large freshmen class, so they resorted to treating "their rushees as though they were gods."[154] According to the article, freshman took full advantage of this turn of events by flagrantly disobeying the rushing rules, attending fraternity dinners to get free meals, then leaving early because they made up their minds to remain independents.[155] Some students pointed out that the elaborate fraternity-sponsored feasts that were designed to attract students to the houses proved to be ridiculously wasteful in a time of economic crisis. Most first-year students were seeking friendship and camaraderie with like-minded individuals; they did not need to be filled up with "feasts and hot air" if they wished to join the Greek system to form true friendships.[156] A student from the George Washington University criticized the amount of money spent on the rush season, stating that a large proportion of the money was wasted when one compared the percentage of students who were accepted to the number who were so "lavishly entertained in a pell-mell, catch-as-catch-can system of rushing."[157]

The lavish spending of fraternities and sororities reached crisis levels in the early 1930s. George Banta, Jr., an authority on college fraternities and publisher of over 80 Greek letter society publications, decreed that fraternities had been "riding for a fall" for several years and had finally taken it.[158] Some critics of the Greek system posited that fraternities lost their relevance on college campuses because students had no interest in "entering a run-down, wasteful, purposeless organization, which is floundering in debt and despair."[159] In the mid-to-late nineteenth century fraternities were not only social groups—they had scholarly, literary and debating interests as well. A trend started in the 1890s when fraternities became "victims of the boom era" and began going into debt and building extravagant houses.[160] In 1932 the situation was desperate and many houses were closing up. Banta posited that if houses wanted to survive they had to ask for outside help and have preceptors from national headquarters offices or from one of the strong chapters come in to take charge. The preceptor would make the young men study so they could stay in school and continue to pay house fees. Preceptors would be responsible for tackling the finances by getting alumni support, bargaining with local merchants and putting each member on a monthly payment schedule.[161] Students had to contribute to the cause of keeping their houses afloat by lowering their expectations about having ostentatious parties, "Poor people have no right to be entertained lavishly and that's what these fraternity members are—poor people."[162]

Sorority houses, too, struggled with financial issues in the early 1930s. University of Michigan Dean Alice Lloyd explained that in the past, sororities had provided female students with "dignified lodgings, unusual opportunities for friendship, comradeship and a certain stability in social life."[163] By the early 1930s most sororities resembled "glorified boarding-houses," and dormitories often offered better living conditions than sorority houses.[164] Banta believed that sororities had better chances of surviving than fraternities because the young women knew how to be sensible, stick to a budget and rent rooms out to non-members in order to make ends meet.[165]

The year 1933 heralded huge changes on college campuses and in the nation as a whole. Franklin Delano Roosevelt was sworn in as the new President of the United States, and quickly bound into action with his New Deal and National Recovery Act.[166] The first phase of the New Deal legislation, launched in 1933, focused on speedy economic recovery, the structure of the market system and the relationship between the federal government and the market.[167] Experts, including campus administrators, deans and national and local members of the Interfraternity and Pan-Hellenic Councils, took the key notions of the New Deal and applied them to saving the Greek system from economic ruin. Greek houses were forced to examine the effects of dwindling membership, lack of student interest and the financial difficulties that plagued them.[168] Fraternity and sorority houses, experiencing the aftereffects of the "sluggishness, the procrastination and the apathy" by which houses had previously conducted their financial business, had to change their ways or perish.[169] Many Greek houses collected only about 70% of the student fees they were owed.[170] Part of what made collection of fees difficult was that the relationship between members was that of "brothers" and "sisters" not landlords and tenants.[171]

University officials took cues from the New Deal and stepped in to help houses weather the economic storm by letting first-year pledges move into Greek houses,[172] establishing rules requiring each fraternity and sorority house to submit budgets and financial reports to a central agency,[173] and installing graduate students as house managers.[174] One student noted that having graduate house managers would solve two problems at once; cutting down on delinquent payments and abolishing fraternity hazing practices. Having an older house manager present would make hell-week rituals obsolete because the practices would no longer be needed as disciplinary measures. The beating of underclassmen would lose its last excuse for existence.[175] These policies of centralization and outside management echoed the key components of the New Deal initiatives.

Some universities embraced National Recovery Act style codes that stated that students who lived in Greek houses would be forbidden from taking their final exams until their house fees were paid in full.[176] The University of Michigan instituted rules in 1934 that any fraternity or sorority that had unpaid accounts receivable amounting to $200 or unpaid accounts payable above $500 after July 1 of any year would be shut down and not permitted to open the next fall. This process was designed to weed out the weaker houses that had only proved "to be parasites to Ann Arbor merchants during their existence."[177] Greek house members resented what they perceived as outside interference from paternalistic organizations, including the Fraternity Judiciary Council and Interfraternity Council. They argued that if the university wanted to enact a "New Deal" for Greek houses, the administration should take responsibility for making students pay their debts rather than closing down the houses.[178]

One adult woman who worked at a fraternity argued that the University of Michigan should help Greek fraternities and sororities survive because the houses employed 300–400 students who worked in the kitchens for their board.[179] By the mid-1930s, the federal government was providing monetary aid to more than 300,000 young people between the ages of 16 and 25, who were attending high schools and colleges throughout the nation.[180] Four thousand of the beneficiaries were in graduate school and received about $25 a month. One hundred thousand undergraduate students attending over 1,600 colleges and universities received average benefits of $15 a month, while 200,000 high school students were awarded $6 a month each. The government funds were not honorariums, but represented "wages earned for constructive work in or about the schools and communities."[181] This system of working in exchange for one's board provided students, who might be undernourished if left to their own devices, with "a standard of food suitable for their welfare."[182] In 1933 the National Student League visited fraternity and sorority houses at the University of Michigan to investigate whether they were living up to NRA restaurant codes, which defined non-profit clubs and organizations that served meals to their members as restaurants.[183] The National Student League officers accused Greek houses of underpaying their dining staff and required them to make immediate adjustments to their practices.[184] According to NRA codes, the university students who worked as waiters and dishwashers for 21 hours a week in exchange for their board at the house should be paid 26 cents an hour, or $5.20 a week. The code automatically evaluated a week's board at $3.00, so Greek houses were accused of underpaying their dining staff by $2.20 a week.[185] Most houses remedied the situation by lessening the hours that students worked each week. This solution helped to alleviate campus unemployment, since more students were needed to fill the kitchen help positions.[186]

Students who initially resisted having New Deal style policies applied to their living situations slowly began embracing the cooperative ethos of Roosevelt's plan. Fraternity houses at the University of Michigan sought to consolidate in order to save themselves from going out of existence.[187] Greek letter houses had a difficult time combining because the national societies did want their membership numbers reduced and the national constitutions prohibited their members from becoming active in another fraternity.[188] Undergraduates sought guidance from the Alumni Interfraternity Council to plead their cases to the national organizations. Amherst looked to Wesleyan for an example of how to install cooperative buying systems for the Amherst fraternity houses. The cooperative buying plans, which were based on sound financial principles, involved having ten houses combine funds to buy food items. The director, Edward G. Stephany, argued that having the houses pool funds would inspire merchants to quote lower prices in order to get that amount of trade. Amherst students were advised to keep abreast of the situation at Wesleyan to see if cooperative buying would be a viable option for Amherst fraternities.[189] One month after the article was published another article appeared in *The Amherst Student* explaining that "largely as a result of the times" people in the business world had recognized the importance of cooperation and group work.[190] This realization moved beyond the business world and into the world of college fraternities and student organizations.[191] Students at Amherst proposed that cooperative buying of standard items such as food, furniture, coal and athletic equipment would help lower expenses of fraternity houses on campus. Sociology and political science graduate students at the University of Michigan embraced the cooperative ethos by creating a cooperative eating house in 1932. By 1933 more than 100 students who "might otherwise be unable to attend the University" could eat for about $3.50 a week at the Michigan Cooperative Boarding House. In 1934, four key organizations at the George Washington University, including the student council and Intrafraternity and Pan-Hellenic councils banded together to sponsor a reception for first-year students. This cooperative endeavor was the first time that the groups worked cooperatively to put on a single impressive event rather than several smaller ones.[192]

By 1935, even the fraternities at Amherst were questioning the values embraced by the Greek system.[193] Amherst fraternities, while not facing financial ruin, needed to recruit new members in order to survive. They conducted a poll to see what their social standing was on campus and how they ranked in levels of prestige. Students from Amherst College recognized that fraternities at Eastern schools were losing status while also facing economic and ideological insecurity. They circulated a questionnaire around several private universities to gauge what problems existed. The questions included: 1) Is there a noticeable element of the student body that criticizes fraternities? 2) Is the administration in harmony with fraternities? 3) Does membership in fraternities retard intellectual progress? 4) What are some weaknesses of the fraternities? 5) How much strength do fraternities have on campus? This questionnaire is reminiscent of ones circulated by a man named Wilson Benton Heller who started the College Survey Bureau in 1912 in order to provide annual rankings of fraternities and sororities on college campuses. Heller based the comparisons on surveys of student opinions about the "importance, prominence and power" of individual Greek chapters on each campus.[194]

The Interfraternity Council did their part to attract more students by regulating the hazing rules. Hazing used to be a semester-long free-for-all where older fraternity brothers could abuse first-year students at whim. With the new rules, during the first six weeks of the college freshman were not allowed to do more than two hours of work at the fraternity house each day. All hazing had to take place in the fraternity house, except for one Saturday night during the first six weeks of school where freshman could be taken off campus and kept out past midnight.[195] Houses that violated the rushing and hazing rules faced having their misdeeds publicized in the student paper and Freshman Handbook. Houses that committed larger infractions faced monetary fines and potential disbarment from the Interfraternity Council.[196] In 1935 all forms of hazing were completely abolished by the Council of Fraternity President. The number of freshmen pledging to fraternities had been dwindling, in part, because hazing traditions were too harsh.[197] The complete termination of hazing represented a fiscal survival mechanism rather than a humanitarian strategy.

Many Amherst students believed the end of fraternity hazing was a sign that all traditions were disappearing and the college was suffering because of it.[198] Similar complaints about a lack of student interest in fraternity life were raised at Howard University when representatives from the fraternities met with first-year students. The freshmen were largely unimpressed with the presentation. When a reporter from *The Howard Hilltop* asked the young men to describe what the meeting was about they responded, "Oh nothing, a few guys just talked about ideals and things."[199]

For Depression-era undergraduates, "ideals and things" related to first-year student hazing, hell week practices and the financial and social status of Greek houses either took on supreme importance or, conversely, barely registered as issues of concern. Undergraduates located in a wide array of social positions strongly voiced their opinions about how traditions should be honored or vanquished from college campuses. The debates elucidate how Depression-era students questioned the common doxa, reconceptualized status, prestige, power and privilege and attempted to gain a sense of personal and collective power in a time of economic crisis.

Chapter Four

The Marketplace of Romance: Rating and Dating, 1935–1940

> Now everybody knows that you have to believe in a product before you can sell it successfully. The product you have to sell is YOU. And, for the most part, you have to be your own press agent.[1]
>
> —*How To Get Your Man And Hold Him*, 1936

> There was a young gal who challenged the Fates.
> By being unfair to her campus dates.
> They disparaged her manner
> And proceeded to pan her.
> Now she finds she no longer rates.[2]
>
> —*The University of Michigan Daily*, 22 October 1936

The excerpts from a mass-marketed manual and a student newspaper illuminate some key aspects of the rating and dating discourse of the mid-to-late 1930s. "Rating and dating," a term coined by sociologist Willard Waller, described systems of courtship and competition for popularity that he encountered while studying undergraduates on the campus of Pennsylvania State University in the mid-1930s.[3] In this system, undergraduates methodically ranked one another on aspects including looks, charm, clothing, conversational acumen and dancing skills as a means to delineate who was worthy of the attention of the opposite sex.

Students attending college in the years of 1935–1940 were exposed to a barrage of messages about rating, dating and moving themselves like merchandise through a dating marketplace in order to gain the esteem of their peers. Rating and dating organized gendered social interaction in a way that enabled middle-class men and women to display their commodity and to determine their market value in the peer-regulated field of campus social life. Young women understood that in order to keep their social stocks high and to achieve good ratings from their peers, they had to envision themselves as commodities and sell themselves as such in the rating and dating marketplace. Youths of both genders fashioned themselves into commodified beings who existed in a heterosexual field of exchange. Experts offered youthful readers advice on how to ensure that their "stock" ratings remained high. Males in the world of rating at dating were essentially viewed as interchangeable commodities who were judged on their appearance, social skills and their economic ability to provide a good time for young women. The students who circulated in the dating marketplace participated in the world of exchange that was mediated by peer norms and expectations about gender roles.

Young middle-class women acted as the primary architects of the rating and dating system, drawing on the gendered imagination to shape their expectations about norms and behavior in the realm of romance. The rating and dating system had the potential to empower women by furnishing them with the tools to rate men for their various attributes or lack thereof. Yet the young women who perpetuated the normative standards were, in a sense, trapped because they too had to abide by the values that they collectively created if they wished to rate dates. The peer-moderated system created interesting power dynamics—where young women set the parameters of who rated but also had to fit into often-narrow normative values themselves. Coeds who wanted to rate had to be wary of alienating their female peers by overvaluing themselves; while also walking a thin line of conforming to the expectations of their peers without exceeding them.[4] This dynamic created a circular set of relations where students could acquire prestige only through the judgment of others.[5]

Dating worked as a process of negotiation between members of both sexes, with clearly-stated rules of performance that could easily be learned by young men and women.[6] Style and performance were key components of the mid-to-late 1930s dating scene. Young women who chose to engage in the world of rating and dating operated as a "public of equals who were also competitors."[7] It makes sense that peer groups defined many of the parameters of the dating field for youths, since most middle-class college students had been immersed in, and forced to adjust to, peer culture since they started elementary school. Peer groups helped shape attitudes, values and habits that could not be completely controlled by adult institutions.[8] The importance of peer guidance increased during the Depression because the rules, restrictions and regulations generated by parents and schools weakened as the adult world crumbled under the weight of the Depression.[9]

Although peers played a significant role in the adolescent socialization process, experts including sociologists, psychologists, educators and etiquette writers took on the role of adult advisors to students in textbooks and advice books. The expert-penned texts contained similar messages that were consistently repeated and constantly reinforced in magazine articles, advice books, etiquette manuals and school texts resulting in the creation of an "extremely coherent discursive universe."[10] Authors encouraged young women to view themselves as commodities by advising readers to look at themselves from the outside, see themselves as others saw them and figure out how best to circulate themselves through the dating marketplace. Both students and experts liberally peppered their writings with marketplace metaphors to describe dating situations. Experts informed youths that people who achieved success in the dating marketplace did so because of their ability to "sell themselves to other people in a favorable light" that would help them attain the cooperation of others.[11] Some experts likened dating to "selling—you must be alert to the other person's responses. An appropriate turn of phrase and everything is won. Too much high pressure, perhaps, and everything is lost."[12] Students who desired "big returns from life in the form of popularity" were required to make big investments in the process in order to reap "high dividends on any social market!"[13] This strategy of self-commodification created a dialectical situation where young women bowed to the expectations of peers and expert authorities, while simultaneously subverting traditional gender roles by becoming savvy "economists" who actively marketed themselves in a volatile dating marketplace.[14]

In order to delineate desirable dates from the crowd, students developed their own informal polls about the attributes of others, and then constructed a hierarchical ladder where people were rated for their overall desirability. In the mid-1930s polls and surveys became important arbiters for measuring and shaping public opinion. In 1935, George Gallup created the American Institute of Public Opinion, which made polling a common phenomenon in American life. Soon surveys, opinion polls and sociological studies became the rage on college campuses. Students and experts began conducting polls of their own to tap into the belief systems of their friends, neighbors and communities.[15]

The courtship practices of the middle-class youths of the late nineteenth and early twentieth had been heavily governed by parents and marriage was seen as the end-goal of dating, but some experts argued that by the mid-1930s dating was done for dating sake. Waller found that while older forms of courtship had prepared young people for marriage by taking them through a series of progressive commitments, dating in the 1930s focused solely on thrill seeking.[16] Most youths in the 1930s were interested in achieving a level of social success and increasing their popularity without forming emotional attachments.[17] The goal of dating was attaining general popularity with peers, not embarking on a serious romance with one partner.[18] Even though many experts contended that dating was solely done to gain social prestige and popularity, I argue that the college campuses of the Depression era functioned as training grounds where youths learned how to enact the heterosexual gender roles that they would be expected to play in the future. During the 1930s the overriding expectations about healthy male and female middle-class citizens centered on men enacting the role of paternal breadwinner and women becoming wives and mothers who supported their husbands' success in the world of work.[19] Although much of the discourse about dating in the mid-1930s focused on playing the field and rating as many dates as possible to prove one's popularity, youths also looked at dating as a means to find a future husband or wife.

Popularity had social currency in the 1930s; youths who were popular had prestige in their peer groups. The symbolic capital of popularity had to be earned on a daily basis.[20] In Depression-era youth culture, the most efficient means for achieving popularity was by engaging in the competitive process of dating, because dating created and confirmed cachet on college campuses.[21] Young people had to prove their worth in the dating marketplace by dating often, visibly and multitudinously. Women attending college in the 1930s dated to elevate their social position because they could gain prestige by dating well.[22]

The fields of cultural production function as "universes of belief" where both products and the desire for products are generated at the same time.[23] Youths of the Depression era embraced the ideals of self production, self-commodification and self-promotion in the symbolic marketplace of dating. Experts and middle-class students used the language of the marketplace, the logic of capitalism and the process of self-commodification to make sense of the world of dating and to reproduce status quo gender norms in an era of extreme economic dislocations.

Dating became commodified and linked with the marketplace during the Depression era. Youths learned to market and sell themselves and to monitor their social stock levels. There was a bit of a cold-hearted edge to the rating and dating system, where control of relationships was based on the "principle of least interest" meaning that whichever party cared less about the other person maintained the power in the heterosexual marketplace.[24] Bourdieu defines interest as being present, willing to participate, admitting that the game is worth playing and that the stakes created as part of the game are worth pursuing. Bourdieu criticizes economists for incorrectly theorizing that "economic interest" is what drives everything because anthropological and historical studies show that the "social magic of institutions can constitute just about anything as an interest."[25]

Students used strategies of accumulation to maximize their symbolic profit by attempting to rate as many dates as possible. A female student's rating depended "upon dating more than anything else," Waller explained, "here, as nowhere else, nothing succeeds like success."[26] A student poll at the University of Michigan found that one of the most important factors for determining the happiness of the college student were the type and number of dates that people had.[27] Experts concurred that dating could be a source of prestige, when a student dated frequently and dated popular high-rated members of the opposite sex. Conversely, dating could function as a source of dissatisfaction for individuals who had trouble attracting acceptable dates and dating enough to rate with peers.[28] The importance of dating mattered more to young women than young men. Male students usually did not judge male peers by the number of dates they went on, but female students were more likely to judge female students by how often they went out with men. Girls who failed to date often began to feel inferior to their peers who dated frequently.[29] Experts contributed to the anxiety about rating dates by having young women ponder whether they were popular or not, and telling them "if you can not rate a date, you are a wallflower; and any girl who has sat at home on Saturday night knows how Cinderella felt when her sisters dressed for the ball."[30] Female students recognized that scoring dates would be key for attaining popularity on campus.

Status in the world of rating and dating also hinged upon avoiding being exploited by the opposite sex.[31] Males and females who engaged with each other in the field of rating and dating became extremely wary of one another. Young men feared that coeds were out to "gold dig" from them while young women worried about taking men's compliments and declarations of love seriously, because they never knew if they were being "taken for a ride" by their date.[32] This system of mutual exploitation raises questions about who was in control of the rating and dating process. On one hand, young women were supposed to appear passive and receptive to male advances, yet they also actively marketed themselves. Females compared the attributes, money spent and dating style of the men they dated, used rigorous standards to rank their suitors, and shared this information with other women. Men exchanged intimate details about their dates in "bull sessions" and competed to go out with the "campus belles."

Male undergraduates who rated the highest level of prestige usually belonged to a fraternity, possessed "smooth" manners, talked a good line, danced skillfully, dressed impeccably and had access to an automobile.[33] Young women who rated "Class A," and were therefore eligible to date the most prestigious men, had nice wardrobes, were articulate, graceful dancers and most importantly had the reputation of being popular dates.[34] Coeds who wanted to win or maintain a high level of prestige on campus had to follow a few extra rules. They "must never be available for last minute dates; they must avoid being seen too often with the same boy, in order that others might not be frightened away or get too discouraged; they must be seen when they go out, and therefore must go to the popular and often expensive meeting places; they must have many partners at the dances." [35] The discourse surrounding rating and dating began on the peer level, but soon spread to the mass media, where experts, youths and parents debated the meanings of rating and dating. Stories in student newspapers illustrate that many undergraduates took these rules to heart and applied them to their own situations in order to succeed in the world of rating and dating.

Clever coeds who wanted to be viewed as valuable commodities quickly learned to "give the impression of being much sought after" even if this was contrary to fact.[36] Since most university students on the campus were very conscious of these social distinctions and of their own position within this tightly organized social hierarchy, they realized that *appearing* popular affected their rating, social standing and the rung that they inhabited on the ladder of popularity. Having a high rating proved incredibly important for a young woman, because being an overlooked commodity in the marketplace led to disastrous drops in a woman's stock.[37]

Since a girl's standing in the marketplace determined her popularity and desirability as a date, she might be tempted to try to raise her own rating by bragging about her social successes. Some mass-market manual authors touted the benefits of acting as one's own press agent, but other writers firmly admonished their readers to forgo the temptation to discuss other dates with the men they were currently seeing, because it was a cheap way to advertise one's popularity and may serve to tarnish a young woman's image.[38] Young women were warned to be wary of "self-appointed press-agents" who attempted to secure notice for themselves, since many times the press agents had hidden agendas or social wounds lurking right below the surface.[39]

Maintaining an image of popularity proved very important for female college students of the late 1930s. In order to rate and ultimately score a date, a young woman not only had to garner male attention, but also had to make her female competitors and compatriots believe that she was popular. One expert explained that young women could keep their ratings high by covering their mirrors with photos of men, writing themselves letters, sending themselves flowers and arranging to have men call them when they knew that their house mates would be around to witness it.[40] This investment seems extreme, but female college students were caught in a vicious cycle of having to rate in order to date and vice versa. A coed had to maintain a guise of constant male attention and approval, lest her rating dip so low that she could never rate a date again. One expert consoled young women who failed to rate by explaining that many forms of popularity were available "on the present social market" and that self-management in the "business of living" was the key to accessing better ratings.[41]

Rating and dating measurement methods spread through college campuses in the mid-to-late 1930s. George Washington University students proposed that the newly-designed social calendar that listed all of the events on campus for the upcoming year could be used to measure a young woman's popularity. Young women wanted "to rate grade A, ultra popular," had to be invited to attend at least 12 of the 16 major functions on the calendar. Female students who attended at least eight but less than twelve events would be called "just plain popular," and the unfortunate young women who were asked to go to only four to eight student functions "would have to be content with semi-popularity."[42] Using quantifiable methods to track one's social status and the success or failure of others provided young women with a sense of empowerment and control, but also served to keep them constantly competing to measure up to the very standards that they created.

Many young women embraced the lighter, humorous side of the rating and dating system and used it to poke fun at both themselves and at men on campus. A group of young women known as the Damda Phi Data society at the University of Michigan developed a scale to rate the Big Men On Campus (BMOC's) according to their dating value. Men who merited a place on the list had to have dated several women from the group. After much discussion and serious consideration the young men were graded alphabetically using the following delineations: "A, smooth; B, okay; C, pass in a crowd; D, semigoon and E, spook."[43] Copies of the list could be found in several locations on the campus and appeared to have been used quite extensively. Women enjoyed the list because it let them know if men possessed the desirable traits of a good personality and dance skills and if the men were tactful, amusing, well dressed, prompt and courteous. The list contained pertinent additional information about the man's level of lasciviousness, designated by plus and minus marks next to the letter grade with "the first designating honorable intentions, the second the opposite."[44] Young female students may have focused on the humorous edge of rating and dating as a defensive measure. They knew that they were likely to be rated by their peers and that their rating would affect their dating status with young men, so they turned the tables and rated males in the same way that young women were being rated.

The "industrious women of Radcliffe" created a color-coded date rating system that was written up in both *The Howard Hilltop* and *The Mount Holyoke News*. Radcliffe women realized that they were spending too much time away from their study desks rehashing what happened on their dates the previous evening, so they developed a new method to rate their dates.[45] When the young women returned to their dormitories after an evening out they had to sign in a big book. "One ingenious student" provided the women with colored pencils and a chart that told them which colors to use to rate their date.[46] Signing in bright red pencil meant that the date provided the young woman with a "perfectly swell time." Harvard men usually averaged a green, meaning that the young woman had "just a plain nice time." Purple signified that the date was "too, too divine." Brown ratings meant that the date filled up an evening, but failed to be especially fun while writing one's name in yellow let the other young women know that the date was an "utter flop."[47] The sign-in rating system helped women to compare notes about desirable escorts and to keep their ratings up using the sign-in book as a vehicle to advertise their quantity and quality of dates. Young middle-class women attending college in the 1930s exchanged information about their dates, whom they appeared to see as mere commodities. The middle-class male students who escorted women on dates had the use value of showing the young women a good time, paying for tickets, meals and cab fare and providing women with someone with whom to be seen, yet the women seemed to value their dates more for the exchange value and prestige they could provide by translating the date into social currency that would pay off in popularity on campus.

BIG MEN ON CAMPUS & CAMPUS BELLES

Having a large number of dates helped boost student ratings, but students were well aware of the fact that quality mattered as much as quantity in the rating and dating system. Wise female students invested their energy in being seen with the most popular men on campus, because dating a BMOC boosted a young woman's rating. Because the sex ratio at many coeducational universities in the mid-1930s was six males to one female, many young women enjoyed "a relatively high position on the scale of desirability."[48] The young women attending schools with skewed sex ratios knew that they held the upper hand in the dating marketplace and many made the most of the cards that were dealt them. Co-eds wanted their dates to be campus stars, BMOCs and men "who stood above the common herd."[49]

BMOCs might be difficult to lure because they had "so many people to greet and be slapped on the back by that getting more than a smile and a 'I'll give you a break' wave is almost impossible," but if a young woman earned a date with a BMOC, her rating and popularity often skyrocketed as a result.[50] One George Washington University writer described the "glamour girls," who dated BMOCs as the ones who assumed a look of disinterest in their own status. Glamour girls walked around campus wearing dirty saddle shoes, cardigan sweaters, ankle socks and nonchalant "I'm doing all right," expressions on their faces.[51] Glamorous coeds arrived at morning classes wearing bright red lipstick and the orchid corsages given to them by their dates the night before.[52] Wearing visible signifiers, like corsages, let others know that a woman had scored a date with a BMOC the previous evening. This strategic maneuver boosted a young woman's popularity quotient and contributed to her prestige in the rating and dating system.

On campuses where the sex-ratio differences were high, non-fraternity men barely stood a chance for rating a date; these dateless men often expressed "widespread antagonism" toward female students. Waller explained that some men in the dateless group coped by taking on the role of misogynists and reading Schopenhauer.[53] One particularly embittered male student at the University of Michigan found it unfair that women benefited from operating in a field of limited competition for dates; he expressed his anguish in an article that contended that co-eds had taken on too much power, become hollow conceited snobs and acquired domineering attitudes toward the men on campus.[54] The sex ratio on campus allowed a young woman to boost herself up onto a "tottering pedestal from which only the sight of a ten dollar bill and a male chest plastered with a BMOC rating can induce her to descend." Male students had to "crawl in respect and obedience" if they wished to go on a date.[55]

Men wanted to be seen out in public with the "campus belles" just as much as women wanted to be noticed out on dates with the BMOCs. At the University of Missouri, the sex ratios were tilted in favor of the men, with many more females on campus than males. Male students, because of their short supply, were much in demand. They could spot a campus queen, discover her name and address and "make a date—all in the course of an hour or so, for there are so many more women than men that even 'slick numbers' may be dated on extremely short notice and meager recommendation."[56] Young men attending the University of Missouri could break dates with little warning and without providing an explanation. Conversely, if a coed foolishly broke a date with a fraternity man the whole fraternity would place not only the young woman, but all of her sorority sisters, on a black list which forbade all fraternity brothers to date any woman from the offending sorority house.[57]

Male undergraduates at the University of Michigan envied their peers at the University of Missouri who had their pick of campus belles. Michigan men also lamented that many of the girls who were worth dating were "mortgaged," meaning that they were going steady with one man rather than dating several men. The popular girls who were still single tended to schedule their dates two to three weeks in advance, so young men had a hard time scoring a date with them. One young man proposed that the men on campus should "boycott" the young women in order to teach them a lesson.[58] In the world of rating and dating, most experts admonished that young women should keep their competitive edge in the marketplace by playing the field rather than settling down with one partner. Young men, especially at coeducational institutions that had skewed sex ratios preferred that female students circulate through the dating marketplace rather than mortgaging themselves in long-term steady relationships. The use of market language in these passages points to the notion that women were seen as wares that could be mortgaged, bartered for and boycotted when they failed to deliver the desired goods.

Young women attending the University of Michigan responded to the boycott proposal by stating that the men who were complaining about the dating situation on campus should wake up, arguing that pure inertia mixed with vanity motivated all of the men to desire dates with the same girls[59] Men, in one female writer's estimation were "not only too lazy to find other girls who are just as nice, but too vain not to make a play for the 'belles.'"[60] Experts supported the contention that "men like girls that other men want" and argued that women should stay in good competitive form by parrying for dates in the open field, keeping their social weapons "sharp and glistening" and finding female opponents against whom to "match their steel."[61] Another expert argued that going steady cramped a young woman's style, arguing that it was "worth money in the bank" to have many young men on their dating calendars.[62] This expert advised that young women "draw up your contracts with a clause that specifies No Monopoly, Part-time Service, All-time Trust and Loyalty and a Big Thrill. Inscribe your names and let it be your policy." [63]

A young woman did not always have to resort to using steel weapons or contractual negotiations to score dates; she could instead appeal to male's inherent "sheep instincts" and herd them in her direction. All young women had to do was be nice to "boys who don't matter."[64] A student at Mount Holyoke described how a young women could be kind to inconsequential men by offering to dance with the shortest man on the dance floor, sweep around the room with him and act like she did not look ridiculous towering over him.[65] The boys would be so grateful that they would form a personal stag line around the girl and worthier males would invariably be drawn to the woman surrounded by stags.[66] The author guaranteed that males would not bother to analyze the caliber of men who composed a woman's personal stag line; they would just notice that the young woman was encircled by males and would be curious to know why.[67] Waller disagreed, stating that low-ranking students had more to gain "by abstaining from dating than from dating a person with his own rank" since being seen with someone unpopular was worse for a student's rating than not being seen at all.[68] Young men and women willingly removed themselves from the rating and dating marketplace rather than enduring the loss of prestige that came with socializing with low-ranked individuals. Being seen with people who failed to rate had the potential to taint a person's high rating with peers or to reify poor ratings.

Women who were unable to rate dates with BMOCs or attract a private stag line could still use the principles of supply and demand to keep themselves on the market. Co-eds could make themselves appear as desirable commodities by refusing to accept late dates. A passage in the advice book *Co-Ediquette* described a typical Saturday evening where the young women who did not have dates wandered aimlessly from room to room watching their friends get ready to go out. If the phone rang during this time there was "a stampede in the house like cattle galloping across the Texas Plains" as all of the females rushed toward the phone:

> A few doors open and voices call, "Was that for me?" This particular time it happens to be a male voice. One of the men at the fraternity house wants to know who hasn't a date, for he wants to "fix someone up" with one of their guests. The message is relayed from room to room. The girls look at each other blankly, and one by one they all refuse. They are eager to go out, but they are a little afraid that the man is shopping; and they would rather vegetate in boredom than admit to the voice on the other end of the wire that they have no date at that hour on Saturday night.[69]

This excerpt illuminates the key tenets of the commodified rating and dating system. Savvy young women, who recognized all other females as competitors in the dating marketplace, showed concern that men who shopped around for dates on a Saturday night might be looking for cheap goods that were left on the shelf. Enterprising females had to manipulate the marketplace to keep their stock and rating up, and accepting last-minute offers for dates lowered their own value in the marketplace. Females quickly learned to create an artificial sense of scarcity in order to keep their value high.

Surveys on college campuses demonstrated that young women heeded the expert advice to decline late dates. Men who called up a sorority or dormitory corridor to ask if there was anyone in the house who would go out faced almost certain rejection; of the one hundred and twenty women surveyed at the University of Michigan 105 responded that they would not accept offers for last-minute dates.[70] Women saw the late-hour phoning as a sign of arrogance and resented it greatly. Mount Holyoke and Smith students explained that, "Amherst boys are so conceited it isn't even funny. They call up on Saturday afternoon for a date on Saturday night and then they act as though they are doing you a favor."[71] Wise women knew not to accept the so-called "favor" because it would mark them as cheap goods and lower their rating in the marketplace. Young women learned from peer- and expert-generated discourse that if their friends found out about someone accepting late dates it would lower their ranking with peers, the first step on the slippery slope of plummeting stock ratings.

DATING BUREAUS

Undergraduates who failed to find dates by conventional means could turn to "dating bureaus" that cropped up on many college campuses of the late 1930s. Dating bureaus represented a complete commodification of the rating and dating system.[72] People of the Depression put their faith in experts to solve many troubling issues, so the scientific management of love was seen as normal and socially acceptable.[73] At most bureaus students filled out cards with their "name, height, coloring, and preferences for a date" and a suitable date would be supplied in accordance with the student's specifications.[74] Students at Mount Holyoke organized an "NRA Date Bureau" for a benefit dance on campus. They charged a five-cent fee over and above the twenty-five cent ticket price with the guarantee that they would supply female students with a "scientifically-chosen date" from a masculine branch of the registration bureau.[75]

A Campus Date Bureau opened for business at the University of Michigan in 1935, offering "to correct the lonely, dateless conditions on campus" for the mere fee of twenty-five cents.[76] The Date Bureau kept a file of personal details about each client, including lists of the social activities in which they wished to participate. The founders of the bureau believed that it would offer a "sure-fire method of bringing kindred souls together," but the sex ratio on campus reared its ugly head again. All of the calls for dates were from men and no women signed up for the service.[77] A date bureau that opened at Michigan State University a few years later took a lesson from the failed enterprise at the University of Michigan. The bureau was run by both a man and a woman who interviewed applicants extensively asking them about their "height, weight, color of hair and eyes, whether they like dancing, bridge, athletics, concerts, lectures, if they are affiliated and what kind of companionship they like—reserved, peppy, shy or talkative."[78] The introductions were "brought about by means of slips which the boy brings to the housemother at the girl's house. The housemother makes the introduction."[79] Students could also let their friends set them up on blind dates, but this option was much maligned as evidenced by the description that "some of the blind dates will be worse than going to a five-hour lab as far as the freshmen are concerned."[80] Students at the University of Michigan gambled a little in the rating and dating field; one survey of 68 women and 70 men found that all of those interviewed had been on at least one blind date. The average number of blind dates per year was 10 for women and 3 for men.[81]

YOU'VE RATED THE DATE, NOW WHERE DO YOU GO?

No matter how they scored their date, students on college campuses of the late 1930s had many options of where to go on dates. The social life on the college campuses varied by location, but events that occurred regularly on most campuses of the 1930s included college or fraternity dances, public lectures, sporting events, movies and informal gatherings for victrola dances and "necking."[82] Some of the most popular events at the George Washington University were football games, dorm-sponsored dances, dramatic performances and the homecoming ball.[83] Students could also partake in the annual Student Fiesta which featured musical comedies, revues, follies and a coronation pageant for the Fiesta Queen.[84] University of Michigan undergraduates attended basketball, football and hockey games, but according to one survey conducted in three dormitories and one sorority, 96 percent of the female students would rather attend dances or movies.[85] Other popular campus events included "hard times" parties, sleigh rides and hay rides.[86] Amherst men and Mount Holyoke women could share an evening having a beer at a local bar or restaurant, attending college lectures, playing bridge or playing record albums in a man's dorm room.[87] Howard University students held scavenger hunts, theater productions, parties and dances.[88] At Howard University each class—freshman, sophomore, junior and senior—sponsored its own individual prom.[89]

A remarkable number of dances were held on college campuses in the mid-to-late 1930s. Mount Holyoke sponsored an informal dance every Saturday night.[90] At the University of Michigan fraternities alone sponsored over 300 evening dance events a year; during football season a record number of 35 dances were held on campus in one night.[91] Amherst students ran into some trouble when six fraternity dances took place on the same evening. Many uninvited guests appeared and "the cold weather forced many a chilled reveler to resort to the bottle in search of artificial weather-stripping."[92] The writer did not go into details of what occurred next, but summarized the story by stating that Amherst students needed to learn how to behave like gentlemen otherwise, "no young lady will ever dare to set a dainty foot within the town of Amherst, and before long we shall be dancing with each other."[93]

The highlights of every school's social season were the formal proms sponsored by fraternities, the universities or separate classes. Prom trotters, especially those at Mount Holyoke and Amherst, covered a great deal of territory in their trotting. Young women from Mount Holyoke often attended five or six proms at well-known schools each year. On the eve of Amherst Lord Jeff Prom *The Amherst Student* performed a survey to see how their dance ranked against other schools. Many young women ranked Amherst third to Princeton and Dartmouth.[94] Most Smith girls liked Dartmouth dances the best and rated the Dartmouth Winter Carnival as "more fun than anything all year." Smith students concurred that in contrast to Dartmouth, dances at Amherst were merely "all right." [95] Women from Smith College appeared to rank first in the hearts of Amherst men the weekend of the Junior Prom of 1936. Of the 170 Junior Prom guests 53 were from Smith. True to form, women from Mount Holyoke placed second on the list of prom guests, with the women from Vassar taking third place. Students traveled from the three aforementioned schools and from seventeen additional women's colleges to attend the event.[96] Men who trotted to the Junior Prom at Mount Holyoke could run into a difficult time finding accommodations. One Mount Holyoke undergraduate quipped that the WPA could profit by constructing a large hotel "down in the button-field to take care of the men who arrive for the weekends." South Hadley lacked a hotel like the Northampton, which set up rows of army cots in its ball room so men could sleep there when they were attending proms at Smith College.[97] The descriptions of proms in the student newspapers illustrate that students who wished to rate dates had to have enough money to spend on clothing, lodging, train fare and other travel expenses if they wanted to prom trot with their friends. Young women were encouraged to share clothing and accessories with friends and sorority sisters, but the clothing items had to be up to a certain standard to make them acceptable formal wear.[98]

Formal dances proved to be the most critical social events of the season, and students often obsessed about them for months in advance. Young women fretted over who would ask them, what they would wear and how they would perform in the very public arena of the dance floor. The dance floor at formal dances represented a site akin to the New York stock exchange where people could observe their peer's social status rise and plummet at alarming rates.[99] Dance etiquette in the 1930s dictated that females assume a passive stance while men took on the role of actively pursuing interaction. Young men, even though they were in the numerical majority on most campuses, had the opportunity to pick from a plethora of female partners. Most campus dances had a system for "cutting in" where men stood in stag lines at the edge of the floor and waited to cut in on dancing pairs by tapping the shoulder of the desired young woman. If a dance was a "cut" affair, it was generally accepted that a young woman had to dance with whoever cut in, even if she would rather stay with her current partner.[100] Young women who resisted this notion were told that "no matter how much you believe in the equality of women, remember that on the dance floor, the man is your master."[101] According to advice and etiquette manuals, young women should revel in this loss of control, because getting "clapped" many times in one evening was a badge of popularity. This badge advertised a young woman's high rating, guaranteeing that her stock would skyrocket.

Some young co-eds disagreed with this advice, and delved deeply into the Emily Post etiquette guide to find a way to circumvent the cutting rules. Several young men at George Washington University were angered by a woman who would not let anyone cut in during the course of the whole evening, "She had made the issue doubly certain by dancing with her eyes closed."[102] When young men unsuccessfully tried to cut in she would say "Young man, can't you see that my eyes were shut?" much to the men's embarrassment.[103] When asked why she did this, she haughtily replied, "If this question is to become a burning issue on campus, ranking in importance with the election of the queen of the Fiasco—I mean Fiesta—and the erection of the flagpole, I suppose that I shall have to explain the matter, though I must say I have never seen such a mass of socially uninformed people in such a small area." The woman then quoted Emily Post saying that it was socially acceptable for a woman to dance with her eyes shut if she wished to communicate that she was not interested in taking cuts.[104]

Emily Post provided some leeway for males in regard to cutting rules as well. Some men raised the question of how long they had to wait before rescuing their beloved dates the men who cut in. Emily Post dictated that cutting was an almost universal practice, so if someone cut in on a man, for the time being he just had to live with it. "However, as soon as someone else cuts in on the first cutter-inner, you are at liberty to cut back."[105] Men were allowed to "rescue" their dates by cutting back in if the young man who cut in was monopolizing her, or she him, for too long a period.[106]

Students who found it difficult to negotiate through all of the cutting rules faced the stiffer challenge of "getting stuck" on the dance floor with one partner and having nobody cut in. Getting stuck was popularly perceived as a massive social failure. Being stuck on the dance floor represented a nightmare for a young woman, because it advertised her unpopularity in a showcase where the eyes of her peers were fixed upon her in rapt attention. A worst-case scenario in an etiquette book depicted a young woman being guided deftly around the floor by one partner, while watching out of the corner of her eye for the next man to cut in. Meanwhile her roommate was being "clapped" on the shoulder and cut in on at a breathless pace. The author described the mounting tension in vivid detail:

> Surely, someone will cut. But no one does. Around the room four times and five. What is your partner thinking? Is he casting eyes at your roommate who is surrounded by a group of eager men? Does he want to be rid of you? At last, that man in the corner is coming to your rescue; but there is no gleam of recognition in his eye as you go past, ten times, twelve. The music ends with a sudden crescendo . . . The music starts again. He looks hopelessly about and starts dragging you around the floor once more and not even his forced politeness any longer conceals the fact that he knows that he is stuck.[107]

Men hated being stuck almost as much as women did, because being seen with an obviously unpopular woman lowered a male's rating in the eyes of his peers. Also, a man was held honor bound by a code of chivalry to continue dancing with a young woman until someone cut in or she suggested that they stop. Males trapped in the precarious situation of being stuck on the dance floor still were expected to fulfill the performative role of a good escort and to obey the traditional rules and norms of dance-floor etiquette, meaning that young men could not abandon a woman on the dance floor for a hotter commodity unless the woman suggested that they stop dancing and go their separate ways. If young women chose not to flee the dance floor, they had little control over who their next partner would be, but most women wanted men to cut in as often as possible. A young woman who got stuck had few options for getting herself out of the situation. She had to wait patiently and passively for another man to come to her rescue and save her from the embarrassing situation. Therefore, her plummeting stock was visible to every evaluating eye on the dance floor. Most young men knew, or could easily tell, which women were popular. Men avoided dancing with unpopular women, not only because it lowered male ratings, but because they feared that clapping the shoulder of an unpopular female could result in "an evening's sentence."[108]

The predicament about being stuck became the fodder for jokes that appeared in campus newspapers and national magazines. One joke involved a young woman from a senior class complaining that a freshman cut in while she was dancing with one of the senior campus big shots. The first-year student explained his supposed breach of etiquette, "Listen, lady, I'm working my way through college and the guy dancing with you was waving a dollar bill at me."[109] An article that appeared in *True Confessions* had a young woman explaining a worst-case scenario of being stuck on the dance floor. She described the utter horror of "knowing that a boy is dancing past the stag line and waving a five-dollar bill behind your back as an offer to anyone who'll come take you away!"[110]

Experts believed that young women with high stock ratings loved stag lines because they could enjoy having men scuffle for their attention and compete in the marketplace for the honor of dancing with a highly-rated female. The stag arrangement invited public humiliation for less popular girls by leaving all of the power of cutting in to the boys.[111] An unpopular young woman, also known as a "tag widow," had one of two choices: she could retreat to the dressing room or to the side of the man who brought her to the dance. Young women who got stuck and escaped to the safety of the powder room were advised not to advertise the fact that they were stranded by the stags. Looking for comfort and commiseration within a community of other young women proved to be a dangerous option that had the potential to haunt a young woman in the future. The "wise prom-trotter," even when she was with her girlfriends, understood the "wisdom of keeping up the fiction of her own popularity."[112] One historian notes that changing standards of emotional management came to the fore in the 1930s, with experts advising young women not to reveal embarrassing secrets about themselves to their female friends.[113] Many expert-penned texts warned that relying on other young women to be emotional crutches in matters of the heart could prove harmful, because women unconsciously disliked each other and saw all other women as potential competitors for men.[114] This belief that young women innately disliked one another resonates with the notion of competitive individualistic sisterhood, where women were supposed to help their female friends, but also engage in constant competition for male approval, even if it meant competing against a "sister."

Even women with high ratings found the presence of stag lines at college-sponsored events to be nerve-wracking. Several students from Mount Holyoke argued that stag lines should be completely eliminated because dances had become a "combination of shoving and toe-smashing, with the male escorts receiving most of the brunt."[115] Totally eliminating stag lines would be the only way to get rid of the problem, but in lieu of that, the stag line should be moved to the background, so the dancing could continue "unchallenged."[116] Students had tried to remedy the situation a year earlier by instituting a new system of cutting and a new location for the stag line. The somewhat complicated solution involved cutting being allowed only during alternate dances, which would be indicated by a placard on the stage, and by having stags on only one side of the room as designated by ropes between columns.[117] The new system represented an "honest attempt to counteract the faults which have led to extensive, if vague, criticism of Saturday night dances."[118]

The pushing and shoving in the stag lines at the University of Michigan had escalated to the point that only people who arrived to dances in couples were allowed to enter the dance hall. Students who came as stags and single females were required to wait in the lobby while people were dancing, and hope that somebody approached them during an intermission.[119] Some students defended the rules by stating that the system was instituted to protect young women from over-aggressive stags. Co-eds who wanted to dance were told to make themselves available in the lobby, not to hide their light under a bushel and not to scurry off into a corner with friends because it would make men too scared to approach them.[120] Experts supported these statements and added that young women should not congregate with the wallflowers of the room because they would be judged by the company that they kept and it was "just plain stupid to get yourself identified with the forgotten girls."[121] In the rating and dating scene, being a "forgotten girl" represented a worse fate than being one of the 1930s forgotten men. Young women had to keep their composure, maintain their poise and manage their social stock rating whenever they appeared in a public realm where they would be visible to their peer group. The discourse about rating and dating on college campuses contains many allusions about women judging other young women. Some of these allusions come from expert-penned texts; others appeared in student newspaper descriptions of dances and social events where young women passed judgment on peers' clothing choices, hair styles and dates. In the peer culture of the Depression era, the young women who constructed and maintained the rating and dating norms were highly unforgiving of social missteps on the part of their female counterparts.

WHO PAYS?

Most people who succeeded in rating and dating had access to expendable cash. Having money to spend on dating was equally important for young men and young women. Men were expected to pay for most of the expenses on a date, but women who wanted to rate with their peers had to dress for the part by constantly keeping up with fashion trends and having the necessary clothing for formal dances.[122]

Consumerism and dating had become intimately entwined in the early twentieth century and the trend continued throughout the 1930s. Even with the national cash flow running at low ebb, most dates still involved a female and a male going to a public place and purchasing something: tickets to a movie or show, admission to a dance, or even a Coke at the corner store. Generally, men were expected to pay for their date's entertainment, transportation and meals. One expert author explained that the old-fashioned courting practice of spending an evening in a woman's family parlor was much cheaper and simpler than modern day customs of going out to movie theaters and restaurants.[123] Collegiate youths had to navigate a veritable minefield of potential social gaffes when it came to deciding who should pay for a date and had to negotiate the power dynamics entrenched in the meaning of paying for a date.

The process of men paying for the evening's entertainment served to reify the gender dynamics of men as providers and women as dependents. Some women enjoyed the dependent role, but others expressed concerns that they would be expected to reward men with sexual favors to balance the scales. Emily Post's book had a whole section about who should pay for a date, arguing that in the modern era of the 1930s young women were competing with men in politics, professions and most every other realm, so it was ridiculous to cling to the notion that men should pay for everything on a date. Post proclaimed that perhaps in the Victorian era young women had to be dependent on men for protection, but in the modern days of the 1930s women's earning power and professional equality created a situation where women could pay for dates without putting the men in positions of embarrassment.[124]

Many males plead for the widespread adoption of the "Dutch treat" plan, where men and women split the costs of dating in half or took turns paying for dates, since campus surveys consistently showed that co-eds had more spending money at their disposal than their male counterparts.[125]

Men's coffers were often drained by dating and by always being expected to pay. One student writer praised the "very brave young man who takes his girl out on a Sunday night with 97 cents or some such restraining sum in his pocket and has her order first so he will know what he can afford for himself," and contended that the strapped-for-cash male "would probably have a definite reaction if he know that rattling in her purse was a sum three times his own.[126] One political science student attending the University of Michigan wrote a letter to the student newspaper explaining how he presented an itemized bill to the woman he was dating at the end of the week. The bill usually included charges like the following:

Movies.	$1.40
Cab fares.	$1.00
The dance Friday.	$2.65
Beer.	$0.90
Hot chocolate.	$0.85

If the total bill for their dates was $6.80 he believed that the woman owed him $3.40 for her half, because she probably had as much fun being with him as he did with her.[127] He added that women probably felt degraded when they leaned on young men for economic support, so shouldering some of the expense on dates would prove empowering for females.[128] Michigan women did not concur with this statement at all; no matter how much fun they had on dates, they still, for the most part, wanted the men to pay. Undergraduate men at the George Washington University warned other men who favored the idea of Dutch dating not let the co-eds know it.[129]

Young women, according to a campus survey conducted at the George Washington University, disapproved of Dutch dating. Several co-eds explained that paying their own way made them lose their dependence on men and if a woman became too independent she would "lose the feeling that she has to please him."[130] An expert author voiced a similar opinion, stating that it went against female instincts to pay their own way, "yet thousands of girls and women are doing it and something in them is shriveling all the time."[131] Most men still believed that they had to pay for theater tickets, meals, taxis and any other expenses lest they be branded as "gigolos or parasites."[132] Young women who were in the early phases of dating believed that if young men asked them out, the men should be prepared to cover all expenses incurred on the date. The dynamics were allowed to shift a bit once a couple began going steady; several girls interviewed stated in cases of steady dates women sometimes "shouldered the entire expense" for a date.[133] Emily Post advised that if a woman was paying for a man's meal at a restaurant she should either order the dinner and pay for it in advance or tell the head waiter to bring the check to her in the ladies dressing room so that the man will not have to endure the humiliation of having a woman pay for him in public.[134] Even though Post stated that she believed women could contribute to paying for dates, this last piece of advice gives the impression that young men naturally were supposed to pay for dates but that in the special circumstances of the Depression young women could pitch in. One author stated that even if females agreed to pay their own way on a Dutch date, they instinctually began to hate the situation. In a properly-ordered gender universe, men were supposed to pay for the pleasure of women's company; when they failed to do this, it "roused all kinds of doubts" in women's minds.[135]

The Howard Hilltop ran a satirical advice column entitled "Anty Toxin" which included a letter from "Disillusioned Dutch Boy," who said that he had written to Anty Toxin earlier that year because his girlfriend would not pay her own way on dates. Anty Toxin said that she would send him a list of women who would pay their own way. The Disillusioned Dutch Boy complained:

> You sent me the list—but you ought to see the girls. I didn't think there were that many ugly women in the world. One is knock-kneed and cross-eyed, one is as big (literally) as an elephant and another is at least seventy years old—and has flat feet. And I can't get rid of them. They call me up at all hours of the day and night and want to take me to the show. They would pay my way anywhere, but I don't want to go. Please, Anty Toxin, please tell me how to get rid of these chicks and get my old girl back.[136]

Anty Toxin's only response to the Dutch Boy was "Ha! ha!" with the implicit message being that young men who tried to shirk their duties of paying for everything in the rating and dating marketplace got what they paid for.

Some experts advised young women not to go Dutch because it might embarrass young men. They insisted that it was much better to date on what a young man could manage to pay for, even if it was nothing. One author explained that considerate girls would never expect their dates to spend more money on them than they could afford, especially since so many young men needed to use their money to pay for college expenses.[137] Conversely, a wise young woman would not embarrass a young man by lavishing him with expensive forms of entertainment that he would be unable to reciprocate.[138]

One method that young people used to navigate the choppy waters economic waters of paying for dates was to make sure to keep the outing as inexpensive as possible. Students at the George Washington University instituted rules forbidding corsages from being worn to the proms of 1933, '34 and '35 so that more students could attend while still remaining within their budgetary constraints.[139] Men at Michigan argued there were many places on campus where students could have a swell time for a dollar,[140] and that most co-eds were easygoing enough that they could enjoy one of the less expensive venues.[141] Experts and students advised young women to keep expenses in mind when they were out on a date, suggesting that youths do things that cost no money, including taking walks together, attending free concerts and sitting in the park.[142] *The Mount Holyoke News* printed a list of the five essential qualities of an ideal female date: "1. She doesn't eat much; 2 She's good looking; 3. She doesn't eat much; 4. She's a good dancer; 5. She doesn't eat much."[143] One expert admonished females who were dating males of modest means not to clamor to go to expensive places and not to order the most expensive items from the menu, stating that, "If you do, he will fly from you like the plague."[144] Another expert framed the same sentiment more positively by assuring female readers who ordered the cheaper items on the menu would be guaranteed of sending their "stock to a new high."[145] Young women had to maintain the delicate balance of valuing themselves as worthwhile commodities, while keeping their expectations in check, in order to avoid being disappointed or to proving disappointing to their dates.

Female students at the George Washington University who were tired of the traditional gender roles of the rating and dating system created a carnivalesque situation by sponsoring a Sadie Hawkins dance in 1939. The tradition of Sadie Hawkins events debuted in the Al Capp comic strip "Li'l Abner" in November 1937. The comic-strip character Sadie was well known in her town of Dogpatch for being "the homeliest gal in the hills." Sadie's wealthy and powerful father feared that his daughter would become an old maid, and tried to prevent this fate by creating a foot race where all of the unmarried women in town could chase down the bachelors and make them marry them.[146] By the late 1930s, events based on the Sadie Hawkins theme where women were allowed to take the initiative to ask men out and pay for the date had "swept the nation." *Life* magazine reported that over 200 colleges held Sadie Hawkins Day events in 1939.[147] For the dance at George Washington University, women were expected to pay for both their own and their dates' admission fees to the dance. Refreshments at the event would only be sold to females.[148] In further contradiction to the standard gender norms of the 1930s, females were expected do all of the cutting in on the dance floor for the entire evening.[149]

Both males and females expressed excitement about the opportunity to turn the tables on the usual gender norms that ruled the dating scene. Young men eagerly agreed to have women foot the bill for the date, while female undergraduates crowed jubilantly about having a chance to usurp gender norms and "get even" with the males who appeared to hold most of the power in the dating field.[150] Girls who usually had to wait to be asked out welcomed the "golden opportunity for all of the so-called popular boys on campus to find out how popular they really are."[151] Young men were excited for women to get a taste of what it felt like to be in the male role in the dating marketplace. One male undergraduate proclaimed that the Sadie Hawkins dance represented a "rare occasion when the mere college male assumes his rightful status of an equal with a coed—a coed who will, once she leaves G Street, begin demanding 'equality' with men."[152] Men would be allowed to enjoy being asked out, rather than doing the asking and having someone pay for the date rather than paying for both of them.

The young women gleefully used the night of the Sadie Hawkins dance to "even up a few scores" by bringing into play some of the same tricks that BMOCs had relied upon throughout their college years.[153] Women especially enjoyed exploiting their power to cut in on the dance floor to torment young men who were used to holding the power to cut in on dancing pairs. A female writer described how one young man, who was stuck on the dance floor for a full 20 minutes, was seen smiling hopefully at an attractive young woman from the Phi Delt sorority who approached him. Instead of rescuing him from being stuck, the Phi Delt just "murmured a mild hello in his direction" and continued to cruise the dance floor to find someone more worthy of her attention.[154] Two women employed the "time-honored method of waving ten dollar bills to save themselves from being stuck with their 'duty cuts.'" Some other female stags walked around the dance floor critically surveying the male goods and finally stating, "after looking them over, I think I'll have to go cut my own date.'"[155] While the males enjoyed having everything paid for by somebody else experiencing the ego-bruising dance floor politics of being stuck proved humbling to say the least. The co-eds fully enjoyed the overturning of usual gender norms, which raises the question of how much the dating marketplace would have been altered if young women paid their own way or paid fully for their dates and themselves.

SEXUAL ETIQUETTE

Young woman knew that their rating as a date would either lead to more dates or being overlooked. They recognized that men discussed their dates and compared notes about young women's levels of responsiveness to sexual advances. Women had to maintain their balance and walk a thin line between being a "hot number" or an "icicle." Getting a reputation for being too forward or too frigid could permanently ruin a young woman's rating. Female undergraduates had to be savvy, because word of mouth advertising was the most effective means of keeping one's stock high. If a young woman was saddled with a reputation for being an unresponsive date, her rating might plummet, never to rise again. Some undergraduates heeded the expert advice and argued that kisses were symbols of affection, but kissing could become a "pretty tawdry and stupid symbol when overworked and used indiscriminately."[156]

When dealing with sticky subjects like sexuality and petting, many experts tended not to overstep the boundary between youth peer culture and authoritarian culture. Instead of voicing rules and regulations about dating and sexual behavior, many manual writers borrowed survey methodology from sociologists, effectively utilizing expert techniques to collect, process and report information from the peer group rather than constructing answers themselves. Therefore, young people who turned to popular publications to read expert advice on issues of gender norms, dating, necking and petting often received responses culled from surveys of their own national peer group.[157] The Depression era saw an emergence of surveys, polls and sociological studies that became the predominant means of collecting "empirical" evidence about normative youth ideals and behavior. Young people and the experts who tabulated and published the results of the polls entered into a dialectical relationship, where young people generated the raw data and opinions that made up the normative statistics, yet the publication of this data exposed and reinforced dominant cultural patterns onto the group that initially generated the norms.

Experts and youths discussed kissing, necking and petting in mass-market manuals, textbooks and student publications. For young people, petting, meaning any sexual contact short of intercourse, was increasingly incorporated into a normative set of behaviors.[158] Experts had a more difficult time accepting the petting practices of young people as normal. Many critics of modern youthful mores blamed the concurrent rise of car culture and the commodification of courtship for making it possible for dates to occur in faraway places, beyond the chaperonage of prying parental eyes. Experts contended that youths of the 1930s conceptualized their cars as "rolling parlors" that could be used as a place for sexual expression, experimentation and even intercourse. Automobiles gave young people a private place to engage in petting.[159]

Depression era manuals and textbooks linked ill-earned popularity with wanton sexual behavior. The highest possible price paid for promiscuous petting was a precipitous drop in a young woman's rating in the dating marketplace. The expert authors, both male and female, who addressed issues of sexuality, placed the burden of "sexual brinkmanship" squarely on the shoulders of young women.[160] Females were held accountable for curbing most sexual activity on their dates, and if they failed for any reason, it was perceived as their own fault. One female expert explained that if women wanted to hold a man's interest, they had to learn to hold them off; females should be cordial and friendly on dates, but should always remember that they held the "reins" in their hands. It was up to women to "steer the course and to know when to put on the brakes."[161] Another female expert explained that most young men were out for a good time, either mentally or physically, so it was the responsibility of the young women to learn how to keep men captivated without "giving it all."[162] She advised female readers to become good listeners and refrain from talking about themselves on dates if they wanted to keep young men interested in them.[163]

When it came to issues of petting, men on college campuses had learned to manipulate both the marketplace and their dates to some degree. Henry A. Bowman, author of *Marriage for Moderns,* advised female readers that collegiate males might attempt to turn the rating and dating system against young women who refuse to comply with male wishes to pet. He explained that young women need not yield to young men's desire to pet, even when the males threatened to use their influence to make it impossible for girls to get other dates. The best a young man could likely do to ruin a woman's chances of getting other dates was "to dissuade a few of his closest friends or fraternity brothers," Bowman went on to contend that "in most cases he is bluffing and his bark is worse than his bite."[164] In his study of rating and dating, Waller found that sorority sisters consistently worried about being blacklisted by fraternity brothers as icy dates because it affected not only the young woman who refused to pet, but her entire sorority house. Many sorority members feared that refusing to pet with fraternity brothers could cause their own ratings to dip with males, while also having the additional negative side effect of their social stock dropping with their female peers as well.

Experts explained to female readers that young men often used talk of their sexual experiences to boost their own ratings with their peer group. Young men, according to experts, liked to exaggerate their exploits in order to impress their male friends. College men, who lived amongst their peers, were especially prone to embellishing the facts in order to gain acclaim during a bull session and to make themselves the center of attention of gullible underclassmen.[165] Waller contended that "verbatim transcriptions from fraternity bull sessions showed that almost all of the participants pretended to have a ruthless attitude toward women that they really did not feel."[166] Even if the men were bluffing and boasting, the gossip they created could have a strong effect on a young woman's reputation, popularity and rating.

Men who enjoyed bragging to their friends about their sexual exploits could "inspire a dangerous run of popularity" for young women.[167] One expert warned that kissing a fraternity man may as well be done on the fifty yard line of the school stadium on the day of a big football game, because men engaged in constant bull sessions and spread the word about fast girls very quickly.[168] Expert authors counseled young women who were interested in keeping high ratings to make sure that their names did not come up too often in young men's conversations, because "Boys like their girls to rank high. No boy likes to hear his girl's name bandied about freely and lightly. . . . Boys don't like second-hand models either."[169] Girls who petted in order to gain popularity often found that they were only popular because they petted on dates and young men found them as "attractive and convenient" means to an end.[170]

The rules and norms of the rating and dating system forced young women to keep constant track of their status in the marketplace and monitor the status of their competitors in order to ensure that they were still rating as hot commodities and not losing their market value when compared to their peers. Manuals and textbooks advised young women to obsess about the status of their social stock and their rating in the dating marketplace. The experts counseled young women to use their intelligence to charm young men, score dates and outwit their female competitors.

The rating and dating system essentially was constructed and maintained by the young women who participated in its practices. But the rating and dating system was built on the foundations of gender norms that had been shaken during the earlier part of the decade. The female undergraduates did their part to resurrect some of the ideologies about men as providers and women as dependents in order to assuage the crisis of masculinity generated by the Great Depression.[171] The female architects of rating and dating empowered themselves by defining the criteria by which they would be judged, by deducing how best to market themselves to the public and by learning to compete for what they desired. The downside of this system was its premise that women had to compete against one another, act in conniving ways and sometimes sell themselves out in order to gain the prize of popularity.

Participants in the rating and dating realm contributed to the maintenance of heterosexual patriarchal normative values and upheld traditional conservative gender roles as the means to access popularity with peers. This system ultimately created dynamics where young women competed with one another and kept other females in check so that males would not have to exert much effort in keeping women preoccupied and disinterested in academic achievement. Males suffered in the rating and dating system by being conceptualized as mere commodities that women would use, discuss and discard without much thought.

The "battle of the sexes" took on a decidedly commercial tone during the economically-constricted years of the Great Depression. Both males and females appeared to embrace the practice of conceptualizing themselves as commodities to be bought, sold, mortgaged, bargained for, shelved, advertised and rated during the mid-to-late 1930s. The language of commerce appeared with stunning regularity in mass-marketed advice manuals, expert-authored texts and in the writings of students themselves. The anxiety generated by the lack of material wealth in the 1930s inspired youths and experts to market the one commodity that they had at their disposal at all times: themselves. The rating and dating system effectively blurred the boundaries between finance and romance, ultimately creating an unclear vision of which gender truly held the reins in the romantic marketplace.

Chapter Five

The Price of Wedded Bliss: Companionate Marriage and Its Discontents, 1935–1940

> Every normal girl, every normal woman, wants a husband. That desire for a mate and marriage is a vital part of her being. It is a fundamental craving, as natural as eating, breathing and wishing to live.[1]
>
> —*How to Win and Hold a Husband*, 1940

> Mr. President, we have been getting a fine technical education, but no preparation at all for what we consider one of the most important relations in life; we mean marriage. We know how to build bridges, but not a happy home life.[2]
>
> —Letter to a college president from five male Midwestern undergraduates, 1935

In 1935 college students from around the nation gathered in Orange, New Jersey to indict American society for failing the country's youth. The young people were angry about the economic situation of the country and the lack of jobs available to young people, but mainly they were angry about marriage. In "The Trial by Jury in the Case of Youth vs. Society" young people accused adult society of being indifferent to and ignorant of the problems of youth in respect to marriage. The students argued that they were unable to marry due to lack of employment and that they were receiving inadequate instruction about choosing a mate and insufficient sex instruction.[3] Members of the American Youth Congress including YMCA leaders, labor union representatives, young Communists and representatives from various religious groups, began meeting regularly in 1934 to debate about the issues that most affected America's youth. On July 4, 1936 the young people created "A Declaration of the Rights of American Youth" in which they declared that their generation was "rightfully entitled to a useful, creative, and happy life" that included access to "educational opportunities, steady employment at adequate wages, security in time of need, civil rights, religious freedom, and peace."[4] These demands covered the spectrum of personal and political issues and demonstrated that youths recognized themselves as a cohesive unit that could make demands on the government.[5]

Students from around the country concurred with the accusations railed at society. Many expressed feeling intellectually and emotionally ill-equipped to create successful marriages. Young people initiated a groundswell of support for university-sanctioned marriage and family courses to be offered to all interested parties. Students demanded that the "marriage problem" be formally addressed through marriage and family courses, weekend-long parleys and campus lectures by professional speakers on the topic of making wise choices for marriage. Most college students had experienced the social whirl of rating and dating; they knew how to flirt, interact and have relationships with members of the opposite sex. By the late 1930s students were searching for something deeper and were ready to make commitments that the Depression had put on hold. Unlike the shallow pursuit of popularity inherent in the rating and dating system, the pursuit of marriage was considered a serious undertaking by many young people. They wanted expert advice about how to proceed and demanded that their concerns be addressed.

Marriage, in the sociopolitical context of the late 1930s, became freighted with multiple meanings. Young people envisioned the ability to marry as a sign of returning prosperity, a means to escape parental authority and a way to establish a sense of emotional and economic stability after years of upheaval. As the 1930s progressed young women described marriage in many different ways including a vocation, a default option and something to pursue with great vigor. No matter what motivated them, students of the 1930s actively sought to improve their futures and make peace with their pasts by preparing for the rite of passage that had been out of reach during the earlier days of the Great Depression. Undergraduates of the late 1930s wanted to get married and demanded that expert adults provide them with the information to proceed.

This chapter explores how improving economic conditions enabled young people to embark on the path toward marriage and what marriage meant to the youths and experts of the late 1930s. Young people worried about finding desirable mates in the marriage marketplace or being overlooked altogether. Experts—including professional psychologists, sociologists and mass-market manual writers—advised young women to inventory their assets and liabilities, raise their caches of symbolic capital and prepare themselves to look for a husband using the same methods that they would have applied to seeking a job just a few years earlier. In most expert texts, young men were portrayed merely as the desirable commodities that women would hunt down and ensnare into marriage. Experts and youths believed that middle-class life was under threat by the decline in marriages and looked to the language of the marketplace, the logic of capitalism and the process of self-commodification to make sense of their situation. This interest in marriage exposes both expert and student investment in reproducing traditional gender norms, family relationships and the heterosexual patriarchal familial social order.

Many middle-class college-educated youths of the mid-to-late 1930s were eager to wed and to begin new chapters of their lives, but they demanded expert guidance because they wanted to have marriages that were different from their parents.[6] Youths wanted to form unions based on sexual attraction, mutual devotion and equal investment from both partners; they wanted companionate marriages.[7] The concept of the companionate marriage was first described by Denver judge Benjamin Lindsey in the mid-1920s and popularized by educators, sociologists and psychologists. Youths embraced the ideal of having marriages where their spouse would be their best friend on whom they could rely for support, understanding, emotional intimacy, romance and fun.[8] The notion of a companionate marriage barely had time to take root before the economic crisis of the 1930s delayed the possibility of the movement bearing fruit.

The college-educated middle-class youths of the 1930s had higher expectations for their marriages than people of previous generations. Modern companionate marriages were conceptualized as voluntary arrangements "based on equality and respect" and a joyous union of two personalities.[9] Many middle-class college-aged women of the 1930s envisioned marriage as the most important event in their lives and had romantic visions of how a companionate marriage would work as a perfect blending of two personalities.[10] The companionate marriage ideal elevated people's expectations of the rewards that marriage could provide, but many couples ended up disappointed with the reality.[11] Marriage and family expert Ernest R. Groves warned young people that they were creating unrealistic visions about the intimacy and emotional fulfillment that being married would provide.[12] Groves explained that in earlier decades the struggle of life was so difficult and the economic advantages of being married were so great that there was no opportunity to overload marriage with expectations.[13] Advice columnist Dorthea Dix also advised young people to lower their expectations about marriage to avoid disappointment in the future.[14]

The economic dislocations and deprivations of 1930s created a rigid and role-bound form of the companionate marriage that focused more on fulfilling traditional gender roles rather than on developing a mutually-fulfilling partnership.[15] Ruth Feldstein explains that during the Depression era members of the public embraced conservative gender roles where healthy, male citizens were expected to be paternal breadwinners for their families and healthy female citizens were delegated the roles of being wives and mothers.[16] In the ideal companionate marriage both the man and the woman would enjoy romance, emotional fulfillment and an egalitarian relationship based on shared ideals and interests. Women often found the reality of married life somewhat lacking. This discrepancy between ideal and real created emotional tensions that were most often felt by and mediated by women, since females were usually held responsible for making marriages work.[17]

Collegiate youths expressed doubts that their middle-class parents and peers could provide adequate answers to the questions they were raising about how to form successful companionate marriages based on love, sex and mutual respect. While collegians seemed satisfied in gleaning information about the world of rating and dating from bull sessions and gossip with their friends, students of the late 1930s took marriage very seriously. Youths demanded concrete advice from experts about choosing the right mate, communicating effectively and having satisfying sexual relations.[18]

The movement for marriage and family instruction represents one of the most blatant examples of pan-campus student organizing the late 1930s. This brand of student activism appears conservative and somewhat retrograde when compared with Marxist movements and anti-war organizing efforts that were occurring on college campuses during the same period. Yet the passion and persistence that students dedicated to learning how to have successful marriages proves remarkable. Late-twentieth century historian Beth Bailey describes the rise of marriage and family courses on college campuses in the 1930s as an expert-contrived movement to centralize their power and to create a marketing niche for a burgeoning field.[19] Marriage educators, in Bailey's estimation, tapped into the national sense of crisis about the crumbling institution of marriage and utilized the mass fear as an intellectual justification to create their new field.[20] The multitude of articles in student newspapers tell a different story, a story of students actively seeking information, organizing weekend parleys and traveling to other campuses to attend meetings. The level of dedication to the marriage cause demonstrated that students, while possibly influenced by experts, took strong initiative to raise questions and seek answers on the marriage and family front.

Student-penned articles in campus newspapers clearly show that middle-class college students demanded marriage and family courses on their own. The pervasive gender conservatism of the 1930s is most visible in this return to the ideal of marriage. William Chafe describes how women's magazines of the 1930s urged female readers to "return to femininity" while creating an "elaborate ideology in support of the home and marriages to facilitate the process."[21] Many students appear to have embraced the ideology that marriage, family and home were the central elements of a fulfilling life. Vocal student activists from colleges and universities around the country appealed to faculty, college administrators and experts in the field to create permanent marriage and family courses.

Prominent marriage and family expert Dr. Ernest R. Groves fully supported college student's petitions for marriage and family preparation courses.[22] He believed that education about marriage and family life needed to spread beyond college campuses so that it would reach all American youths. William F. Bigelow, the editor of *Good Housekeeping* magazine and *The Good Housekeeping Marriage Book* was inspired to edit the book of essays about marriage after reading a small news item about students at a large university in California asking that courses in marriage and family be offered.[23]

Marriage and family courses fit in with a larger curriculum that had been built in the early years of the twentieth century which understood home as the center of women's competence.[24] In the 1930s there was a growing interest in parent-education programs; six universities and two schools of social work offered professional training for parent education workers. Lectures, discussion groups, magazine articles and university-sponsored correspondence courses offered advice to parents, especially on subjects regarding personality formation, character development and social adjustment.[25] Marriage and family courses fit in with this widespread cultural interest in educating youths for productive and reproductive home lives.

Students who wanted to get married demanded professional guidance to help them form successful partnerships.[26] There was an extensive literature about marriage and family, so much so, that Lewis M. Terman wrote that the subject of marriage and marital happiness had been treated by so many writers, both lay and professional, that the market was flooded with "hopelessly jumbled confusion of information and misinformation" about the topic.[27] Students wanted more than access to literature; they insisted that courses be offered on campus and that speakers come to lecture and teach at marriage parleys organized by undergraduates. Mount Holyoke students organized a marriage parley that focused on the psychological, sociological, physical and spiritual phases of marriage, contending that the parley should inspire a "permanent academic course in marriage, such as the one recently begun at Vassar."[28] A poll at the University of Michigan found 90% of the 523 students surveyed favored a course in preparation for the problems of married life.[29] Even if males had reasons to be less enthusiastic about the idea of getting married than females, students of both genders expressed interest in having marriage and family courses taught on their campuses. Men were often less interested in getting married right after college because many males had concerns about being able to support themselves, a wife and possible offspring during a time of economic crisis.[30] An editorial writer for *The Michigan Daily* stated that marriage and family classes would prove beneficial to students because "marriage has physiological, psychological and economic aspects which cannot be learned in the usual college curricula. And despite their attempted insouciance, college students have little enough knowledge of such matters."[31]

Many experts concurred with the students' conclusions that professional intervention was needed to educate students about marriage. Paul Popenoe argued that parents, the church and schools failed to prepare youths for married life. In their desperation for information, young people turned to movies, magazines and radio shows to get their ideas about the meaning of love and romance which resulted in sexual and economic misconceptions that created unsuccessful unions.[32] To remedy this situation, Popenoe conducted speaking tours at colleges and universities around the country. In the late 1930s he visited the campuses of George Washington University, Mount Holyoke and the University of Michigan to present lectures about how to find a mate and have a successful marriage. He presented three separate lectures at Mount Holyoke that focused on different aspects of marriage. The first was "How to Know When You're In Love," the second centered on new morality, which described how humans mature from adolescent attraction to the opposite sex to adult monogamous relationships. Popenoe's final lecture, "Looking Forward to Marriage," described how to have a good attitude toward marriage and how to find the proper mate while also imparting technical knowledge about sexual intercourse.[33]

Using the companionate marriage ideal as his model, Popenoe explained that undergraduates should envision marriage as a cooperative adventure not a competitive one. Mature relationships were based on five components including the biological mating impulse, economic relations, a sexual relationship, companionship and mutual interest in home and children.[34] Popenoe's list of elements was quite similar to the elements that mass-marketed marriage manuals touted as the most important aspects of married life. Although Lindsey, the original proponent of companionate marriage, believed that external pressures from the church, one's family or the state could not keep a marriage intact, many experts, youths and popular writers proposed that the church, family and state band together to contribute their time and resources to resurrect the institution of marriage to its previous level of primacy.[35]

Members of the middle class noted that economic conditions had improved by the mid-1930s. By 1935 the economy appeared to be on an upswing, marriage became a viable option for youths again and the rates finally climbed back to 10.6 per 1,000 for the first time since the crash of the stock market.[36] By the mid-to-late 1930s students were ready to embark on a quest for marital happiness, and they placed their faith in experts to provide them with rational means for developing meaningful martial relationships. In the early years of the twentieth century marriage had represented an important rite of passage where middle-class children embraced adult roles, embarked on a domestic path with a partner and set up a private residence away from their family. In the early years of the Great Depression, youths often were deprived of these opportunities because the lack of jobs made it financially impossible to marry. 1935 appears to be the year which experts and youths decided that the economy had improved enough to make marriage a possible venture again.[37] Experts and students looked to marriage as a stabilizing institution that could bring normalcy back to a country that had suffered the ravages of the Depression. During the early years of the Depression a large number of young people were forced to forestall marriage due to a lack of economic resources. In 1929 there were 10.6 marriages per thousand population; by 1932 the rate had decreased to 7.9 per thousand.[38] The national marriage rate rose to 9.7 by 1934, still short of the pre-Depression average.

For many young people being able to marry represented more than an ordinary rite of passage—it signified victory over circumstance and the dawning of a new era in which they could finally function as full-fledged adults. In the mid-to-late 1930s young people not only began getting married at a rapid pace, they also appeared to value the institution of marriage more than youths of the 1920s ever had. During the 1920s a fair number of young people held scornful attitudes toward marriage, but by the late 1930s it seemed that the absence of the ability to marry had made students hearts grow fonder of the concept.[39] One survey of college students conducted in the mid-1930s found that 90–95% of college women said that their main career goal was to become a wife and mother. The young women also stated that helping a husband establish himself in his career was more important than pursuing career success for themselves.[40]

The ability to get married, for many youths, signaled the end of the economic strife generated by the Depression and the chance to establish independent homes away from parental authority. During the early years of the Depression young people often remained dependent on economic support from their parents for years on end because the youths could not find employment. One sociologist estimated that almost one million youths who would have gotten married had there not been a Depression postponed getting married for year after year in vain hope that the economy would improve.[41] Studies compiled in the late 1930s detailed the detrimental psychological impact on young people who experienced discouragement and delays in attaining financial independence and embarking on careers of their own.[42] Texts from the era describe frustrated male youths who wished to strike out and find a place of their own in the world but were forced by circumstance to live under their parental roof in a state of protracted adolescence.[43]

Many middle-class youths who had chosen to marry despite the Depression were forced by economic circumstances to "double up" by taking up residence in a spare bedroom, attic or other corner of a relative's house, usually one of the married youth's parental homes, for an indefinite amount of time.[44] Residing with in-laws often proved to be a less-than-ideal way to start a new marriage, since it tended to create marital discord rather than harmony.[45] A property inventory conducted in 64 cities in January 1934 found that 2% to 15% of families were doubled up due to the Depression.[46] Even though the practice of living with in-laws became more common during the early years of the Depression, it was still frowned upon by 68% of young men and women who were surveyed about the option.[47]

Young people who did not want to live with their in-laws after wedding put off getting married until they felt capable of affording a domicile of their own. The people who were most likely to wait to marry were from business-class families who felt insecure about their class position and feared that they might be teetering on the brink of economic disaster.[48] Young people who grew up in homes where a college education was valued as something "to be striven for at all costs," even if it caused financial hardship for their families, tended to postpone marriage more markedly than any other group.[49] For whites, the more education they had, the later they tended to get married. This occurred because college graduates of the 1930s had a difficult time accumulating economic resources immediately following graduation.[50] Within a few years of graduating, most college-educated youths began to acquire economic resources quickly so that by their mid-twenties college-educated married men were much more likely to have their own households than young white men who had never attended college.[51] Experts advised against newly-wedded couples living with their in-laws because "interference, irritation and nervous tension" usually accompanied living with one's folks.[52]

While white college-educated youths who married young often paid the "Depression penalty" of having to live with in-laws for the first few years of marriage, some experts contended that African-American youths had few incentives to forestall matrimony since their financial situation was perilous whether they waited or wedded very young. Although students at Howard University described their economic situation in the late 1930s as "a blank wall of economic insecurity," since positions for college-educated African-Americans were almost completely nonexistent, they did not tend to marry earlier or more often than their white counterparts.[53] Male graduates took jobs as porters and elevator operators while female graduates worked in tea rooms and kitchens.[54] Howard students' concerns moved beyond the realm of being able to afford their own homes and start their own families. They understood that the economic insecurity faced by most African-Americans was linked with larger social and political problems that needed to be addressed before focusing on personal concerns.

EXPERT INVESTMENT IN MARRIAGE

Marriage, in both mass-market advice manuals and marriage and family textbooks, was depicted as a stabilizing force where men and women could fulfill their biological reproductive destinies and enact proper gender roles.[55] Experts were extremely invested in the concept of white, middle-class college-educated youths getting married as soon as possible. Many experts argued that the Depression had gotten men out of the habit of marrying and that it was up to the middle-class white women who wanted preserve society to cajole men into getting married and starting families as soon as they were able.[56] Popenoe expressed concern that marriages were not taking place between prudent educated middle-class white people but between "Negroes . . . certain foreign born groups, or in the strata of the population with low educational standards."[57] Youthful marriages between the so-called "inferior classes" constituted a threat to the American populace; people who were married early in life tended to reproduce rapidly, having three or four children before college graduates had even become betrothed.[58] In Popenoe's estimation, this trend proved to be a fearsome handicap for the educated classes of people who would be forced to carry the economic burden for the "excess of eugenically inferior children" who came from the unions of non-college educated people.

Popenoe's opinions about eugenics were far from unique, Homer P. Rainey, Director of the American Youth Commission of the American Council of Education warned Americans that "college graduates, professional people, men of science and several other favored groups" were failing to attain the minimum reproduction rates of 2.62 births per marriage. Meanwhile, Popenoe mused, feeble-minded people and the "dull normals" were multiplying rapidly and decreasing the value of American stock.[59] Middle-class women who continued to work outside of the home after getting married were popularly perceived as "menaces to the race" because they posed a threat to the definition of family, the birthrate and the economic system.[60] Getting married was deemed not just a personal choice, but a moral imperative for middle-class white women to pursue. The common line of argument was that college-educated white women owed it to their country to get married and to reproduce themselves, a sense of middle-class social order and the normative values that had been shaken from their sturdy foundations during the early years of the Depression.

The ideologies that the eugenics movement promoted bore some striking similarities to the ideologies of competitive rugged individualism, in that eugenics placed the blame for society's economic, social and political problems on "defective germ plasmas" that were carried by individuals and ethnic groups, instead of blaming the structure of society itself.[61] A historian later succinctly surmised that eugenicists cleverly used "the cover of science to blame the victims for their own problems."[62] Some of the United States most prestigious universities including Harvard, Columbia, Cornell and Brown offered courses on eugenics; by the late 1920s eugenics was part of the curriculum in 376 separate college courses, which enrolled approximately 20,000 students.[63] These college courses upheld notions about the differential birthrates between the biologically "fit" and "unfit," and trained students that segregation, immigration restrictions and sterilization were "worthy policies to maintain in American culture."[64] College courses also emphasized that white middle-class women should be careful about tracing their ancestral lines and should choose a worthy mate with care.[65]

Eugenicists valued white college-educated middle-class women of the 1930s for their intelligence and breeding and expected these women to do their duty for the nation by getting married and reproducing. Educated white females could increase the value of American stock by marrying well and passing their genes onto the next generation. Women who appeared to be too intelligent received stern warnings from experts that they were diminishing their chances for finding husbands. The myth that earning a Phi Beta Kappa key doomed a woman to a lonely life of spinsterhood received attention in many venues. A student from Mount Holyoke wrote an editorial explaining that earning a Phi Beta Kappa key did not necessarily condemn young women to futures of being greasy grinds who spent the rest of their lives working "and never getting anywhere."[66] She argued that while some women who belonged to Phi Beta Kappa took jobs in the business world, many had others had successfully and happily answered "the call of love and marriage."[67] An alarming number of experts admonished young women who wished to be marriage bound to safeguard themselves by hiding their Phi Beta Kappa keys and wearing some swank costume jewelry instead.[68] Women who earned a Phi Beta Kappa key were advised to profess that winning the honor was a total surprise. If a young woman could not resist reading her textbooks and racking up a "regrettable number of A's" she would have to use ruses to pretend that it was not intentional in order to avoid being condemned as a greasy grind.[69] One mother wrote an editorial for *The University of Michigan Daily* contending that an "all 'A' scholastic record with a Phi Beta Kappa key loses much of its significance if the owner is socially offensive" so young women should focus more on etiquette and the social graces and less on academic achievement if they wished to find husbands.[70]

Experts postulated that young women who were too intelligent—Phi Beta Kappa key or not—hindered their chances of ever getting married. Authors warned "highbrow" girls that they might "pay the penalty of life-long celibacy" for the "spurious culture which is foisted upon them" during their years at college."[71] Experts advised highbrow girls that they might temporarily enjoy the advantages of being brilliant, outspoken and able to "take a job, any job and keep it;" they might even "earn more money than their boyfriends," but behind their backs all of their friends secretly hated them.[72] Young women who constantly paraded the fact that they went to college opened themselves up to "the suspicion that this information is her only stock in trade."[73] One author stressed that the only way to avoid the "terrible mistake" which would make people laugh at a young woman behind her back was to "forget the fact that you ever went to college!"[74]

The fact that several experts advised women to underplay their intelligence and educational achievements points to the anxiety that authors felt about young women having access to university education and professional training that could prepare them to earn their own livings, rather than planning to be dependent on their husbands for financial support.[75] Economic independence gave women more bargaining power on the marriage market, especially if they had jobs that paid well.[76] A single young working woman enjoyed the benefits of having professional interests and economic independence, two things that might encourage them to delay getting married.[77] Psychologist Laura Hutton, author of *The Single Woman: Her Adjustment to Life and Love* argued that women who had interesting careers, economic independence and freedom from familial responsibilities might turn their thoughts away from marriage.[78] According to Hutton, career women were, in fact, unaware that they were victims of arrested emotional development and were shrinking either "consciously or unconsciously, from the implications and responsibilities of marriage."[79] These misguided women, in Hutton's view, were using work and professional success as a means to escape the emotional, sexual and psychological issues that they felt too ill-equipped to face directly.[80]

Marriage, in the context of the mid-to-late 1930s, performed the cultural work of rebalancing gender roles by repositioning married men as sole wage earners for their families and married women as support systems for the men.[81] Most expert authors encouraged women to focus on emotionally supporting their husbands rather than economically supporting themselves. Experts espoused the belief that young women would attain both personal happiness and financial fulfillment by "finding and marrying the right man and inspiring him to achieve greater financial success."[82] Young women were advised to offer their strength, courage, tenderness and sacrifice in order to assure that the men they married could achieve greatness. Sacrificing one's own career, and to some extent one's identity, was viewed as a worthwhile endeavor because the knowledge that a woman had contributed to a man's fulfillment purportedly provided females with "richness and satisfaction" that far surpassed achieving their own success.[83]

Lisa Lowe's theoretical framework in *Immigrant Acts* proves useful for understanding the mission of the standard marriage and family curricula, which served to "universalize the values and norms of the 'common' national culture" in order to create a individual generic subjects who would, in turn, reproduce the values of the state.[84] During the monetary crisis of the 1930s, the state valued women who were content to remain in the background and support the men who were faltering under the huge weight of the economic pressures brought about by the Depression. Married women who worked for wages outside of the home were popularly perceived as wretched beings who had stolen their jobs from deserving men. Young women who competed in college classrooms for academic accolades and good grades were described by expert marriage and family textbook authors as annoyances to males in the academic realm and as potential threats to male job security in the future.

Some experts portrayed marital harmony as the key element for shaping efficient producers in the marketplace.[85] An essay entitled "It Pays to be Happily Married" explained that a woman who wanted to be a good wife should be willing to adjust herself and her personality to help her husband's career; this was deemed a wise investment since the economic outcome would affect both parties. Young women were advised to treat the job of being a housewife as seriously as they would a position in an office that paid a monthly salary.[86] The prescriptive literature of the late 1930s admonished young married women to look to other office wives as examples, to copy their manners, to dress and act like wives of associates, to develop poise and interests that mirrored the other women and to entertain people who could help their husband's career.[87]

Women attending Teachers College at Columbia University in the mid-1930s were required to sign a business creed that encouraged them to be ambitious, hard-working, frugal, and committed to their education and careers. One of the final stipulations of the creed read:

> I believe that while every woman should be able to care for herself in some outside gainful employment, homemaking is the natural vocation for woman just as earning money income for a home is the natural vocation for man. I believe that, for the woman who marries, woman can make her best contribution to her family's support by skillful management and personal service within the home rather than by trying to continue outside gainful employment after marriage.[88]

This oath exemplifies the pervasive environ of gender conservatism in the 1930s. The pledge upheld strictly-demarcated gender roles for women and men who wished to marry. It also prescribed that married women quit their jobs as teachers in order to devote themselves to reproducing the social order, while potentially opening up another job for an unemployed male.

The socially-prescribed role of husband-as-provider could be as crippling to men as the role of wife-as-support-system was for women. For men, marriage was a huge financial obligation fraught with expectations about being a strong economic provider for his family. The role of provider took on enormous importance and created great anxiety during a time when the economy was still on shaky ground. A survey of university students conducted in 1936 found that 65% of undergraduate women required a man to earn at least $3,000 a year to be considered a potentially marriageable mate. Only 16% of the women interviewed would be willing to marry a man who had annual income of $1,500.[89] Many young men of the 1930s admitted that they were avoiding getting married until they were earning a big enough salary to enable them to cover the bills that came along with wedded life.

Students at all-male colleges and universities were strongly discouraged or implicitly forbidden to marry during their undergraduate years. The basis for this rule was that the administration feared that male students might marry impulsively, attaching themselves to some "non-entity" who would ruin their future.[90] Waller voiced the opinion that for the average male college student a "love affair which led to immediate marriage would be tragic because of the havoc it would create in his scheme of life."[91] Princeton and Yale both prohibited undergraduate marriages, with the rule at Yale reading "any undergraduate who marries removes himself automatically from the college."[92] Students from Dartmouth and Harvard were only allowed to get married with express permission from their dean.[93] Dean Porter of Amherst College stated that the administration did not encourage their students marrying, but were willing to consider each marriage on a case-by-case basis. "The question of undergraduate marriages at Amherst College is not a problem at the present time, and we hope it will not develop into a problem in the future."[94]

Women's colleges, one the other hand, usually were supportive of female students who wed while still in school. In 1934 Vassar, an all-women's college, adopted a liberal policy regarding student marriages that permitted undergraduates to marry and continue as students in "perfect harmony with the rules."[95] Eleanor Dodge, the warden of Vassar, stated in 1934 that the new policy was a radical departure from the rules previously upheld at Vassar and all other women's colleges. Dodge refused to comment when asked if Vassar's policy changes would have an impact on the rules of Mount Holyoke, Smith and Wellesley. Within a couple of years, the impact was felt as several women's colleges adopted lenient policies akin to those at Vassar. By 1936 female undergraduates attending Barnard, Vassar, Smith and Mount Holyoke were allowed to remain in college and even live in the dormitories after getting married.[96] Administrators tacitly believed that for females, being married while still an undergraduate provided them with emotional stability.[97]

Marriage was seen as a wonderful opportunity for undergraduate women but a burden for college men; even so, most expert authors advised undergraduates of both genders to wait until they finished school to get married. Some prescriptive literature authors recommended that young people forego marriage until all of their professional training was completed because the challenges of attending law school, medical school or engineering programs often created conflicts for newly married couples.[98] The vast differences in the rules regarding male and female undergraduates getting married while still in school undoubtedly were connected to the economic expectations for each party in a late-1930s marriage. Married men were expected to support themselves and their wives, a responsibility that could be a cumbersome burden to a college student. Married women were often banned from working for wages, so the husband would be expected to assume all financial responsibilities before landing his first job. The situation for women made it much easier to marry while in school because there were no additional financial burdens and there were few expectations that she would use her education to find a lucrative job after graduation.

MARRIAGE AS A CAREER

The Great Depression created a sociopolitical climate ruled largely by conservative gender norms where marriage and family were conceived of as a full-time career commitment for women.[99] Eleanor Roosevelt contributed to the discourse that few women were talented enough to have careers in the work world and supported the idea that marriage should be the career of choice for most women. In an essay entitled "Should Wives Work?" Roosevelt raised the question of whether it was possible for a woman to get married and still have a career. She argued that the question was poorly worded since very few women of the 1930s had real careers. "Most women marry and work, and work will not be a 'career.' The question put this way also seems to imply that marriage itself is not a career. Anyone who believes that has no real understanding of marriage."[100] The essay provided examples of different types of married couples, but concluded by stating that "just a few women who have special gifts, who have established careers before they meet the men they wish to marry" might want to continue working after wedding.[101] Roosevelt stressed that the women who pursued careers after marriage held the responsibility for finding competent staff to manage their homes in their absence. Roosevelt's comments about educated middle-class women working outside of the home or choosing to make marriage a career fit into the theoretical framework developed by Phyllis Palmer in *Domesticity and Dirt: Housewives and Domestic Servants in the United States, 1920–1945*. Palmer contends that Depression-era-middle-class housewives could hire domestic workers to perform some of the more arduous household tasks so the middle-class women could hold onto the belief that they had escaped a life of domestic drudgery.[102] Some young women at Mount Holyoke expressed frustration that thousands of college-educated couples who wished to marry would be unable to afford it unless both the man and the woman continued to work for a few years. Female students expressed resentment that "the nation as a whole" was telling young women that they had to chose between having a marriage or a career, since the majority of citizens had decided that females should not try to hold a husband and a job at the same time.[103]

The realization that most Americans believed that women should either be married or employed, but not both, proved somewhat shocking for the young women who had been exposed to the career and marriage feminism of the 1920s. During the 1920s feminists touted the emotional rewards that women experienced when they worked for wages. Many contended that the personal satisfaction derived from working outweighed the economic aspects and that working after marriage was critical to "individual esteem as well as to enhance economic status."[104] In the early 1930s many middle-class women were forced to take jobs out of economic necessity and found out that they enjoyed working and earning a paycheck. Feminist ideals of the emotional and economic rewards that came from having a career were tossed out the window as one of the necessary sacrifices for marriage. One expert wrote that although women excelled in certain occupations they were often denied employment because employers suspected that women would likely marry and leave positions opened to them. The author explained that even if potential marriage was not an issue, young women had to realize that "certain qualities such as woman's cattiness, petty jealousies and her frequent inability to be a good sport, all stand in the way of her success in reaching her goal. These are your problems. See to it that you face them wisely and that you make the most of the opportunities that are yours in the new economic and social order."[105] While this expert recognized that there was a new social order, she still used old arguments about the essential nature of women in order to blame them as a sex class for their economic and social situation.

The tension surrounding a woman's earning her own living and developing a sense of identity through work rather than marriage came to the fore in the later half of the 1930s.[106] The subtext of many marriage manuals was that the financial difficulties of the Depression created a crisis in confidence for men that could only be assuaged by women assuming an emotionally supportive stance as stay-at-home wives. In so doing, women could contribute to rebuilding the collective male ego that had been crushed by the setbacks of the previous years. Expert authors explicated that marriage would be emotionally fulfilling for women and men because they could live out their biologically predetermined destinies with husbands as the providers and wives as the dependents. As an added benefit, a collective female return to the home front would, in theory, open up job opportunities for men who had been shut out of the work force by women who chosen career over marriage.[107] The sacrifice of a woman's career ambitions was seen as a fair trade off and a wise economic choice for most women to make. In the discourse of the late 1930s, marriage and career were often presented as mutually-exclusive options for young women. One psychologist argued that a large obstacle to marriage in the 1930s was that women were reluctant to sacrifice their economic independence and personal freedom for married life.[108]

Young women attending Smith and Mount Holyoke stated that they were willing to sacrifice having a career in order to have a marriage. In the spring of 1937 Professor Ralph Harlow presented a speech to the Amherst College students that outlined the psychological elements and adjustments of marriage. Harlow stated that a strong marital bond could be achieved through *mutual* sacrifice, yet the headline that ran in the *Amherst Student* read: "College Girl is Willing to Sacrifice." The women from Smith and Mount Holyoke who were in attendance at the lecture did not seem to mind that the male students overlooked the word "mutual" before sacrifice. Young women made it clear that they were happy to make many compromises in order to attain a good marriage and establish a home and family life.[109] While the apparent lack of resistance proffered by the women of Smith and Mount Holyoke might seem surprising, young women of the late 1930s were exposed to a barrage of mainstream messages that were rife with the notion that women had to be prepared to pay a price should they wish to be married.

One of the prices women were expected to pay was giving up any plans to pursue professional goals. Married women who continued to work for any reason beyond mere survival were popularly perceived as selfish and immoral.[110] National polls and surveys found that the public strongly favored married women staying out of the work force. An American Institute of Public Opinion poll conducted in 1937 found that only 18% of those surveyed believed that a married woman should hold a job if her husband was capable of supporting her.[111] A full 85% of *Fact* magazine readers responded with a resounding "no" when they were asked if married women should be allowed to work for wages.[112] Other popular magazines contributed to the national discourse, not with survey results but with equally-powerful renderings of how gender roles should look. In 1938 *Life* magazine published side-by-side photographs of college students with the captions: "Boy's goal: a profession." and "Girl's goal: still a home."[113] Writers for *Fortune* magazine gently mocked female undergraduates of the previous decade who had sat up late into the night discussing career plans with friends, getting excited about living on their own and making arrangements to head off to Greenwich Village after graduation.[114] According to the journalists for these national publications, by the late 1930s young women no longer craved adventure, travel, careers or independence. Instead female college students embraced the prospects of marriage, children and domesticity as the dreams that were within their grasp.[115]

Opinions expressed in the national discourse were echoed in student surveys on college campuses of the late 1930s. It is difficult to gauge whether young women gave up exciting career plans because of the national discourse about women's work or if young women truly looked forward to getting engaged and married right after graduation. Regardless of their motivations, students surveyed for the *George Washington Hatchet* in 1938 agreed that women—married or single—should be allowed to hold jobs only "if their survival depended on it."[116] The majority of students believed that married women who kept jobs even though their husbands could afford to support them were selfish and deprived men of opportunities. Women who continued to hold jobs to enhance their sense of independence or to have "something to do" were chastised for lacking a "sense of justice."[117]

During the earlier years of the Depression many women were the sole wage earners in their families because unskilled low-paying jobs that were defined as women's work remained available, while higher paying positions that were conceptualized as men's work were difficult to find. Many married women worked for wages in the struggle to uphold a semblance of their family's previous standard of living. Women earning wages created a sense of gender imbalance that fostered pervasive fears that working wives would have too much power in their homes.[118] The student belief that women who worked "lacked a sense of justice" illustrates widely-held opinion that the economy would improve if women retreated to the home and men became the sole breadwinners for their dependent wives and children.[119] Historians have shown that the Depression-era cultural fears about patriarchal dominance being usurped when wives earned wages proved largely unfounded. Most households remained male-dominated even when husbands were jobless and wives were the sole breadwinners of the family. Even so, the cultural response to this shift in wage-earning roles created tensions that lasted throughout the Depression. A young woman who fully dedicated herself to a life of marriage and family would assist the nation in restoring gender roles to their proper pre-Depression order.

College-educated young women were privy to a plethora of mixed messages about whether to work or to wed that were delivered via various venues including student newspaper articles, marriage manuals and speeches by experts. Mixed messages were sometimes contained in the same article. Some articles stated that female students of the Victorian era felt squeamish about the idea of combining marriage and a professional career, but that women of the late 1930s saw the two realms as inseparable.[120] Female undergraduates supposedly craved a well-rounded education because it would prepare them for their futures as wives as mothers. Young women could "plan on having four or five years for an active career after graduation" but then "nine out of ten plan to marry."[121] The article finished by stating that girls who hoped to "get nothing out of college life other than an intellectual background for a life-long career is an exception rather than the rule."[122]

The notion that four or five years represented the time period that most young women set aside as their "career" exposes the widely-embraced belief that females were allowed to be "working girls" but not career women. Working girls were seen as employees who could manage to get by without equal pay for equal work since they were only passing through a fleeting phase of their lives.[123] This meant that working girls did not earn the same respect, pay or say that working men enjoyed.[124] Young women were repeatedly advised to set their sights on working only until they met the right man. Experts stated that nothing could replace the love of a good man, even a recent graduate was "the most independent woman that ever terrorized an office force."[125] During the 1930s, many Americans still embraced the notion that middle-class women who pursued a college degree were merely training for pre-marriage careers and home life.[126] This political, economic and social construction of women's work in the 1930s made it difficult for young women who wanted to pursue both a career and marriage to figure out how to proceed. Getting married represented the overriding ambition for many young women who attended college in the 1930s.[127] One female college student wrote to her parents in 1936 to explain that she needed to devote a large amount of time to her social life in order to avoid the dreaded fate of becoming a career girl.[128] She believed that economic circumstances would force her into the career girl role, but becoming one was "definitely second choice" compared to meeting an eligible man to marry.[129]

One expert explained that young women who wanted "nothing out of college life" other than intellectual training for a life-long career were obviously missing out on the most important aspect of the college experience: finding a husband.[130] In fact, many female students, especially those attending coeducational schools, married soon after graduation.[131] A national survey conducted by the Stewart Howe Alumni Services in 1936 showed that 80% of college women got married within three years of graduation, with 82% marrying men from their *alma mater*.[132] A young woman from George Washington University joyfully embraced the prospect of meeting her future husband on campus and marrying soon after graduating.[133] Some students from Mount Holyoke readily admitted, to the chagrin of some of their classmates, that they wanted only to get married after graduation. A woman from the class of 1937 stated that "I'm telling you that though they won't admit it, the majority of girls in college are just marking time until they can get married." A female student at the University of Michigan sarcastically suggested that all of the ambitious women who wanted to get ahead by competing with men in some field would be better off taking home-making and domestic science courses, since about "80 percent of all the ambitious co-eds turn out to be housewives."[134] Experts of the late 1930s promoted the notion that college-educated youths, especially those who attended coeducational universities, had lower divorce rates than people who lacked college degrees.[135] Many feminist historians have questioned the validity of survey data where overwhelming majorities of women declared that they preferred getting married over having a career. Young women of the 1930s knew that they faced diminished occupational opportunities and may have set their academic pursuits aside, dropped career goals and sought security in marriage as a result.[136]

During the late 1930s social scientists, writers for romance magazines and authors of marriage manuals "rehabilitated marriage as an exciting adventure" for both members of the couple and reconfigured the role of wife into a "vocation."[137] Nancy Cott persuasively argues that because women were *allowed* to work for wages, being a wife and mother looked like a chosen vocation rather than a socially-prescribed mandate.[138] Most young women were under a lot of social pressure to marry, and many educated middle-class women also felt that it would be unfair for them to work for wages. Being a married woman was elevated to vocational status just in time to convince women that staying home would benefit both males and females. The romantic discourse extolling the emotional and sexual rewards inherent in the companionate marriage often obscured the cold economic fact that the lifelong vocation of wife, and possibly mother, was unpaid. A woman's choice of a marriage partner almost fully determined the class position she would hold in the future. For women marriage could represent a risky economic venture, where the woman, after placing her bid, was dependent on her male mate to deliver the economic goods. Just a few years earlier psychologists were warning women to take their time in pursuing marriage. A professor from the University of Wisconsin explained that if women were able to have even a few years of a vocational apprenticeship before getting married, it would allow her to emancipate herself from having "adolescent dependencies" on her future mate.[139] In the early 1930s women were told that they could not continue to play "the ancient role of an infantile and adolescent personality under male protection" if they wanted to survive in the "open field of adult competition."[140] By 1935 onward, it appeared that many experts did not want women out in the field at all, and requested that they please reestablish themselves in the ancient infantile role of passive dependency.[141]

Some students from Mount Holyoke appeared to have embraced the marriage-as-vocation argument wholeheartedly. The young women took the marriage issue very seriously, attended weekend-long marriage parleys at other colleges and organized a parley of their own in 1937.[142] The weekend-long event at Mount Holyoke featured talks about birth control, family planning, choosing a mate and having a strong companionate marriage. Students who attended the parley argued that the college should immediately institute a permanent marriage and family course because the course would offer female undergraduates "practical vocational training" for the roles of wife and mother.[143]

Prominent educators, feminists and professional women were displeased with the spreading notion that marriage was the key vocation for women and expressed disappointment with the growth of marriage and family education on college campuses. In the spring of 1936 the New York League of Business and Professional Women discussed how colleges were being lax in preparing young women to meet the real complexities of daily life. Members of the League believed that the point of women attaining college education was to cultivate a sense of personal responsibility during a time of moral anarchy. Female students needed to be encouraged to think independently, embrace personal responsibility, take initiative and be courageous. A college administrator who attended the meeting argued that colleges were failing in this mission and that marriage and family courses only trained women for a life of domesticity. Members of the New York League of Business and Professional Women concurred that women who wanted to learn to cook, sew or perform domestic tasks could learn these things, but should only seek out domestic studies after building a firm structure of a liberal arts education beneath them.[144] Members of the Alpha Pi Epsilon professional home economics sorority argued that if women were expected to learn about domestic tasks as part of their preparation for marriage and adult life, men should be expected to do the same. Alpha Pi Epsilon proposed implementing a course at George Washington University that would train the male undergraduates as well as females about how to cook, select a wardrobe, deal with family problems and prepare for a "model existence after graduation."[145]

Frances Perkins, United States Secretary of Labor and Mount Holyoke graduate, believed that women needed an education that expanded their roles beyond the four walls of the home. Women required training for jobs that paid wages, vocational guidance and assistance finding jobs; after these needs were met, women could also receive instruction about home making and motherhood. Perkins demanded nursery school facilities, playgrounds and state-sponsored character-building programs so that mothers who had received schooling and vocational guidance could continue to work outside of the home after having children.[146] *Mademoiselle* magazine, in direct contention to the New York League of Business and Professional Women statement, believed that marriage and family courses, home economics classes and domestic science curriculum provided women with the exact training they required, since college-educated males preferred women schooled in the art of domesticity.[147]

MARRIAGE IN MASS-MARKETED MANUALS

If the psychological, political and survey-based discourses about marriage, family and career were not enough to convince young women that they would be best off finding a husband and raising children, a deluge of mass-marketed advice books flooded the marketplace in the years of 1935–1940. Even with the marriage rates rising, authors of mass-marketed manuals were compelled to spend several pages of their texts convincing young women that they naturally craved matrimony and family life above all else. While manuals from the earlier years of the Depression rarely bothered to propose marriage as an option for young readers to consider, texts from the latter half of the 1930s tell a very different story: essentially a tale that emphasizes that venturing forth to find a life mate as soon as possible represented the crucial challenge for young women to undertake. Authors portrayed romance that led to marriage as an empowering adventure on which all young women should embark. Marriage manuals, magazine articles and newspaper columns provided detailed commentary about why young women should pursue marriage over career. The mission of winning and holding a husband was presumed to be the preferred path for most young women, since it was tacitly assumed that few females could find satisfaction in the work world. Authors utilized political, economic and biological arguments to make their points, stating that women were innately less talented than men, their contributions to the work world were essentially meaningless, that success in a career revealed failure in the realm of romance, that getting married was a fundamental biological urge and that women needed to fulfill their biological destiny by becoming wives and mothers. The advice contained in the vulgar mass-marketed manuals often contained contentions similar to those posited by sociologists and psychologists of the Depression era. Popenoe argued in *Modern Marriage* that for 100,000 years women's main goal was "getting and holding a man" and that biologically this still held true in the twentieth century.[148]

Many mass-marketed marriage manual writers employed the argument that women were best suited to be homemakers since most females lacked any particular gifts or talents. The fact that "merely normally intelligent girls far outnumber the feminine geniuses or women of special abilities" meant that average young women should not "hope for nor plan for a brilliant professional career."[149] Undoubtedly, men of merely normal intelligence far outnumbered male geniuses as well, but one would not gather that from reading marriage manuals. While marriage manuals described average women as lacking the skills to find success in the workplace, average men were depicted as having a stunning myriad of qualities including the "idealism and vision that changes the course of nations" and the "humanitarianism that creates Utopias out of chaos."[150] Males also had cornered the market on "the genius that produces the great art, literature, music and architecture of the world" and the technical skills necessary to build "giant dams, bridges and skyscrapers."[151] While the average woman could barely hold down a job, the average man possessed pure genius; logically, men should pursue careers while women were "really fitted only for marriage."[152]

Young women who believed that they had the intelligence and drive necessary to pursue a professional career learned from some manuals that they were deluded if they believed that their career would have any worth. One manual writer informed young women that their contributions to the work world were essentially meaningless; women workers were underpaid dupes who were being worked over by the capitalist system. According to this author, most women who worked were not hired because they possessed any special skills, but because they could be paid less than men would have to receive for the same job.[153] While this author was brutally honest about the economic inequity faced by most female employees, he went on to deliver a blow to women who wanted to work for the emotional fulfillment and esteem it gave them. He stated that some working women labored under the delusion that having careers might afford them opportunities to impress their friends later in life by reminiscing about how important they were. The author offered the cautionary quip that a female's career "meant nothing to her boss, who let her go as soon as he saw the possibility of getting a younger girl at a lower salary."[154]

Should the warnings about women's work being meaningless fail to deter females from the work force, many authors put forth the notion that a woman's success in the work world only served to highlight her failure in the realm of romance. One male author confidently asserted that only a very small number of women could possibly fulfill their emotional needs through career or social activities. The women who tried to convince themselves or others that they enjoyed working and living alone were informed that they were merely rationalizing an unfortunate situation and resorting to using "the lazy woman's answer."[155] The message that career success was a meager compensation for failing at husband hunting was reiterated in multiple marriage manuals in the late 1930s. Single women, even those with successful careers, were popularly portrayed as pathetic spinsters who worked all day only to return home to lodgings that were "chosen for cheapness rather than charm" and who night after night prepared solitary meals for themselves.[156] Marriage was naturalized as the proper choice that normal women made, while abnormal women who wanted to work were either delusional or lying. This passage from *How to Win and Hold a Husband* elucidates the key tenets purported by most mass-market marriage manual authors:

> So, if you are a career girl, don't be ashamed of your natural desire to find a husband and put an end to your business life. You aren't really fooling anyone, if you state loudly that you are interested only in your profession and that you wouldn't consider marriage under any conditions. Such statements are only an admission either that you haven't found the right mate or that you have failed in the game of husband-winning.[157]

The language used in these texts echoes the "scare copy" that Roland Marchand describes in *Advertising the American Dream: Making Way for Modernity, 1920–1940.* Experts, like the advertisers, wrote alarming accounts in order to raise the anxiety of the reader, only to offer a purchasable solution to a probing problem. Experts advised career girls that time was short and the supply of potential mates scarce, so they better put their best foot forward to find a suitable mate before it was too late.[158]

The impact of the marriage and family discourse of the late 1930s appeared to resonate most heavily on the campus of Mount Holyoke. In the early 1930s articles in *The Mount Holyoke News* focused on studies, career goals, travel and philosophical issues. By the late 1930s, poems about marriage, gossip columns about proposals and engagements and stories about how to avoid spinsterhood began appearing in the paper.[159]

Young women who were truly invested in pursuing marriage were encouraged to find out more about themselves and their true calling in life by performing a variety of self-assessments. To assist with this goal, many manuals included personality inventories that promised to aid women in finding husbands by helping them to see themselves as others saw them.[160] The inventories, for the most part, were hybrid creations that blended measures and methods used in psychological tests with mainstream language to make them palatable to the public. Several large tomes about making good marital matches were published during the Depression era; for example, a team of psychologists banded together to produce *Psychological Factors in Marital Happiness* which used 400 variables—under the subheadings of personality factors, background factors and sexual adjustment factors—to calculate the marital happiness of 792 couples.[161] During the 1930s personality became a larger arbiter of a person's value, possibly because personality was one asset that people could carry with them regardless of the larger economic situation. In the inventories one's personality was depicted as a reified commodity that had the necessary plasticity to be molded into something more appealing. One author defined personality as the organization of individual characteristics that could be improved upon, built up, striven for and achieved through conscientious labor.[162]

Experts prescribed personality inventories to women by explaining that any woman who could adequately inventory her personality, evaluate the results, take stock in herself and then follow steps toward self-improvement would attain a reasonable level of success in the game of husband winning. Once young women performed self-evaluations on their personalities and tallied up their faults, they were advised to invite their friends to enumerate their failings too. One author explained that the shock of finding out what others thought was "good psychological medicine" for young women because seeing oneself through other's eyes immediately broke bad habits. Besides, the author argued, the effect of shocking revelations was one of the important discoveries of psychoanalysis.[163] Another author who also suggested that young women have their friends rank them explained that although it could prove painful to hear criticism from friends, it was the lack of self-knowledge that prevented women from getting what they truly desired. The writer assured readers that a bit of psychological anguish was a small price to pay for snaring a husband.[164]

One writer likened the self-inventory process to the practice in some countries of rating one's own property. He invited female readers to ponder their various attributes including looks, charm, wealth, strength of character, breeding, family tree and disposition. Once the young woman performed this task, she was advised to decide what minimum reciprocal qualities she expected from a husband.[165] Women were counseled not place too low an estimate on themselves because it might lead them into making a poor marital bargain that they would regret for the rest of their lives. The writer stated that this usually was not an issue because most women tended to "evaluate themselves at too high a rate."[166] One female writer, unlike other mass-market manual authors, advised against altering one's interests and personality in order to attract a marriageable mate. Instead, self-knowledge was depicted as an asset that would help women make wise choices. The promise of the personality test was that it would help women ferret out their faults, highlight their "assets and disguise their liabilities in order to lead a man to the altar."[167] Personality tests and inventories were taken quite seriously in the late 1930s. Two dissertations, both written by women, questioned the validity of personality tests and took issue with their use by both professionals and lay people. Both critiqued the notion that personality was a quantifiable entity and raised concerns about testing procedures, the consistency and validity of ratings and discrimination in rater attitudes.[168]

The personality inventory and taking stock of oneself spread to college campuses in the later years of the Depression. During the mid-to-late 1930s the Mount Holyoke campus became a site for a flurry of self-improvement talks and stock-taking opportunities. Elizabeth Arden traveled to the campus in the fall of 1936 to inform women that their success hinged upon their personal appearance and that they should work on their looks, charm and personality in order to overcome their innate inferiority complexes.[169] Another beauty consultant, Miss Osborne, spoke at Mount Holyoke in November 1936. She explained that young women should conceptualize college as training school for poise and personality. Every girl possessed the power to fashion herself into "a very decorative person." In order to appeal to the serious Holyoke crowd, Osborne contended that making oneself decorative would lead to greater career success. Nevertheless, each female student was advised to take it upon herself to acquire the necessary knowledge to make the best of her assets and disguise her liabilities.

HUSBAND HUNTING

Once a woman had an accurate blueprint of herself, based on knowledge garnered from personality inventories, the husband-hunting mission could begin.[170] A "man-hunting expedition" was best pursued with vigor but without the "benefit of a gun, camera, or unpleasant publicity," because even if a woman was being the aggressor, she still had to pretend that the man was in control of the process.[171] Good huntresses never let men know that they were being pursued. A skilled female huntress appeared sweet, modest and maidenly, on the surface, but when "she stalks, she stalks to kill."[172] One author described a young woman who sidled up to a man at a dance, asked him to escort her home, introduced him to her mother and four months later they were married. The young woman accomplished this feat by never letting the man know that she was predatory, and by letting the man think that he was pursuing her. This game of conquest could only be won by letting the man think that he was the person calling the shots.[173] Another expert offered advice in the same vein, saying that young men were flattered by being pursued a little bit, but that "the old hunter instinct is an inherent part of the masculine nature and is stronger than the desire to be hunted."[174] If women were planning on doing the pursuing they had to be clever enough to make men think that they were the ones leading the pursuit.[175]

An intriguing aspect of the mass-marketed marriage manuals was that they portrayed husband hunting as empowering to women. The women who were willing to engage in the husband-hunting quest were told that they were smart and strong, two things young women of that era barely heard. Husband hunters were portrayed as powerful aggressors who could use their wits, charm and cunning to lure in and capture the mate of their choice. Some mass-market marriage manual authors likened husband hunting to job hunting; females who had interviewed for jobs knew to prepare themselves for the interview by finding out as much as they could about the position. Authors noted that these skills could be applied to husband hunting, so before setting out to find a man, women were advised to find out all that they could about men and "the requirements of marriage."[176] Husband hunting was likened to military maneuvers in several texts with young women being compared to wise generals who carefully train, equip and prepare themselves before setting forth on military campaigns.[177]

Potential husbands, on the other hand, were described as essentially interchangeable commodities. The individual characteristics of the potential husband were not all that important; the key was to procure the hot commodity as quickly as possible.[178] Some authors described marriageable men as scarce natural resources that women should set their sights on acquiring before the limited supply ran out. Many authors naturalized marriage as an inevitable outcome, describing how normal people had yet to discover a satisfactory substitute for marriage. Even so, a large number of unmarried men were "industriously engaged in the business of avoiding marriage" because they were in mortal fear of being led by the nose to the altar.[179] Most men believed that they would likely marry at some point, but most wished to postpone the "evil day as long as possible."[180] Meanwhile, almost every young woman who was unmarried was expected to spend a good deal of energy, time, intelligence and attractiveness trying to find a desirable husband.[181]

Some male students were aware that they were conceived of as commodities; a humorous article in the *George Washington University Hatchet* warned young men that they were being described as "E.B.'s—or Eligible Bachelors—" in publications like *Mademoiselle*. Writers for *Mademoiselle* explained to female readers that eligible bachelors had to be caught off guard and lured into marriage before they turned 30. After men had passed "that fateful milestone, it is a bitter, bitter struggle to make him give up his life of pampered ease and freedom, and by the time he is 35 nothing short of a shotgun is apt to introduce matrimony into his way of life."[182]

Allusions to shotguns and hunting down mates appeared in several mass-marketed marriage manuals of the late 1930s. Authors described young females as big-game hunters who craftily stalked potential mates. Big-game hunting required women to "camouflage" their intentions, to bait their prey and never to let the young men they were pursuing see the "huntress gleam" in their eyes.[183] One author explained that men's attitudes toward marriage were very much like that of a "fox in the hunt," the chances were that they would be caught, but there was always a small chance that they might get away after enjoying the fun of being chased.[184] While males were likened to foxes, women were advised to be cat-like in their pursuit of male prey. Emily Post explained that young women should not chase men, but they were allowed to do a little cat-like stalking. Young women who wanted to be cat-like had to learn to disguise their intentions and act nonchalant about their prey. Females who obviously bounded in pursuit of male mates, "like puppies let loose," lost their prize at the start.[185]

The license to hunt came with some responsibilities. While most authors condoned females stalking males, they advised against being an immature or restless huntress who sought male attention or who flitted from partner to partner because they feared making a commitment to one man.[186] These unscrupulous types of huntresses did not really care for individual men, but just enjoyed the thrill of the chase and the feeling of conquest.[187] They relished the "sport of love" and had no interest in long-term commitments, loyalty or devotion.[188] Huntresses who were only interested in racking up conquests were advised to "join a gun club and shoot for sport, start collecting Indian relics from the West, get into politics, athletics and organization work" or pursue other activities that would give them the thrill of glory they enjoyed.[189] One author summarized the whole hunting process by stating that it was "a pity that we should be at such cross purposes; that so much scheming and contriving, flight and pursuit, eluding and outwitting, should be necessary to bring about that which usually happens anyway in the natural course of events. But bear this fact in mind: most young men do not want to marry, particularly when the net result is only a wife, however charming she might be."[190]

The marriage and family debates, like the debates about rating and dating, contained some humorous elements as well. Even though women's pursuit of young men and marriage were believed to be the cornerstones for recovering national normalcy, there were some concerns about female agency going awry; hence the male fear of leap year. During leap years, women were allowed to propose marriage to men. The tradition, based on a Scottish law established in the thirteenth century, was that women could woo and propose marriage to any unmarried male whom they desired. In Scottish law a man who received a leap year proposal either had to accept or pay a hefty fine.[191] The United States had no such legal mandates, but tradition deemed that it was socially acceptable for women to pop the question during a leap year. Men from the University of Michigan were told not to worry about too many leap year proposals since the co-eds of 1936 were "as ineffective man-catchers as the bearded women of the itinerant circuses."[192] Men attending George Washington University, on the other hand, received many proposals in 1936. One writer described the "epidemic of engagements, marriages and female proposals" that occurred during the past year. Using quasi-military imagery that commonly appeared in mass-market marriage manuals, he took stock of the leap year "casualties" who were lured over to the "enemy's camp" by female "enchantresses schooled in the wiles of wooing man's weakness." Men who had escaped unscathed were allowed to "plod along in another three years of uninterrupted male aggression, prescribed by natural law."[193] The assumptions about women wanting to trap men into marriage, thereby taking away men's natural role as aggressor echo the biologically-deterministic sentiments expressed in most marriage manuals. Male students at Howard joked that they feared that aggressive young women who attended Howard "to learn pursuing" instead of "to pursue learning" were very likely to take the leap year prerogative and propose marriage to male classmates.[194] The only advantage that leap year gave young women, according to the *Howard Hilltop* writer, was the opportunity to "jump into a well of trouble."[195]

For the most part, expert authors and mass-market marriage manual writers encouraged young female readers to focus their energy toward securing the ultimate prize of a husband. The female power of captivation, where a woman could literally hold a man captive with her charm, was depicted as the ultimate weapon women wielded to ensnare a marital mate. Wise young women were advised to remember it was their responsibility to take the active role in romance and to keep working at the job of captivation.[196] This unpaid assignment of influencing men via the invisible force field of feminine allure was ranked by experts as a worthy pastime for young women to pursue. Authors advised female readers to direct their efforts toward keeping men interested in them in order to reap benefits of her labor in the future.

This emotional investment in the imminent success of men proved to be a risky venture akin to playing the marriage stock market. Young women could invest their romantic capital in one man with the hope that the emotional investment eventually would pay off in a lifetime of financial support and marital mirth. Females who grew up during the Depression era must have realized the risks involved in the endeavor, but the experts pushed the marriage as the primary means to access riches, stability and happiness for all. The images of women hunting men down, captivating and capturing them in the net of matrimony are the strongest representations of women exercising individual agency in Depression-era texts. Husband hunting and wedded bliss were upheld as the finest occupation for young women to pursue in the mid-to-late 1930s.

Experts depicted marriage as the only source of female happiness, which made the marriage market more competitive in the latter part of the 1930s.[197] By the end of the Depression era, a young woman's success in college could be measured by obtaining an engagement ring before graduation. For many women, getting married was upheld as the main means for proving their worth and desirability. The *Mount Holyoke News* ran a jubilant account of the fact that two Mount Holyoke women were getting married to Amherst men and only one woman from Smith was. The Amherst adage that the males should "date Smith girls and marry Mount Holyoke girls" held true "since two girls from over the notch plan to take the vows with Amherst seniors while only one Smith girl has such plans."[198] For many young women of the late 1930s college shifted from being a place to learn about oneself, pursue academic excellence and prepare for a future career to being a stopping point at which to kill time before finding a husband and settling down to a life of domesticity.

The mid-to-late 1930s represented a time of brightened economic outlooks for the nation as a whole, but dimming prospects for many young women. After the beating that the institutions of marriage, male economic dominance and patriarchal privilege took in the early 1930s men seemed ready and women seemed resigned to reinstate gender normalcy by any means necessary. It appears that a mass fit of nostalgia overtook the youths of the late Depression era, causing them to reach back to an imagined past when life was predictable, marriages were stable and abundance was the middle-class norm. Young people experienced so much economic and emotional turmoil in the early years of the Great Depression that marriage must have appeared as an oasis, a haven and the first stop on the planned trajectory of a life of normalcy. The romantic element of wanting to enter wedded bliss represents part of the human condition, yet this element seemed heightened during the later years of the Depression. Young people, forced to postpone marrying their beloved, may have found an increased sense of romanticism in the yearning process. Undergraduates were extremely pragmatic in their demands for marriage and family courses; they wanted clearly-stated rules, matter-of-fact outlines and proven methods to woo and win a matc. While the romanticism and pragmatism appeared well balanced, the tinge of fatalism laced throughout much of the discourse cannot be ignored. Without question, youths wanted to wed, but women who had tasted the financial fruits of their wage-earning labor had a difficult time giving it up for marriage. For the most part, life in the business world was likely no more romantic or exciting than life as a married woman; yet women who had earned college degrees wanted to have choices about how to use their skills and education. Unfortunately, the discourse surrounding marriage and family courses silenced some of the main players, leaving little room for discussion.

Notes

NOTES TO CHAPTER ONE

1. "A Sense of Values" *The University of Michigan Daily,* 3 July 1932.
2. Loren Baritz, *The Good Life: The Meaning of Success for the American Middle Class* (New York: Alfred A. Knopf, 1989), 109.
3. See Barbara and John Ehrenreich, "The Professional-Managerial Class," *Radical America,* Part 1, 11 (March-April 1977): 7–31 and Part 2, 11 (May-June 1977): 7–22 and Barbara and John Ehrenreich, Eds. "The Professional Managerial Class," *Between Labor and Capital* (Boston: South End Press, 1979), 5–45.
4. Frederick Lewis Allen, *Since Yesterday: The Nineteen-Thirties in America, September 3, 1929-September 3, 1939* (New York: Harper & Brothers Publishers, 1940), 57–9.
5. The apparent randomness of how and where misfortune struck deeply disturbed members of the middle class. Economic defeat visited upon people "without rhyme or reason" and struck the "feckless and hardworking, the virtuous and the irresponsible" alike. Frederick Lewis Allen, *The Big Change: America Transforms Itself, 1900–1950* (New York: Harper & Brothers Publishers, 1952), 148–149.
6. David Tyack, Robert Lowe, and Elisabeth Hansot, *Public Schools in Hard Times: The Great Depression and Recent Years* (Cambridge: Harvard University Press, 1984), 3.
7. Robert S. McElvaine, *The Great Depression: America, 1929–1941* (New York: Times Books, 1984), 90.
8. The Depression era is often conceptualized as an historical moment when people instantaneously disposed of all of the frivolous trappings of the roaring 1920s, picked up their pens, wrote manifestos and joined the communist party. Historian Paula Fass notes that the decade of the 1920s is often treated as if it can only be understood in cultural rather than political terms. Paula S. Fass, *The Damned and the Beautiful: American Youth in the 1920s* (New York: Oxford University Press, 1977), 4. The 1930s have suffered a similar fate of being conceptualized as a decade dominated

by economic decline and government programs. The crisis of capitalism undoubtedly shaped the culture of the 1930s, but social and cultural history marched on in tandem with political and economic history. Exploring the lives of middle-class experts and college students shines light on some of the unexplored cultural territory of the Depression era.

9. Several authors address the issue of the hostility working women faced during the Depression era. See Lois Scharf, *To Work and To Wed: Female Employment, Feminism, and the Great Depression* (Westport, CT: Greenwood Press, 1980), Susan Ware, *Holding Their Own: American Women in the 1930s* (Boston: Twayne Publishers, 1982) and Lynn Y. Weiner, *From Working Girl to Working Mother: The Female Labor Force in the United States, 1820–1980* (Chapel Hill: University of North Carolina Press, 1985).
10. Michael Denning, *The Cultural Front: The Laboring of American Culture in the Twentieth Century* (New York: Verso, 1996), xvi.
11. Johanna Brenner, "On Gender and Class in U.S. Labor History," *Monthly Review,* (New York: Monthly Review Press) Vol. 50, No. 6, November 1998.
12. These schools and their newspapers were carefully chosen to represent a degree of demographic, gender and racial diversity while also providing some basis of comparison based on the schools' proximity to each other in the cases of Amherst and Mount Holyoke and The George Washington University and Howard University. All of the newspapers—*The Amherst Student, The George Washington University Hatchet, The Howard Hilltop, The Mount Holyoke News* and *The University of Michigan Daily* are available on microfilm.
13. Winifred D. Wandersee, *Women's Work and Family Values, 1920–1940* (Cambridge: Harvard University Press, 1981), 21.
14. William Leach, *Land of Desire: Merchants, Power and the Rise of a New American Culture* (New York: Vintage Books, 1993), 3.
15. Ibid.
16. Beginning in the late nineteenth century middle-class workers had become quite adept at closing their ranks to outsiders without forming labor unions. They accomplished this by forming professional associations to limit entrance into certain fields. In the 1870s the first state bar examinations for lawyers were installed and medical licensing became the norm. By the 1930s licenses were required for accountants, architects, engineers and pharmacists. C. Wright Mills, *White Collar: The American Middle Classes* (London: Oxford University Press, 1951), 139.
17. It is important to emphasize that business people were upheld as somewhat heroic figures by members of the middle-class during the 1920s. It appears that middle-class undergraduates and experts shared a fondness for the language of the marketplace and that they had an equally difficult time letting go of the rhetoric embraced by the iconic experts of the previous decade. In the early 1920s a recent Yale graduate named Dwight MacDonald met with the owners of Macy's department store and was awed by their pecuniary prowess and business acumen, stating that "The power is all in business. . . . These men I saw were keener, more efficient, more

sure of their power than any college prof I ever knew." Leach, *Land of Desire*, 281.

18. Ashley Frank, "Liberalism as Intellectual Leadership," *The Philosopher*, Volume LXXXVI, 1998. During the latter part of the nineteenth century, progressive social workers professionalized their endeavors, reformed old professional categories and carved out new ones for themselves. The professional category of experts was further refined with a scientific twist in the late 1920s and early 1930s. Sociological research found new problems and created new categories of employees to contend with them. Experts residing in their newly-justified professional categories enjoyed their prestige, power and privilege and desired to hold on to them. Experts, who were crafty about creating markets for their expertise, could maintain significant control over those markets.
19. Ibid.
20. Pierre Bourdieu, *The Field of Cultural Production: Essays on Art and Literature* (New York: Columbia University Press, 1993), 7.
21. Ibid, 75.
22. Elliot B. Weininger, "Class Analysis and Cultural Analysis in Bourdieu," *Economic Sociology European Electronic Newsletter*, Vol. 4, No. 2 (March 2003).
23. "Success Based on Material Goods," *The George Washington University Hatchet*, 14 February 1933. A professor of journalism from University of Alabama named C.E. Cason stated in an address to students that the main valuation of success in America had been based upon the ability to accumulate material goods. "The unripe mind can measure only in terms of size and numbers. Greater maturity is necessary before one can understand that the realities of life consist of such intangibles as friendship, beauty, integrity, harmony, truth, and understanding." Cason believed that Americans would soon learn this through the struggles encountered during "the painful era through which we are now passing."
24. Baritz, *The Good Life*, 56.
25. Michael Kimmel, *Manhood in America: A Cultural History* (New York: Free Press, 1996), 84.
26. Ibid, 396.
27. My method to explore how middle-class experts and college students articulated their middle class status in a time of economic crisis involved reading 200 advice books from the Library of Congress and the full run of student newspapers from five colleges published between the years of 1930–1941. The publishers of the 200 books ranged from mainstream to highly-specialized. The final 65 used as exemplary texts were mostly produced by well-known publishing houses in New York City. D. Appleton & Company (8); MacMillan (7); E.P. Dutton Company (6); Abingdon Press (5); Farrar & Rinehart (5); McGraw Hill (5); Scribners Sons (5); Christopher Publishing House (4); J.B. Lippincott (4); Less than three titles: Bantam Publishing, Dell, Doubleday, Dorrance and Company, Eugenics Press, Harcourt Brace, Hillman-Curl Incorporated, Home Institute Incorporated, Little, Brown & Company, Prentice-Hall, Random House, Womans Press.

28. Beth L. Bailey, *From Front Porch to Back Seat: Courtship in Twentieth-Century America* (Baltimore: Johns Hopkins University Press, 1988), 6.
29. College professors had an advantage in selling knowledge as a commodity. They "brought to the market" the prestige of a university background coupled with a "halo of disinterestedness." Mills, *White Collar,* 133.
30. One obstacle in using college newspapers as a means to access the voices of Depression-era youths is that in the 1930s many educational institutions could not afford to publish a daily or weekly paper. Hence, my sample is drawn from prominent private colleges and one large public university. Three of the schools in the sample were coeducational during the 1930s, while two were single-gender colleges. Most of the schools had predominantly white students in attendance while Howard University boasted an African-American student body.
31. Roland Marchand, *Advertising the American Dream: Making Way for Modernity, 1920–1940 (*Berkeley: University of California Press, 1985), xv.
32. There is a sense of cross-pollination between student newspapers around the country. This phenomenon becomes apparent when reading the papers against one another over time and seeing that the same issues arise and similar opinions are expressed. Part of this phenomenon can be attributed to the rise of mass media and the ability for rapid cross-country communication. By the mid-1930s *The George Washington University Hatchet* and *The Michigan Daily* both regularly ran columns containing bits of news from other college campuses from all of the regions of the country including the West, Northwest, Midwest, South, Southwest, East Coast and Mid Atlantic states. *The Amherst Student* and *The Mount Holyoke News* published stories of happenings on other campuses, but mainly focused on the East Coast Ivy League and Seven Sisters schools. *The Howard Hilltop* contained some stories from other campuses, but most articles that focused on the outside world looked at political issues and conflicts rather than news from other campuses.
33. "The Student and the Outside World," *The Amherst Student,* 16 April 1936.
34. "Intellectual, Sociology Conscious Amherst Students Satirized in Broadway Production," *The Amherst Student,* 2 March 1936.
35. "A Cooperative Welcome," *The George Washington University Hatchet,* 31 July 1934.
36. A survey conducted in 1932 showed that of the one hundred colleges for African-Americans in the South, only six were doing grade A work. Major foundations that contributed to improving educational opportunities for African-American students decided to concentrate on developing four centers for African-American graduate and professional training. Howard University was one of the institutions chosen and was maintained by the federal government. Gould Beech, "Schools for a Minority," *Survey Graphic,* October, 1939, Vol. 28, No. 10.
37. "Farewell Editorial," *The Howard Hilltop,* 5 June 1936.
38. Gould Beech, "Schools for a Minority," *Survey Graphic,* October, 1939, Vol. 28, No. 10.

39. Patricia A. Palmieri, "Women's Colleges," *Women in Academe: Progress and Prospects,* Mariam K. Chamberlain, ed. (New York: Russell Sage Foundation, 1988), 107–131.
40. Ibid.
41. Pierre Bourdieu and Jean-Claude Passeron, *Reproduction in Education, Society and Culture,* Translated by Richard Nice (London: Sage, 1990), 153.
42. Barbara Ehrenreich, *Fear of Falling: The Inner Life of the Middle Class* (New York: Pantheon Books, 1989), 15.
43. Ibid, 13–14.
44. Before the New Deal was in place "rugged individualism" was embraced as the key to social progress in the United States. The ideals of rugged individualism and acquisitive striving lost some of their golden sheen during the Depression years. When the economy and job market were in good shape, the "winners" could argue that life in the United States was a meritocracy, with systems that were fair, equitable and accessible to all. The winners could blame the losers for being losers because if they just tried harder in the equitable system they could step into the winners circle. The disruption brought on by the Depression dissevered this notion.
45. Tyack, et al., *Public Schools in Hard Times,* 111.
46. Bourdieu, *The Field of Cultural Production,* 2.
47. Ibid, 24.
48. "Mount Holyoke Graduates Defy Business Depression," *The Mount Holyoke News,* 17 October 1931.
49. "Graduate Work, Secretarial Study Claim Majority of 1938; Many Are Now Teaching," *The Mount Holyoke News,* 11 November 1938.
50. "Class of 1939 Will Scatter from Boston to Persia in Variety of New Occupations," *The Mount Holyoke News,* 12 June 1939.
51. "Public Opinion," *The Mount Holyoke News,* 24 March 1938.
52. Lucy D. Slowe, "Higher Education of Negro Women," *The Journal of Negro Education,* Vol. 2, No. 3, July 1933, 352–328.
53. Ibid.
54. Ibid.
55. "What After College?" *The Howard Hilltop,* 22 December 1934.
56. "The Question of Jobs," *The Howard Hilltop,* 30 April 1933.
57. Wandersee, *Women's Work and Family Values,* 32.
58. Glen H. Elder, Jr., *Children of the Great Depression: Social Change in Life Experience,* 25th Anniversary Edition (Boulder, CO: Westview, 1999). The people who interviewed middle-class and working-class people about the impact of the Depression on their families rated middle-class mothers who had unemployed husbands as having higher levels of fatigue, feelings of inadequacy and feelings of insecurity than their working-class counterparts. Middle-class unemployment was associated with heavy drinking and reduced participation in social life outside the family. The authors interpreted these effects as defensive responses to loss of status.
59. Warren Susman, *Culture as History: The Transformation of American Society in the Twentieth Century* (New York: Pantheon Books, 1984), 165.

60. Ehrenreich, *Fear of Falling*, 13.
61. Susman, *Culture as History*, xxi.
62. Bourdieu, *The Field of Cultural Production*, 4.
63. Steve Kangas, "A Review of Keynesian Theory," from "The Great Depression: Its Causes and Cure," *Liberalism Resurgent* (1997).
64. Bourdieu explains that a small group of experts and producers monopolize the field of cultural consecration; that is areas of culture in which the formation of canons and the creation of trends occur. Pierre Bourdieu, *Distinction: A Social Critique of the Judgment of Taste*, Translated by Richard Nice, (Cambridge: Harvard University Press, 1984), 386.
65. Bourdieu, *The Field of Cultural Production*, 7.
66. Thorstein Veblen, *Theory of the Leisure Class: An Economic Study of Institutions* (New York: B.W. Huebsch, 1899).
67. Pierre Bourdieu, "Social Space and Symbolic Power," *Sociological Theory*, Volume 7, Issue 1 (Spring 1989), 19.
68. Bourdieu, *The Field of Cultural Production*, 23.
69. Willard Waller, "The Rating and Dating Complex," *American Sociological Review*, Volume 2, Issue 5, October 1937, 729.
70. Helen Lefkowitz Horowitz, *Campus Life: Undergraduate Cultures from the End of the Eighteenth Century to the Present* (New York: Alfred A. Knopf, 1987), xi.
71. David Tyack and Elisabeth Hansot. *Managers of Virtue: Public School Leadership in America, 1820—1980* (New York: Basic Books, 1982), 106.
72. Ibid, 107.
73. Judith Butler, *Gender Trouble: Feminism and the Subversion of Identity* (New York: Routledge, 1990), 19.
74. Brenner, "On Gender and Class in U.S. Labor History."
75. Steven Seidman, *Romantic Longings: Love in America, 1830–1980* (New York: Routledge, 1991), 68.
76. Caroll Smith-Rosenberg, *Disorderly Conduct: Visions of Gender in Victorian America* (New York: Oxford University Press, 1985), 245–96.
77. Kimmel, *Manhood in America*, 87.
78. Seidman, *Romantic Longings*, 68.
79. Clark Davis, "The Corporate Reconstruction of Middle-Class Manhood," *The Middling Sorts: Explorations in the History of the American Middle Class*, eds. Burton J. Bledstein and Robert D. Johnston, (New York: Routledge, 2001), 205.
80. Victoria Wolcott, *Remaking Respectability: African American Women in Interwar Detroit* (Chapel Hill: University of North Carolina Press, 2001), introduction.
81. Paula Giddings, *When and Where I Enter: The Impact of Black Women on Race and Sex in America* (New York: Bantam Books, 1984), 205.
82. William A. Sundstrom, "Last Hired, First Fired? Unemployment and Urban Black Workers During the Great Depression," *The Journal of Economic History*, Vol. 52, No. 2 (June 1992), 415–429. Drawing on data from several sources, including the federal census from 1930, which included a special report about unemployment; a special census conducted in 1931

that measured unemployment rates in 21 selected urban areas; a National Health Survey taken in the winter of 1935–1936 that collected both health and employment data for heads of households; and the U.S. Census of Partial Employment, Unemployment and Occupations that canvassed almost 510,000 households on randomly-selected postal routes during the months of November and December 1937. The statistics cannot distinguish labor from managerial jobs, so I will have to infer that holding on to a middle-class existence was more difficult for African-American families than for white families during the Depression era.

83. *Fifteenth Census: Unemployment* (Washington, DC: U.S. Bureau of the Census) Vol. 2, 232–233, 370–373. By January 1931 the unemployment rates in seven northern cities—including Cleveland, Chicago, Detroit, Manhattan, Philadelphia, Pittsburgh and St. Louis—had skyrocketed, with 27.8% of white males being unemployed and 40.5 of African-American men being unemployed. White women dwelling in northern urban environments faired much better than their counterparts, facing only a 16.9% unemployment level, while African-American women felt the worst effects of the depression with a whopping 45.6% unemployment rate. The 1931 census also measured unemployment in three southern cities including Birmingham, Houston and New Orleans, where 18.6% of white men and 35.9% of black men were unemployed. White women in the three southern cities had an unemployment rate of 14.4% while black women had a rate of 36.2% unemployment.
84. Sundstrom, "Last Hired, First Fired?" 415–429.
85. Ibid, 419.
86. Ruth Feldstein, *Motherhood in Black and White: Race and Sex in American Liberalism, 1930–1965* (Ithaca: Cornell University Press, 2000), 3.
87. Alice Kessler-Harris, *In Pursuit of Equity: Women, Men, and the Quest for Economic Citizenship in 20th-Century America* (New York: Oxford University Press, 2001).
88. Julia Hanna, "Women as Wage Earners," *The Radcliffe Quarterly,* Fall 2001.
89. "Casual Essays," *The University of Michigan Daily,* 13 July 1934.
90. Ibid.
91. Ibid.
92. Wolcott, *Remaking Respectability,* introduction.
93. Michael Kammen, *American Culture, American Tastes: Social Change and the 20th Century* (New York: Knopf, 1999), 53.
94. Susan J. Matt, "Frocks, Finery, and Feelings: Rural and Urban Women's Envy, 1890–1930,"*An Emotional History of the United States,* eds. Peter N. Stearns and Jan Lewis (New York: New York University Press, 1998), 389.
95. Susan J. Matt, *Keeping Up with the Joneses: Envy in American Consumer Society, 1890–1930* (Philadelphia: University of Pennsylvania Press, 2003), 41.
96. Seidman, *Romantic Longings,* 67.

97. Carol Ascher, "Selling to Ms. Consumer," *American Media and Mass Culture: Left Perspectives*, Ed. Donald Lazere (Berkeley: University of California Press, 1987), 44–5.
98. Ibid, 45.
99. Giddings, *When and Where I Enter*, 205.
100. Davis, "The Corporate Reconstruction of Middle-Class Manhood," 202.
101. Ascher, "Selling to Ms. Consumer," 44
102. Davis, "The Corporate Reconstruction of Middle-Class Manhood," 206.
103. Ibid, 202–5.
104. Elder, *Children of the Great Depression*, 50.
105. Ibid.
106. Dana D. Nelson, *National Manhood: Capitalist Citizenship and the Imagined Fraternity of White Men* (Durham: Duke University Press, 1998), ix.
107. Bourdieu, "Social Space and Symbolic Power," 22.
108. Homer P. Rainey, *How Fare American Youth?* (New York: D. Appleton-Century Company, 1937), 47.
109. Robert Cooley Angell, Lowell Julliard Carr, and Charles Horton Cooley *Introductory Sociology* (New York: Charles Scribners Sons, 1933), 167.
110. The majority of books and magazines, 90% in Angell's contention, "tended to define the world in stereotyped patterns" the press was less interested in transmitting new ideas to the world than in "drumming home old ones" which inevitably produced "a certain uniformity of mental outlook." Angell, et al. *Introductory Sociology*, 167.
111. Janice A. Radway quoting Harry Scherman, The Book of the Month Club founder in A *Feeling for Books: The Book of the Month Club, Literary Taste and Middle-Class Desire* (Chapel Hill: University of North Carolina Press, 1997), 199.
112. Olivier Zunz, *Why The American Century?* (Chicago: University of Chicago Press, 1998), 57.
113. Ibid, xii.
114. David J. Hoff, "Pioneers of Modern Testing," *Education Week*, June 16, 1999.
115. Ibid.
116. All major national tests in the United States, including SAT college-entrance exams, compare individual test-takers and groups of students against such norms. Thorndike also collaborated with Robert M. Yerkes and Lewis M. Terman to develop the Alpha-Beta tests that were used on people in the U.S. Army in World War I. Hoff, "Pioneers of Modern Testing."
117. Ibid.
118. Ibid.
119. Zunz, *Why The American Century?* 39.

NOTES TO CHAPTER TWO

1. "What the Public Doesn't Know," *The University of Michigan Daily*, 20 November 1934.

2. Frederick Lewis Allen quoting the editors of *Fortune* magazine in *Since Yesterday: The Nineteen-Thirties in America, September 3, 1929—September 3, 1939* (New York. Harper & Brothers, 1940), 160.
3. One survey of 1,286 families taken in 1932 in Detroit found that only one third of the respondents were regularly employed, while 75 percent of them were looking for jobs. The median income had dropped by two thirds since the stock market crash in 1929. Ten families lost their mortgaged homes while 28 were evicted for missing rent payments. Almost half of those interviewed lost their entire savings accounts while others surrendered life insurance policies and had items that were bought on installment plans repossessed. David Tyack, Robert Lowe, and Elisabeth Hansot, *Public Schools in Hard Times; The Great Depression and Recent Years* (Cambridge: Harvard University Press,1984)
4. John Modell, *Into One's Own: From Youth to Adulthood in the United States, 1920–1975* (Berkeley: University of California Press, 1989), 160.
5. Homer P. Rainey, *How Fare American Youth? A Report to the American Youth Commission and the American Council on Education* (New York: D. Appleton-Century Company, 1937), 36–7.
6. "The Cash Market Value of Higher Education," *The University of Michigan Daily*, 16 October 1932.
7. Ibid.
8. *Courageous Living in Times of Crisis* (New York: The Woman's Press, 1933), 13.
9. "Another Senior" *The Amherst Student*, 5 December 1932.
10. Pierre Bourdieu, "Social Space and Symbolic Power," *Sociological Theory*, Volume 7, Issue 1, (Spring 1989), 21.
11. "Another Senior" *The Amherst Student*, 5 December 1932.
12. Loren Baritz, *The Good Life: The Meaning of Success for the American Middle Class* (New York: Alfred A. Knopf, 1989), 56.
13. Willard Waller, "The Rating and Dating Complex," *American Sociological Review*, Volume 2, Issue 5 (October 1937), 728–9.
14. Carol Tomlinson-Keasey and Charles Blake Keasey, "Graduating from College in the 1930s: The Terman Genetic Studies of Genius," *Women's Lives through Time: Educated Women of the Twentieth Century*, Kathleen Day Hulbert and Diane Tickton Schuster, eds. (San Francisco: Jossey-Bass Publishers, 1993), 89. The Terman longitudinal study followed the lives of 672 girls and 856 boys with a mean IQ of 151 from the 1920s through the 1980s. The study found that the women in the group who did not complete college suffered from higher levels of stress, marital dissatisfaction, emotional disturbances, nervous tendencies and health problems than their female peers who finished college.
15. Ibid.
16. Paula Giddings, *When and Where I Enter: The Impact of Black Women on Race and Sex in America*, (New York: Bantam Books, 1984), 248.
17. "Educational Prosperity" quoting Dean Raymond Walters of Swarthmore College, *The University of Michigan Daily*, 16 December 1931.

18. Louis M. Hacker, *American Problems of Today: A History of the United States since the World War* (New York: F.S. Crofts & Company, 1938), 153.
19. Frederick Lewis Allen explained that the 1930s were a strange time in which to graduate from high school or college. "High schools had larger attendance than ever before, especially in the upper grades, because there were few jobs to tempt any one away. Likewise college graduates who could afford to go on to graduate school were continuing their studies-after a hopeless hunt for jobs-rather than be idle." Allen, *Since Yesterday,* 65.
20. "Educational Prosperity," *The University of Michigan Daily,* 16 December 1931.
21. "Our Costs of Living," *The Mount Holyoke News,* 24 May 1930.
22. Pierre Bourdieu, *Distinction: A Social Critique of the Judgment of Taste,* Translated by Richard Nice (Cambridge: Harvard University Press, 1984), 114.
23. E. Anthony Rotundo, *American Manhood: Transformations in Masculinity from the Revolution to the Modern Era* (New York: Basic Books, 1993), 212.
24. Steven Seidman, *Romantic Longings: Love in America, 1830–1980* (New York: Routledge, 1991), 69.
25. Helen Lefkowitz Horowitz, *Campus Life: Undergraduate Cultures from the End of the Eighteenth Century to the Present* (New York: Alfred A. Knopf, 1987), 197.
26. Rotundo, *American Manhood,* 209.
27. Horowitz, *Campus Life,* 202.
28. Jeanne Westin, *Making Do: How Women Survived the '30s* (Chicago: Follett Publishing Company, 1976), 84.
29. Susan Ware, *Beyond Suffrage: Women in the New Deal* (Cambridge: Harvard University Press, 1981), 22.
30. Ibid.
31. Jana Nidiffer, "Crumbs from the Boy's Table: The First Century of Coeducation," *Women Administrators in Higher Education: Historical and Contemporary Perspectives,* Ed. Jana Nidiffer and Carolyn Terry Bashaw (Albany: State University of New York Press, 2001), 19.
32. Elizabeth Eldridge, *Co-Ediquette: Poise and Popularity for Every Girl* (New York: E.P. Dutton, 1936), 28.
33. "Social Activity at New High as Coed Enrollment Jumps" *The University of Michigan Daily,* 28 June 1934.
34. "Give Us More Women" *The University of Michigan Daily* reprinted from *The Daily Illini,* 18 September 1934.
35. Ellen Lupton, *Mechanical Brides: Women and Machines from Home to Office* (New York: Cooper-Hewitt National Museum of Design Smithsonian Institution and Princeton Architectural Press, 1993), 44.
36. Horowitz, *Campus Life,* 197.
37. Nidiffer, "Crumbs from the Boy's Table," 23.

38. Robert Cooley Angell, *A Study in Undergraduate Adjustment* (Chicago: University of Chicago Press, 1930), 40.
39. Pierre Bourdieu, *The Field of Cultural Production: Essays on Art and Literature,* edited and introduced by Randal Johnson, (New York: Columbia University Press, 1993), 83.
40. "Alpha Nu Defends Right to Bar Women From Union Front Door," *The University of Michigan Daily,* 22 November 1932.
41. "The Union's Sanctity Violated by Feminine Swarms Tonight," *The University of Michigan Daily,* 8 November 1932.
42. Ibid.
43. "On Other Campuses," *The University of Michigan Daily,* 16 October 1932.
44. Ibid.
45. Ibid.
46. Abram de Swaan, *The Management of Normality: Critical Essays in Health and Welfare* (London: Routledge, 1990), 170.
47. At George Washington University in 1933, fraternity men had a grade point average of 2.10, while non-affiliated men had a 2.22. The University average for all men was 2.18. Sorority women had a collective grade point average of 2.47 compared to the 2.68 average of unpledged women. "Scholastic Statistics," *The George Washington University Hatchet* 10 October 1933.
48. "Be Just," *The Howard Hilltop,* 27 February 1931.
49. Ibid.
50. Ibid.
51. "Women Are Here to Give Men What They Want, Admit Coeds," *The University of Michigan Daily,* 15 January 1932
52. John H. Holcombe, a male from Massachusetts sent a letter to *The Mount Holyoke News* noting that the brains of women weighed less than men, but that the size of the brain failed to determine intellectual capacity. Holcombe, like the Alpha Nu men, also recognized that women who attended public coeducational colleges took the lead in attaining higher grades and scholastic honors than their male peers. "A Man's Idea of the Modern College Girl," John H. Holcombe, *The Mount Holyoke News,* 23 May 1931.
53. Pierre Bourdieu, *Outline of a Theory of Practice* (Cambridge: Cambridge University Press, 1977), 161.
54. Bourdieu, "Social Space and Symbolic Power," 21.
55. Bourdieu, *Outline of a Theory of Practice,* 161.
56. An example of a gold-digger joke was a poem sent in by an undergraduate at the University of Michigan, who wrote: "Eanie, meanie, miney, mo/ Don't ever take a co-ed's "no"/If she hollers let her know/There is just one way to get your dough." The same day, a quip about women's fickle nature appeared in the same column, "If a co-ed does it, she exercises the feminine privilege of changing her mind. If a man does it, he is a cock-eyed liar." "Collegiate Observer," *The University of Michigan Daily,* 25 September 1934. The column in the George Washington University paper also ran

jokes at women's expense, including, "Purely in a detached scientific fashion it was pointed out that the girls at Barnard college had emotionally, considerable in common with little nursery children of ages two to six." "On Other Campuses," *The George Washington University Hatchet*, 30 January 1934.

57. "Co-Eds—Blah," *The University of Michigan Daily*, 6 October 1934.
58. Curtis Humes, "Pierre Bourdieu, Reflexive Practice," [http://themargins.net/fps/links.htm], 1999.
59. "Brains," *The University of Michigan Daily*, 28 September 1933.
60. Ibid.
61. Angell, *A Study in Undergraduate Adjustment*, 40.
62. Ibid.
63. Horowitz, *Campus Life*, 199–201.
64. "Fascinating Womanhood Again . . ." *The Mount Holyoke News*, 8 November 1930.
65. Ibid.
66. Ibid.
67. "Please Cash My Check," *The Mount Holyoke News*, 9 March 1933.
68. "Our Rating" *The Mount Holyoke News*, 5 March 1932.
69. Ronald L. F. Davis, "Surviving Jim Crow: In-Depth Essay," [http://www.jimcrowhistory.org/history/surviving2.htm], 2005.
70. Ibid.
71. Ibid.
72. Jerrold M. Packard, *American Nightmare: The History of Jim Crow* (New York: St. Martin's Press, 2002).
73. Youth File from Group I (1909–1939) of the NAACP collection, Manuscripts Division of the Library of Congress, Washington, D.C.
74. Speech by Eleanor Roosevelt printed in *The Journal of Negro Education* 3 (October 1934): 573—575. Address delivered at the National Conference on Fundamental Problems in the Education of Negroes, Washington, D.C., May 11, 1934.
75. Rainey, *How Fare American Youth?*, 10.
76. *The Journal of Negro Education* 3 (October 1934): 573—575. Address delivered at the National Conference on Fundamental Problems in the Education of Negroes, Washington, D.C., May 11, 1934.
77. Ibid.
78. Ibid.
79. Ibid.
80. "Does Higher Education Pay?" *The University of Michigan Daily* reprinted from *The Salem Republican Leader*, 29 June 1932, quoting Mary R. Beard, co-author of *The Rise of American Civilization*.
81. Bourdieu, *The Field of Cultural Production*, 97.
82. Ibid.
83. Maxine Davis, *The Lost Generation: A Portrait of American Youth Today* (New York: The MacMillan Company, 1936), 114.
84. "A Business Creed for School and College Girls," written by Benjamin R. Andrews from Teachers College at Columbia University, quoted in Adelaide

Laura Van Duzer, *Everyday Living for Girls* (Philadelphia: Lippincott, 1936), 251.

85. "Our Costs of Living," *The Mount Holyoke News*, 24 May 1930.
86. "Statistics," *The Mount Holyoke News*, 16 March 1934.
87. Ibid.
88. "87 Percent of Student Body Employed, Statistics Reveal in Searching Query," *The George Washington University Hatchet*, 30 January 1934.
89. Ibid.
90. "The University and Student Finances . . ." *The University of Michigan Daily*, 12 August 1932.
91. Ibid.
92. One student wrote that after figuring out that college is worthwhile, university students were forced to confront its corollary—if studying was worth while. The authors cited statistics compiled by the expert researchers who studied 3,806 employees from the American Telephone and Telegraph Company. The assessment was that scholarship had a dollars and cents value, and that people who got good grades were the most successful on the work force. In a survey of 3,806 ATT employees who attended college the study showed that employees who graduated in the first tenth had four times as good a chance of making a success in the business world as a people who finished in the lowest third. Walter S. Gifford, the President of AT&T stated that "The time is coming when the low scholarship man, like the non-college man, will be shut out of better opportunities in the professions and in business. "Studying Is Worth While," *The George Washington University Hatchet*, reprinted from the *South California Daily Trojan*, 3 October 1933.
93. "We Talk It Over With A Senior," *The George Washington University Hatchet*, 22 May 1933.
94. Ibid.
95. "The Value of an Education," *The University of Michigan Daily*, 21 February 1933.
96. "The Value of an Education" *The George Washington University Hatchet*, reprinted from *The Carnegie Tartan*, 3 October 1933.
97. "Wanted: A Job" *The Mount Holyoke News*, 4 May 1933.
98. Ibid.
99. "Women Face Wage Reduction" *The Mount Holyoke News*, 9 January 1932.
100. Ibid.
101. Ibid.
102. The national marriage rate in 1932 was the lowest ever recorded in the United States. Robert S. Lynd and Helen Merrell Lynd, *Middletown in Transition: A Study in Cultural Conflicts* (New York: Harcourt, Brace and Company, 1937), 149.
103. Lupton, *Mechanical Brides*, 44.
104. The following headlines from autumn 1931 illustrate that women were being told that they did not need to earn a college degree in order to attain a job: "College Education Not Necessary for Authors, Says Ellen Glasgow,"

The University of Michigan Daily, 30 September 1931; "Aviation Attracts Many Women Who Prove Themselves Skilled," *The University of Michigan Daily,* 14 October 1931; "Woman Poet Declares Marriage Is More Important Than Career," in which poet Ann Campbell, speaker at the Press Convention banquet stated, "Don't think that I take myself too seriously. I don't. I try always to remember what Havelock Ellis once said, 'Man is the genius.'" She went on to tell young women, "Don't give up marriage for a career. If you can't combine them, then don't have a career. After all, life is more important than poetry." *The University of Michigan Daily,* 21 November 1931. Another story ran in *The University of Michigan Daily* in the autumn1931 under the headline "Conformity to Social Convention Necessary Is Opinion of Author" quoted Susan Lee a contributor to the *North American Review* who stated that modern bachelor girls might have "an ideal existence" compared to women from past generations in that they had economic independence, "the first step towards happiness and self-respect." But while professional training opened up "worlds of self-expression for young women" being married proved far more important than independence and self-support ever could. "Conformity to Social Convention Necessary Is Opinion of Author" *The University of Michigan Daily,* 17 November 1931.

105. Robert S. McElvaine, *The Great Depression: America, 1929–1941,* (New York: Times Books, 1984), 182.
106. Ibid.
107. Ibid.
108. "Teaching Favored by College Women After Graduation" *The University of Michigan Daily,* 8 November 1932.
109. "Medicine and Law Most Profitable Professions," *The University of Michigan Daily,* 16 October 1932.
110. By 1940 about one third of all employed white women worked in the clerical sector, while only 1.2 percent of black women labored in these fields. Conversely, a full 60 percent of employed black females worked as domestic servants, compared to 10 percent of white women. Jacqueline Jones, *Labor of Love, Labor of Sorrow: Black Women, Work and the Family, From Slavery to the Present* (New York: Vintage Books, 1986), 200.
111. Giddings, *When and Where I Enter,* 147.
112. Ibid.
113. McElvaine *The Great Depression,* 183.
114. "What After College?" *The Howard Hilltop,* 22 December 1934.
115. McElvaine, *The Great Depression,* 187.
116. Ibid.
117. William A. Sundstrom, "Last Hired, First Fired? Unemployment and Urban Black Workers During the Great Depression," *The Journal of Economic History,* Vol. 52, No. 2 (June, 1992), 415–429.
118. Ibid.
119. Ibid.

120. "The Good Life," *The Howard Hilltop* 13 May 1936. Although this article was published after the time parameters of this chapter—1930–1934—it illustrates that even after the job market improved for white college graduates in the mid-1930s, African-American students still faced enormous obstacles when seeking to attain employment.
121. Ibid.
122. Myron D. Hockenbury, *Make Yourself A Job: A Student Employment Handbook* (Harrisburg: Dauphin Publishing Company, 1936), 20.
123. Rainey, *How Fare American Youth?*,132.
124. Ibid.
125. Ibid.
126. *The Journal of Negro Education* 3 (October 1934): 573—575. Address delivered at the National Conference on Fundamental Problems in the Education of Negroes, Washington, D.C., May 11, 1934.
127. Ibid.
128. "What After College?" *The Howard Hilltop,* 22 December 1934.
129. Karl Marx, *Capital: A Critique of Political Economy,* Translated by Samuel Moore and Edward Aveling; Edited by Frederick Engels (New York: The Modern Library, 1936).
130. Clark Davis, "The Corporate Reconstruction of Middle-Class Manhood," *The Middling Sorts: Explorations in the History of the American Middle Class,* eds. Burton J. Bledstein and Robert D. Johnston, (New York: Routledge, 2001), 207.
131. C. Wright Mills, *White Collar: The American Middle Classes* (London: Oxford University Press, 1951), xvii.
132. John Modell, *Into One's Own: From Youth to Adulthood in the United States, 1920–1975* (Berkeley: University of California Press, 1989), 69.
133. "The Age of Ballyhoo—Is It Waning?" *The University of Michigan Daily,* 27 November 1932.
134. "National Psychology," *The George Washington University Hatchet,* 11 April 1933.
135. "The Age of Ballyhoo—Is It Waning?" *The University of Michigan Daily,* 27 November 1932.
136. Bourdieu, *The Field of Cultural Production,* 4.
137. On the surface it appears bizarre and somewhat surprising that students from the different universities would express concern about their public image. Students appeared to be drawing on the works of Bruce Barton believed that countries should advertise themselves. He envisioned each nation explaining its achievements and ideals to the rest of the world as a means for promoting understanding and peace. Warren Susman, *Culture as History: The Transformation of American Society in the Twentieth Century* (New York: Pantheon Books, 1984), 127.
138. "What the Public Doesn't Know," *The University of Michigan Daily,* 20 November 1934.
139. In *The Damned and the Beautiful* Paula Fass describes how "national agencies like movies, magazines, and advertising which spread the influence of college fashions and styles turned the idea of youth into an eminently

salable commodity. A new genre, the movie about college life, flourished in the twenties, and a new technique for selling clothes that emphasized the prestige of the 'collegiate' style was introduced," *The Damned and the Beautiful: American Youth in the 1920s* (New York: Oxford University Press, 1977), 126.

140. "Students: Just Humans After All," *The University of Michigan Daily,* 25 March 1933.
141. "The College Myth," *The University of Michigan Daily,* 26 January 1932.
142. "Collegiate-ism Returns to High School," *The University of Michigan Daily,* 13 October 1931.
143. "Undergraduates Lauded By Campbell for Seriousness," *The University of Michigan Daily,* 28 January 1933.
144. "The New Deal College Student," *The University of Michigan Daily,* 7 August 1934.
145. "The College Myth," *The University of Michigan Daily,* 26 January 1932.
146. "Preserve the Illusion," *The University of Michigan Daily,* 19 January 1932.
147. Ibid.
148. "The College Myth," *The University of Michigan Daily,* 26 January 1932, reprinted from *The Indiana Daily Student.*
149. Ibid.
150. Gould Beech, "Schools for a Minority," *Survey Graphic,* October, 1939, Vol. 28, No. 10.
151. "What After College?" *The Howard Hilltop,* 22 December 1934.
152. Davis, *The Lost Generation,* 123.
153. "Student Advocates Raising Tuition Fee," F.D. Hunt, *The George Washington University Hatchet,* 17 January 1933.
154. Ibid.
155. "Headline Hash," *The Mount Holyoke News,* 16 November 1934.
156. David Tyack, Robert Lowe, and Elisabeth Hansford, *Public Schools in Hard Times: The Great Depression and Recent Years* (Cambridge: Harvard University Press, 1984), 92–138.
157. At the time the article was published, 36 schools including Bryn Mawr, Sarah Lawrence and Haverford also declined accepting government aid and support. "Relief: Hopkins Answers Critics of Federal Aid for Students," *Newsweek,* 1 December 1934.
158. "Relief: Hopkins Answers Critics Of Federal Aid for Students," *Newsweek,* 1 December 1934.
159. "Men Used To Monopolize Jobs—Now Women Are Muscling In," *The University of Michigan Daily,* 27 November 1932.
160. Ibid.
161. "140 Applications for Women's Work Effectively Handled" *The University of Michigan Daily,* 27 September 1933.
162. "Over $77,000 Earned by Women Working Way Through College" *The University of Michigan Daily,* 7 January 1933.

163. "87 Percent of Student Body Employed, Statistics Reveal in Searching Query," *The George Washington University Hatchet*, 30 January 1934.
164. Ibid.
165. During the Depression, many males at the University of Wisconsin-Madison took on the previously undesirable domestic work that had once been the sole domain of women. *The George Washington Hatchet* ran a story stating that 200 male students applied to work as domestics in Madison homes, performing tasks like cleaning, washing dishes, serving food, and acting as butlers and chauffeurs. Alice King, the director of the student employment bureau explained 1933 was the "first time in the seven year history of the bureau that men have outnumbered the women in their applications for work in a field formerly thought to belong to women alone." "Male Students Earn Cash by Housework," *The George Washington University Hatchet*, 10 November 1933.
166. Ibid.
167. "Over $77,000 Earned by Women Working Way Through College" *The University of Michigan Daily*, 7 January 1933.
168. Ibid.
169. "Margaret Whittemore Explains Rights for Women in Industry" By Elsie G. Feldman, *The University of Michigan Daily*, 4 November 1931.
170. "Statistics," *The Mount Holyoke News*, 16 March 1934.
171. "Who Wears the Pants?" *California Daily Bruin*, reprinted in *The University of Michigan Daily*, 6 October 1934.
172. Ibid.
173. Ibid.
174. "On Other Campuses," *The University of Michigan Daily*, 18 October 1932.
175. "The Coming of the Amazons" *The Amherst Student*, 1 May 1933.
176. "Control of Nation's Wealth By Women Reaches High Point," *The University of Michigan Daily*, 28 November 1931.
177. Ibid.
178. Paul Popenoe, *Modern Marriage: A Handbook for Men* (New York: The MacMillan Company, 1940), 70.
179. Ibid.
180. Ibid, 72.

NOTES TO CHAPTER THREE

1. "Black Friday Tradition Finds Little Support; Freshman Discover No Victims In Search For Wandering Sophomores," *The University of Michigan Daily*, 29 October 1932.
2. "Amherst Traditions and the Freshmen," *The Amherst Student*, 29 September 1932.
3. Pierre Bourdieu, *The Field of Cultural Production: Essays on Art and Literature*, Edited and Introduced by Randal Johnson, (New York: Columbia University Press: 1993), 83.

4. Pierre Bourdieu, *Distinction: A Social Critique of the Judgment of Taste*, Translated by Richard Nice, (Cambridge: Harvard University Press, 1984), 476.
5. "Youth in College," *Fortune*, June 1936, 100.
6. Bourdieu, *The Field of Cultural Production*, 83.
7. Abram de Swaan, *The Management of Normality: Critical Essays in Health and Welfare* (London: Routledge, 1990), 176.
8. Bourdieu, *Distinction*, 479.
9. Bourdieu, *The Field of Cultural Production*, 28.
10. Loren Baritz, *The Good Life: The Meaning of Success for the American Middle Class* (New York: Alfred A. Knopf, 1989), 10.
11. Johanna Brenner, "On Gender and Class in U.S. Labor History," *Monthly Review*, (New York: Monthly Review Press) Vol. 50, No. 6, November 1998.
12. Pierre Bourdieu, "Social Space and Symbolic Power," *Sociological Theory*, Volume 7, Issue 1 (Spring 1989), 19.
13. Theodore M. Newcomb's *Personality and Social Change: Attitude Formation in a Student Community* (New York: Dryden Press, 1943) as cited in Stephen R.G. Jones, *The Economics of Conformism* (New York: Basil Blackwell Inc., 1984), 16–17.
14. Stephen R.G. Jones, *The Economics of Conformism* (New York: Basil Blackwell Inc., 1984), 17.
15. "A New Question in Hazing," *The Amherst Student*, 30 September 1935.
16. Ibid.
17. "The Sophomore Begins to Graduate," *The University of Michigan Daily*, 20 September 1931.
18. Ibid.
19. "Hazing Differs Somewhat in Forty Years But Freshman Still Indulge in Faux Pas," *The Mount Holyoke News*, 8 October 1932.
20. Ibid.
21. Ibid.
22. "Freshman Bow to Mighty Seniors: Wear Queer-Looking Lampshades Sing and Recite for Benefit of Dignified Upperclassmen," *The Mount Holyoke News*, 11 November 1933.
23. "Upper Class Await Date of Freshmen's Humiliation," *The Mount Holyoke News*, 4 November 1933.
24. Ibid.
25. "Neophytes," *The Mount Holyoke News*, 8 October 1932.
26. "Pots and the Freshman," *The University of Michigan Daily*, 9 October 1931.
27. "Survey Reveals First-Year Students Everywhere Favor Freshmen Rules," *The George Washington University Hatchet*, 27 September 1932.
28. "Stop! Freshmen!!! Look!: Freshmen Rules," *The Howard Hilltop*, 15 October 1931.
29. "Freshmen and Amherst Traditions," *The Amherst Student*, 5 October 1933.

30. Hank Nuwer, *Wrongs of Passage: Fraternities, Sororities, Hazing and Binge Drinking* (Bloomington: Indiana University Press, 1999), 54.
31. David Roediger's discussion of minstrelsy and blackface points to similar issues of sublimated homoerotic sexuality and violence being played out in a forum that makes it safe for white males to participate. David Roediger, *The Wages of Whiteness: Race and the Making of the American Working Class* (New York: Verso, 1991), 116–127.
32. "Amherst Traditions and the Freshmen," *The Amherst Student*, 29 September 1932.
33. "Freshmen and Amherst Traditions," *The Amherst Student*, 5 October 1933.
34. "Survey Reveals First-Year Students Everywhere Favor Freshman Rules: Forced Attendance at Games, Show of Respect to Upperclassmen, Wearing of Buttons Among Regulations Objected to by Faculty," Karl Dieffenbach, *The George Washington Hatchet*, 27 September 1932.
35. Nuwer, *Wrongs of Passage*, 40.
36. "Freshmen Not Loyal to HU," *The Howard Hilltop*, 12 October 1933.
37. "Letter to the Editor," Raymond L. Reben, *The University of Michigan Daily*, 27 Oc^tober 1931.
38. Ibid.
39. "Petition To Be Made Against Pot Tradition, *The University of Michigan Daily*, 18 November 1932.
40. "Freshmen Not Loyal to HU," *The Howard Hilltop*, 12 October 1933.
41. Ibid.
42. Ibid.
43. "At Other Campuses," *The University of Michigan Daily*, 18 October 1932.
44. "The Sophomore Begins to Graduate," *The University of Michigan Daily*, 20 September 1931.
45. "Sophomore Heaven and Unclassified Morons," *The University of Michigan Daily*, 2 March 1933.
46. Ibid.
47. "Take Hell Out of Hell Week, *The University of Michigan Daily*, 21 February 1934.
48. "Regulating the Freshmen," *The Howard Hilltop*, 9 November 1934.
49. "Slightly Sour Grapes," *The George Washington University Hatchet*, 14 March 1933.
50. Ibid.
51. "Freshmen—Amherst Men or Schoolboys?" *The Amherst Student*, 4 May 1934.
52. Ibid.
53. Nuwer, *Wrongs of Passage*, 110.
54. "Finis To The Pot Tradition . . ." *The University of Michigan Daily*, 25 September 1934.
55. Ibid.
56. "College Humor—And Sense," *The Amherst Student*, 25 September 1933.

57. Helen Lefkowitz Horowitz, *Campus Life: Undergraduate Cultures from the End of the Eighteenth Century to the Present* (New York: Alfred A. Knopf, 1987), 131.
58. Ibid.
59. Elizabeth Eldridge, *Co-Ediquette: Poise and Popularity for Every Girl* (New York: E.P. Dutton,1936), 25.
60. "Understanding of Fraternities, Sororities Essential to Satisfactory Membership: Before Pledging Freshmen Should Investigate Thoroughly," *The George Washington University Hatchet,* 18 September 1934.
61. Horowitz, *Campus Life,* 138.
62. Eldridge, *Co-Ediquette,* 45.
63. Letter from University of Michigan Dean James A. Bursley to former student Gene Reichert describing the historical import of the fraternity system. Dated 5 February 1937. Office of Student Affairs Collection, Box 1, Folder 1937, Bentley Historical Library, University of Michigan, Ann Arbor.
64. Horowitz, *Campus Life,* 128.
65. de Swaan, *The Management of Normality,* 176.
66. Randal Johnson, "Introduction" to Pierre Bourdieu, *The Field of Cultural Production: Essays on Art and Literature,* Edited and Introduced by Randal Johnson, (New York: Columbia University Press, 1993), 24.
67. *Baird's Manual of American College Fraternities* (Menasha, Wisconsin: The Collegiate Press, George Banta Publishing Company, 1949).
68. Horowitz, *Campus Life,* 135–8.
69. Eldridge, *Co-Ediquette,* 44.
70. Ibid, 45.
71. Horowitz, *Campus Life,* 128.
72. Robert Cooley Angell, *A Study in Undergraduate Adjustment* (Chicago: University of Chicago Press, 1930), 112–114.
73. Ibid.
74. "More About Pledging," *The George Washington University Hatchet,* 18 October 1932.
75. Ibid.
76. "To The Unpledged," *The University of Michigan Daily* reprinted from the *University Daily Kansan,* 16 October 1932.
77. Ibid.
78. Regina Westcott Wieman, *Popularity* (Chicago: Willet, Clark & Company, 1936), 131.
79. Ibid.
80. Eldridge, *Co-Ediquette,* 54.
81. Ibid.
82. Horowitz , *Campus Life,* 7.
83. "Fraternities on the Spot?" *The Amherst Student,* 16 October 1933.
84. Dana D. Nelson, *National Manhood: Capitalist Citizenship and the Imagined Fraternity of White Men* (Durham: Duke University Press, 1998), 187.
85. Bourdieu, *The Field of Cultural Production,* 117.
86. Ibid.
87. Ibid.

88. E. Anthony Rotundo, *American Manhood: Transformations in Masculinity from the Revolution to the Modern Era* (New York: Basic Books, 1993), 63–68.
89. Ibid.
90. Michael Kimmel, *Manhood in America: A Cultural History* (New York: Free Press, 1996), 170–1.
91. Ibid.
92. Ibid.
93. "Sophomore Heaven and Unclassified Morons," *The University of Michigan Daily*, 2 March 1933.
94. Nelson, *National Manhood*, 186.
95. Rotundo, *American Manhood*, 69.
96. Horowitz, *Campus Life*, 119.
97. Kimmel, *Manhood in America*, 103.
98. Pierre Bourdieu, *Outline of a Theory of Practice* (Cambridge: Cambridge University Press, 1977), 161.
99. Caroll Smith-Rosenberg, *Disorderly Conduct: Visions of Gender in Victorian America* (New York: Oxford University Press, 1985), 53–76.
100. Linda W. Rosenzweig, *Another Self: Middle-Class American Women and Their Friends in the Twentieth Century* (New York: New York University Press, 1999), 67.
101. Ibid, 71.
102. Eldridge, *Co-Ediquette*, 200.
103. Ibid., 205–10.
104. Ibid., 211.
105. Rosenzweig, *Another Self*, 71.
106. Ibid., 205–10.
107. Regina Westcott Wieman, *Popularity* (Chicago: Willet, Clark & Company, 1936), 32.
108. "Columbia Spectator on Fraternities," *The University of Michigan Daily*, 16 October 1934.
109. Eldridge, *Co-Ediquette*, 54.
110. "Sisterly Love," *The University of Michigan Daily*, 7 November 1934.
111. Frances Angell, *Compete!* (Philadelphia: Dorrance & Company, Inc., 1935), 102.
112. Ibid, 102–3.
113. "Sisterly Love," *The University of Michigan Daily*, 7 November 1934.
114. "Snobbery and the Sororities," *The University of Michigan Daily*, 31 October 1934.
115. Angell, *Compete!*,101.
116. "Fraternities," *The University of Michigan Daily*, 27 September 1933.
117. "Rushees—Be Careful!" *The George Washington University Hatchet*, 27 September 1932.
118. "Fraternities on the Spot?" *The Amherst Student*, 16 October 1933.
119. "The Idea Behind Going to College" *The University of Michigan Daily*, 8 November 1931.
120. "Freedom and Conformity" *The University of Michigan Daily*, 12 November 1932. Reprinted from *The Daily Princetonian*.

121. Janice A. Radway, *A Feeling for Books: The Book of the Month Club, Literary Taste and Middle-Class Desire* (Chapel Hill: University of North Carolina Press, 1997), 209–10.
122. Paul K. Conkin, *The New Deal: The Crowell American History Series* (New York: Thomas Y. Crowell Company, 1967), 28.
123. Ibid.
124. "Snobbery and the Sororities," *The University of Michigan Daily*, 31 October 1934.
125. "Fraternities and Realities," *The Amherst Student*, 27 December 1933.
126. Ibid.
127. "Putting A Question Up to Howard Students," *The Howard Hilltop*, 29 April 1932.
128. Ibid.
129. Ibid.
130. Ibid.
131. Ibid.
132. "Columbia Spectator on Fraternities," *The University of Michigan Daily*, 16 October 1934. *The Amherst Student* put a different spin on the ousting of fraternities from places like Yale and Harvard by stating that economic troubles created situations where the houses "had no choice but to relinquish active existence." "Another Rung in the Ladder," *The Amherst Student*, 16 December 1935.
133. "Columbia Spectator on Fraternities," *The University of Michigan Daily*, 16 October 1934.
134. Ibid.
135. "About Joining Fraternities, Sororities . . . ," *The University of Michigan Daily*, 19 September 1933.
136. Ibid and "Yale: Two Fraternities Fall Before the Residence System," *Newsweek*, 13 October 1934.
137. "Non-Fraternity Group Has Mine of Material: Overwhelming Majority Available For New Organization," Verna Volz, *The George Washington University Hatchet*, 14 May 1935.
138. Ibid.
139. "Student Council Advocates a Club Room for Amherst Group of Non-Fraternity Men," *The Amherst Student*, 28 February 1935.
140. Ibid
141. "The Jeff Club Proves Its Worth," *The Amherst Student*, 22 September 1935.
142. Ibid
143. Nuwer, *Wrongs of Passage*, 41.
144. Eldridge, *Co-Ediquette*, 53–4.
145. Ibid.
146. Ibid., 54.
147. "Fraternal Snobbishness," Evelyn Seeley, *New York World Telegram*, 18 October 1934.
148. Ibid.
149. Ibid.

150. At the University of Michigan 1933 Panhellenic Banquet, the Dean of Women, Miss Alice Lloyd contended that sororities were "on trial for their existence" because of financial and social issues. "Snobbery and the Sororities," *The University of Michigan Daily* 31 October 1934.
151. "Fraternity System Faces Crisis As Houses Seek To Consolidate," *The University of Michigan Daily,* 24 February 1933.
152. "Sororities Are Struggling For Existence, Dean Lloyd States," *The University of Michigan Daily,* 29 April 1933.
153. "Yale: Two Fraternities Fall Before the Residence System," *Newsweek,* 13 October 1934.
154. "Frosh, Pots, and Fraternities," *The University of Michigan Daily,* 15 January 1932.
155. Ibid.
156. "The Human Cost of Rushing," *The University of Michigan Daily,* 10 October 1933.
157. "Rushing," *The George Washington University Hatchet,* 17 September 1932.
158. George Banta, Jr. and his family had a long history of participation in fraternal life. Fifty members of the Banta family, from the grandfather down, were active in Greek life. The grandfather of George Banta, Jr. began the publishing business of Greek letter houses in the 1850s. By 1932 George Banta, Jr. issued publications for 80 Greek letter societies as well as 80 publications for educational and scientific societies. He also was the national president of Phi Delta Theta and his wife was the national president of her sorority, Kappa Alpha Theta. "Crisis Is Faced By Fraternities," *The Washington Evening Star,* 19 December 1932.
159. "Crisis Is Faced By Fraternities," *The Washington Evening Star,* 19 December 1932.
160. Ibid.
161. Banta unsympathetically stated "If the brothers don't pay their house fees, kick them out!" "Crisis Is Faced By Fraternities," *The Washington Evening Star,* 19 December 1932.
162. Ibid.
163. "Sororities Are Struggling For Existence, Dean Lloyd States," *The University of Michigan Daily,* 29 April 1933.
164. Ibid.
165. "Crisis Is Faced By Fraternities," *The Washington Evening Star,* 19 December 1932.
166. The National Recovery Act (NRA) was often conceptualized as government interference into private business matters. Paul Conkin contends that the NRA never tried in "any cohesive or coherent way, to force public goals upon an unwilling business community. It was the businessmen who dominated the early NRA, both in the writing of codes and in the operation of the enforcing code authorities." Paul K. Conkin, *The New Deal; The Crowell American History Series* (New York: Thomas Y. Crowell Company, 1967), 35.
167. Ibid, 22.

168. "Fraternities Must Take Stock," *The University of Michigan Daily,* 7 January 1933.
169. Ibid.
170. "Greeks Look Forward," *The George Washington University Hatchet,* reprinted from *The Wisconsin Daily Cardinal,* 31 July 1934.
171. Students proposed taking a cue from other universities and withholding class credit to inspire students to pay their house bills and help the houses survive. "Fraternity and Sorority Finance . . ." *The University of Michigan Daily,* 12 October 1934.
172. "University Recommends Letting Freshmen Move Into Fraternity Houses," *The University of Michigan Daily,* 15 November 1933.
173. "Fraternity Compliance With the New Rules," *The University of Michigan Daily,* 29 November 1933.
174. "Greeks Look Forward," *The George Washington University Hatchet,* reprinted from *The Wisconsin Daily Cardinal,* 31 July 1934.
175. Ibid.
176. Ibid.
177. "Fraternity and Sorority Finance . . ." *The University of Michigan Daily,* 12 October 1934.
178. Ibid.
179. "Landladies vs. The University," *The University of Michigan Daily,* 8 January 1933.
180. Aubrey Williams, "The Problem of Unemployment," Franklin D. Roosevelt Library, Hopkins Papers, Box 13, Speech given January 16, 1935.
181. Ibid.
182. "Landladies Vs. The University," *The University of Michigan Daily,* 8 January 1933.
183. "Fraternities and Sororities May Be Asked to Join the NRA," *The University of Michigan Daily,* 3 October 1933.
184. Ibid.
185. Ibid.
186. Ibid.
187. Ibid.
188. Ibid.
189. "Cooperative Buying," *The Amherst Student,* 15 January 1934.
190. "Cheap Meals at Co-Operative Now Served to More Than 100," *The University of Michigan Daily,* 1 October 1933.
191. "The Power of the Group," *The Amherst Student,* 22 February 1934.
192. "A Cooperative Welcome," *The George Washington University Hatchet,* 31 July 1934.
193. "The Eastern Fraternity—And Amherst," *The Amherst Student,* 17 January 1935.
194. During the 1920s and 1930s, Heller was a Hollywood press agent, but gave up that career in 1945 to devote full time to his interest in the fraternity world. University of Illinois Archives. Box 10: Fraternity and Sorority Chapter Ratings, 1943–82.

195. "Enforcement Rules Passed for Hazing, Women Regulations: Fraternity Heads Meet," *The Amherst Student,* 27 September 1934.
196. "Teeth for Rushing Rules," *The Amherst Student,* 7 May 1934.
197. "Pre-Initiation Hazing of Freshmen Abolished: Council of House Presidents Adopts Rule Effective in September 1935" *The Amherst Student,* 21 February 1935.
198. "A Sign of Decay?" *The Amherst Student,* February 23, 1935.
199. "Fraternities and Freshmen," *The Howard Hilltop,* 12 December 1935.

NOTES TO CHAPTER FOUR

1. Dorothy Hoover Downs, *How To Get Your Man and Hold Him,* (New York: A.L. Taylor, 1936), 44.
2. "Advice To Women," *The University of Michigan Daily,* 22 October 1936.
3. Willard Waller, "The Rating and Dating Complex," *American Sociological Review,* Volume 2, Issue 5, October 1937, 727–728. Both money and sexuality functioned as forms of currency in the rating and dating system; described the system as one of mutual exploitation between young women and men where females used males for the sake of "presents and expensive amusements" and males sought their thrills from the bodies of their dates
4. Phyllis Chesler, *Woman's Inhumanity to Woman,* (New York: Thundermouth Press/Nation Books, 2001), 82.
5. Pierre Bourdieu, *The Field of Cultural Production: Essays on Art and Literature* (New York: Columbia University Press, 1993), 116.
6. Ibid, 96.
7. John Modell, *Into One's Own: From Youth to Adulthood in the United States, 1920–1975* (Berkeley: University of California Press, 1989), 95.
8. Paula S. Fass, *The Damned and the Beautiful: American Youth in the 1920s* (New York: Oxford University Press, 1977), 57.
9. Robert S. Lynd and Helen Merrell Lynd, *Middletown in Transition: A Study in Cultural Conflicts* (New York: Harcourt, Brace and Company, 1937), 168.
10. Beth L. Bailey, *From Front Porch to Back Seat: Courtship in Twentieth-Century America* (Baltimore: Johns Hopkins University Press, 1988), 8.
11. Rosa Lee Hill, *How to Attract Men and Money: An Intimate Revelation for Women Past Eighteen,* (Meriden, Connecticut: Ralston Society, 1938), 339.
12. Frances Bruce Strain, *Love at the Threshold: A Book on Dating, Romance and Marriage* (New York: D. Appleton-Century, 1939), 11–12.
13. Regina Westcott Wieman, *Popularity* (Chicago: Willet, Clark & Company, 1936), 41.
14. In her book about the impact of the Great Depression Caroline Bird noted that during her undergraduate years at Vassar a remarkable number of her female classmates majored in economics, which was the major of choice second only to English. Caroline Bird, *The Invisible Scar* (New York: D. McKay, 1966), 139.
15. George Gallup, creator of the Gallup Poll, explained that public opinion polls provided swift and efficient methods by "which legislators, educators, experts and editors, as well as ordinary citizens throughout the length and

breadth of the country can have a more reliable measure of the pulse of democracy." George Gallup and Saul Forbes Rae, *The Pulse of Democracy: The Public-Opinion Poll and How It Works* (New York: Simon & Schuster, 1940), 14.

16. Waller, "The Rating and Dating Complex," 727–728.
17. Rodney M. Cate and Sally A. Lloyd, *Courtship* (London: Sage, 1992), 24.
18. Bailey, *From Front Porch to Back Seat,* 29.
19. See Ruth Feldstein, *Motherhood in Black and White: Race and Sex in American Liberalism, 1930–1965* (Ithaca: Cornell University Press, 2000) for descriptions of healthy middle-class citizens during the Depression era.
20. The notion of popularity and how to attain it received much attention in the mid-to-late 1930s. In 1937 Emily Post added three chapters about popularity and rating to the revised edition of her classic text *Etiquette: The Blue Book of Social Usage.* Cas Wouters, "Etiquette Books and Emotion Management in the Twentieth Century: American Habitus in International Comparison," *An Emotional History of the United States,* eds. Peter N. Stearns and Jan Lewis (New York: New York University Press, 1998), 297.
21. Helen Lefkowitz Horowitz, *Campus Life: Undergraduate Cultures from the End of the Eighteenth Century to the Present* (New York: Alfred A. Knopf, 1987), 208.
22. Ibid., 128.
23. Bourdieu, *The Field of Cultural Production,* 82.
24. Waller, "The Rating and Dating Complex," 733.
25. Richard Swedberg, "Bourdieu's Advocacy of the Concept of Interest and Its Role in Economic Sociology," *Economic Sociology—European Electronic Newsletter,* Vol. 4, No. 2 (March 2003).
26. Willard Waller, *The Family: A Dynamic Interpretation* (New York: Cordon, 1938), 232.
27. "Peak of Student Joy Reached Saturday Night, Survey Shows," *The University of Michigan Daily,* 5 May 1935.
28. Henry A. Bowman, *Marriage for Moderns* (New York: McGraw-Hill, 1942), 212.
29. "Men Dominate Campus, Women Not Well Adjusted, Says Angell," *The University of Michigan Daily,* 27 March 1936.
30. Elizabeth Eldridge, *Co-Ediquette: Poise and Popularity for Every Girl* (New York: E.P. Dutton, 1936), 185. Eldridge's advice book received some publicity at the University of Michigan in the summer of 1936. Two sorority sisters, Lee Penock and Marjorie Stefan, did a live dramatic reading and book review of Eldridge's *Co-Ediquette* on the campus radio station. The young women contended that some of Eldridge's advice about "what not to do" just didn't stand up on the modern campus. "But all in all, aside from the fact that the best way was to try four years at college yourself, Miss Eldridge's book was given faithful support and recommended for incoming co-eds." "University Broadcast Advises Michigan Co-Eds, Vacationers," *The University of Michigan Daily,* 17 July 1936.
31. Waller, "The Rating and Dating Complex," 731.
32. Ibid.

33. Waller, *The Family,* 231.
34. Ibid., 232.
35. Waller, "The Rating and Dating Complex," 730.
36. Waller, *The Family,* 233.
37. Even high school girls were expected to get involved in the competition for dates. Manual authors advised their readers to hone their competitive skills early in preparation for college days of rating and dating. An article published in a 1940 issue of *Women's Home Companion* demonstrates that the rating and dating system that began on college campuses had siphoned down to the masses, "Dates are the hallmark of personality and popularity. No matter how pretty you may be, how smart your clothes—or your tongue—if you have no dates your rating is low. . . . The modern girl cultivates not one single suitor, but dates, lots of them . . . Her aim is not too obvious romance but general popularity." Beth L. Bailey, *From Front Porch to Back Seat: Courtship in Twentieth-Century America* (Baltimore: Johns Hopkins University Press, 1988), 29.
38. Eldridge, *Co-Ediquette,* 195.
39. Wieman, *Popularity,* 23.
40. Eldridge, *Co-Ediquette,* 197. It appears that many young women at Mount Holyoke began heeding Eldridge's advice by the late 1930s. A gossip column entitled "Much Ado About Nothing" ran stories including: "Barbara Landon has a pin too, but we don't know which of the six pictures on her bureau is guilty; while Becky Ganot can't decide between two lockets and a pin!" "Much Ado About Nothing," *The Mount Holyoke News,* 18 January 1939.
41. Wieman, *Popularity*, 131.
42. "Society Calendar Valuable As Gauge For Co-ed's Popularity," *The George Washington University Hatchet,* 31 July 1934.
43. "Damda Phi Data Sorority Rates BMOC's By Their Dating Value," *The University of Michigan Daily,* 25 March 1936.
44. Ibid.
45. "Colors To Rate The Co-ed's Date," *The Howard Hilltop,* 13 April 1939.
46. Ibid.
47. "Beyond the Blue," *The Mount Holyoke News,* 23 March 1939.
48. Waller, *The Family,* 230–231.
49. "The Michigan Coed," *The University of Michigan Daily,* 15 January 1938.
50. "All Types Of The Stronger Sex Discussed By Your Correspondent: For Women Only," *The George Washington University Hatchet,* 21 November 1939.
51. "College Women Classified On Basis of Who Does What: For Men Only," *The George Washington University Hatchet,* 5 December 1939.
52. Ibid.
53. Waller, "The Rating and Dating Complex," 732.
54. "The Michigan Coed," *The University of Michigan Daily,* 15 January 1938. Some students argued that being a big man or woman on campus did not only entail enjoying collegiate social life. They contended that many

BMOCs and BWOCs belonged to honor societies, literary circles, speech groups, journalism sororities and national education societies. "Honor Societies Are Key Stone for Role of Campus BWOC," *The University of Michigan Daily,* 15 August 1936.

55. "The Michigan Coed," *The University of Michigan Daily,* 15 January 1938.
56. "Men Of Michigan Come To Defense Of Coeds, Outraged By Accusations," *The University of Michigan Daily,* 21 January 1938.
57. Ibid.
58. "Collegiate Observer," *The University of Michigan Daily,* 10 January 1935.
59. Ibid.
60. Ibid.
61. Frances Bruce Strain, *Love at the Threshold: A Book on Dating, Romance and Marriage* (New York: D. Appleton-Century, 1939), 23.
62. Elizabeth Woodward, *Personality Preferred!: How To Grow Up Gracefully* (New York: Harper and Brothers, 1935), 203–204.
63. Ibid.
64. Downs, *How To Get Your Man,* 28.
65. "Advice To Seniors" *The Mount Holyoke News,* 6 March 1936.
66. Downs, *How To Get Your Man,* 29.
67. Ibid.
68. Waller, "The Rating and Dating Complex," 731.
69. Eldridge, *Co-Ediquette,* 199.
70. "Cupid Is Blind On Dates Here, Survey of Students Indicates," *The University of Michigan Daily,* 11 May 1937.
71. "Army Buttons Bother Smith Girls; Amherst Men Both Cocky and Happy Medium in Poll," *The Amherst Student,* 9 March 1936.
72. One expert compared dating bureaus and introduction services to a credit reporting agency where like-minded people could find mates. Credit agencies gathered "all the available data in any particular case and clears that information through to the party it serves." Elmer U. Gross, LL.B., *Meet Your Mate the Modern Way: A Present-Day Practical Solution To An Age-Old Personal Problem* (Boston: The Christopher Publishing House, 1940), 53.
73. David R. Shumway, "Something Old, Something New: Romance and Marital Advice in the 1920s,"*An Emotional History of the United States,* eds. Peter N. Stearns and Jan Lewis (New York: New York University Press, 1998), 314.
74. "Hostel Enthusiasts Sponsor Date Bureau and Dance for Benefit of Holyoke Branch," *The Mount Holyoke News,* 19 April 1935.
75. Ibid.
76. "Local 'Lonely Hearts' Bureau Organized; Co-Eds At Premium," *The University of Michigan Daily,* 13 November 1935.
77. Ibid.
78. "Date Bureau Booms At Michigan State," *The University of Michigan Daily,* 29 April 1938.

79. Ibid.
80. "On The Level," *The University of Michigan Daily,* 1 October 1937.
81. "Cupid Is Blind On Dates Here, Survey of Students Indicates," *The University of Michigan Daily,* 11 May 1937.
82. Waller, *The Family,* 231.
83. "News . . . In Retrospect; Pickens Plans Co-op With Greater Value Which Will Be Offered At Lower Price Than Previously," *The George Washington University Hatchet,* 6 July 1936.
84. "Erection of Fiesta Stage Will Be Started Thursday," *The George Washington University Hatchet,* 5 May 1936.
85. "Survey Reveals Co-Eds Prefer Dances, Movies Over Athletics," *The University of Michigan Daily,* 7 March 1937.
86. "Dance Survey Reveals Socialites Among Fraternities on Campus," *The University of Michigan Daily,* 19 May 1938.
87. "Sunset Gun?" *The Amherst Student,* 28 October 1937. Amherst had "women's rules" which stated that "all women shall be out of fraternity houses by 7:30 on week nights and 11:30 on Saturdays. It is also provided that women shall not be allowed upstairs or in private studies after 7:30 P.M. except upon the occasion of a dance, when special permission can be obtained by the house." The men of Amherst believed that the rules represented an outdated attempt to conform to obsolete moral standards and that "Amherst needs to liberalize the rules and bring the College socially up to date." "Morality By The Clock," *The Amherst Student,* 28 October 1937.
88. "This Thing Called Swing," *The Howard Hilltop,* 13 April 1939.
89. "Act, Don't Wait!" *The Howard Hilltop,* 13 May 1936.
90. "Dance Routine," *The Mount Holyoke News,* 1 November 1935.
91. "Dance Survey Reveals Socialites Among Fraternities on Campus," *The University of Michigan Daily,* 19 May 1938.
92. "Unbecoming A Gentleman," *The Amherst Student,* 22 May 1936.
93. Ibid.
94. Some women disliked Yale dances and were unimpressed by Harvard proms. "Opinions of Veteran Prom Trotters Place Amherst Fall Dance High Up On List," *The Amherst Student,* 19 November 1936.
95. "Army Buttons Bother Smith Girls; Amherst Men Both Cocky and Happy Medium in Poll," *The Amherst Student,* 9 March 1936.
96. "180 Beauteous Guests Invade Amherst Campus for Festivities of Junior Prom Weekend," *The Amherst Student,* 1 May 1936.
97. "Jazz Jittery Juniors Joyously Hail Prom; Holyoke To Be Invaded By Heart Throbs," *The Mount Holyoke News,* 8 April 1938.
98. In addition to the clothing that young women wore to classes, they were expected to have "several afternoon dresses" for Sunday dinners, a couple of formal dresses for afternoon teas, more than one evening gown, a swagger coat, a dress coat and a fur coat for those attending college in cold climates. Eldridge, *Co-Ediquette,* 37–39.
99. One student from Mount Holyoke warned her classmates that whether they were aware of it or not underclassmen sat "in hundreds" in the balcony above

the dance floor and "could observe all corners." "Dictates for Seniors," *The Mount Holyoke News*, 21 February 1936.

100. Dorothy Constance Stratton, *Your Best Foot Forward: Social Usage for Young Moderns* (New York: McGraw-Hill, 1940), 149.
101. Eldridge, *Co-Ediquette*, 208.
102. "Big Shot Campus Men Irked; Youthful Cutie Refuses Cut Ins," *The George Washington University Hatchet*, 9 April 1935.
103. Ibid.
104. Ibid.
105. "Emily Dictates Cutting Rules," *The George Washington University Hatchet*, 16 April 1935.
106. Ibid.
107. Eldridge, *Co-Ediquette*, 202.
108. Ibid. Cutting etiquette at Mount Holyoke was a bit different, with women sometimes being allowed to take the initiative to cut in. Being able to cut in meant that the young women also risked getting stuck with a less-than-desirable partner. An issue of *The Mount Holyoke News* included a hilarious one act tragedy set in a hall of torture, otherwise known as the dance floor. A young woman from Mount Holyoke asks to cut in.

    He: "It's a pleasure. Baby, when you said those words it was the luckiest minute of your life."
    She: "Oh, you're from Amherst?"
    Man makes some stale jokes, she comments that he must read *College Humor*, he responds "Not me, Baby. *College Humor* has spies following me all the time. It keeps their stuff up to date and snappy."
    She: "I'll bet you are a busy man at Amherst, aren't you? Popular and all that, I mean."
    He: "You've no idea, Baby, no idea at all. Being the president of the YWCA is no joke."
    She: "YWCA? You wouldn't kid me, would you?"
    He: "Sure, little one, the Young Women's Crush Association, and I'll put you down with the charter members." "One Act Tragedy," *The Mount Holyoke News*, 4 May 1935.

109. "On The Level," *The University of Michigan Daily*, 15 October 1937.
110. "We Are The Bachelor Girls of 30," *True Confessions*, June 1935.
111. John Modell, "Dating Becomes the Way of American Youth," *Essays on the Family and Historical Change*, Leslie Page Moch, Ed., (College Station: Texas A & M University Press, 1983), 116.
112. Eldridge, *Co-Ediquette*, 206.
113. Rosenzweig, *Another Self*, 68–9.
114. Ibid.
115. "Public Opinion," *The Mount Holyoke News*, 9 October 1936.
116. Ibid.
117. "Dance Routine," *The Mount Holyoke News*, 1 November 1935.
118. Ibid.

119. "Hospitality At The League," *The University of Michigan Daily,* 28 July 1936.
120. "To A Southern Lady," *The University of Michigan Daily,* 30 July 1936.
121. Downs, *How To Get Your Man,* 50.
122. Linda W. Rosenzweig, *Another Self: Middle-Class American Women and Their Friends in the Twentieth Century* (New York: New York University Press, 1999), 84.
123. Margaret Culkin Banning, *Letters to Susan* (New York: Harper & Brothers Publishers, 1936), 122.
124. Emily Post, *Etiquette: The Blue Book of Social Usage* (New York: Funk & Wagnalls Company, 1937), 365.
125. Ibid.
126. "Collegiate Observer," *The University of Michigan Daily,* 1 May 1935.
127. "Have You The Money, Honey?" *The University of Michigan Daily,* 15 January 1936.
128. Ibid.
129. "Boys Favor Dutch Dates, Girls Have Different Ideas," *The George Washington University Hatchet,* 13 December 1938.
130. Ibid.
131. Banning, *Letters to Susan,* 125.
132. Post, *Etiquette,* 365.
133. "Intelligence Is Main Requisite Demanded By Michigan Women," *The University of Michigan Daily,* 26 January 1936.
134. Post, *Etiquette,* 367.
135. Banning, *Letters to Susan,* 122.
136. "Every Campus Has Its Lonely Hearts, But Howard's 'Anty Toxin' Has The Remedy," *The Howard Hilltop,* 28 February 1939.
137. Adelaide Laura Van Duzer, *Everyday Living for Girls* (Philadelphia: Lippincott, 1936), 386.
138. Elizabeth Eldridge, *Etiquette For Teens* (New York: Home Institute Incorporated, 1937), 27.
139. "Former Proms' Faded Glories Recalled By Gala 1935 Affair," *The George Washington University Hatchet,* 26 February 1935.
140. "On The Level," *The University of Michigan Daily,* 1 October 1937.
141. "Intelligence Is Main Requisite Demanded By Michigan Women," *The University of Michigan Daily,* 26 January 1936.
142. Banning, *Letters to Susan,* 128.
143. "Borrowed Bon Mots," *The Mount Holyoke News,* 22 October 1937.
144. Frances Angell, *Compete!* (Philadelphia: Dorrance & Company, Inc., 1935), 35.
145. Downs, *How To Get Your Man,* 30.
146. "Tradition of Sadie Hawkins Endures," Renee Andrews, *The Oklahoma State Daily O'Collegian,* 14 February 1997.
147. "Sadie Hawkins Day," Li'l Abner website http:\www.lil-abner.com/sadiehawk.html] 2005
148. "Girls Pay Bill on Sadie Hawkins Day," *The George Washington University Hatchet,* 25 April 1939.

149. Ibid.
150. "Girls Get Big Chance on Sadie Hawkins Day" *The George Washington University Hatchet*, 2 May 1939.
151. Ibid.
152. "'Sadie Hawkins,' Or, The Underdog Has His Day," *The George Washington University Hatchet*, 2 May 1939.
153. "Campus Girls Turn The Tables On Boy Friends," *The George Washington University Hatchet*, 9 May 1939.
154. Ibid.
155. Ibid.
156. "Sweet Vulgarity," *The University of Michigan Daily*, 30 April 1937.
157. In a sense, expert textbook authors and writers of mass marketed manuals greatly resemble Roland Marchand's advertising copywriters in *Advertising the American Dream: Making Way for Modernity, 1920–1940*. Marchand argues that advertisers became "town criers" of youthful modernity who taught people how to consume correctly and how to evaluate new products in an expanding marketplace. Expert writers utilized statistics, norms, and illustrative narrative to teach young people how to be youthful.
158. Modell, "Dating Becomes the Way of American Youth," 98–9.
159. Ellen K. Rothman, *Hands and Hearts: A History of Courtship in America* (New York: Basic Books, 1984).
160. The term "sexual brinkmanship" comes from Elaine Tyler May's *Homeward Bound: American Families in the Cold War Era* (New York: Basic Books, 1988).
161. Woodward, *Personality Preferred!*, 194.
162. Angell, *Compete!*, 39.
163. Modell, "Dating Becomes the Way of American Youth," 95.
164. Henry A. Bowman, *Marriage for Moderns* (New York: McGraw-Hill, 1942), 223.
165. Ibid, 215.
166. Waller, "The Rating and Dating Complex," 731.
167. Eldridge, *Co-Ediquette*, 184.
168. Ibid.
169. Woodward, *Personality Preferred!*, 193–4.
170. Bowman, *Marriage for Moderns*, 217.
171. Modell, *Into One's Own*, 95.

NOTES TO CHAPTER FIVE

1. Lucille Martin, *How to Win and Hold a Husband* (Los Angeles: Bantam, 1940), 5.
2. Homer P. Rainey, *How Fare American Youth?: A Report to the American Youth Commission and the American Council on Education* (New York: D. Appelton-Century Company, 1937), 134.
3. Wayland D. Towner, "The Case of Youth vs. Society," *Journal of Social Hygiene*, October, November, December 1935, Vol. 21, 331–348. A few

months later, in June 1936, young delegates from 24 religious denominations and 44 states gathered in Lakeside, Ohio for the North American Christian Youth Conference and condemned adults for their almost total failure to provide the marriage instruction that young people needed. Rainey, *How Fare American Youth?*, 144.

4. "The Declaration of the Rights of American Youth," American Youth Congress, Robert Cohen Personal Collection, 4 July 1936.
5. Results from a survey conducted by the Roper Organization in 1937 found that 40% of respondents believed that the government should give financial aid to young people to assist them in getting married and establishing homes. John Modell, *Into One's Own: From Youth to Adulthood in the United States, 1920–1975* (Berkeley: University of California Press, 1989), 143.
6. A survey conducted in 1936 found that almost equal percentages of male and female college students wished to wed within a year or two of graduating from college, with 60 percent of the young women and 50 percent of the men wanting to marry that quickly. Frederick Lewis Allen, *Since Yesterday: The Nineteen-Thirties in America; September 3, 1929-September 3, 1939* (New York: Harper and Brothers, 1940), 135.
7. David E. Kyvig, *Daily Life in the United States, 1920–1939; Decades of Promise and Pain* (Westport, CT: Greenwood Press, 2002), 116.
8. Steven Seidman, *Romantic Longings: Love in America, 1830–1980* (New York: Routledge, 1991), 77.
9. Ibid.
10. Winifred D. Wandersee, *Women's Work and Family Values, 1920–1940* (Cambridge: Harvard University Press, 1981), 104.
11. John S. Spurlock, "The Problem of Modern Married Love for Middle-Class Women," *An Emotional History of the United States*, eds. Peter N. Stearns and Jan Lewis (New York: New York University Press, 1998), 321.
12. Ernest R. Groves, "When He Comes A-Courting," *The Good Housekeeping Marriage Book: Twelve Ways to a Happy Marriage*, William F. Bigelow, Ed. (New York: Prentice-Hall, Inc., 1938), 8.
13. Ibid.
14. Spurlock, "The Problem of Modern Married Love for Middle-Class Women," 329.
15. Francesca M. Cancian, *Love in America: Gender and Self-Development* (New York: Cambridge University Press, 1987), 35.
16. Ruth Feldstein, *Motherhood in Black and White: Race and Sex in American Liberalism, 1930–1965* (Ithaca: Cornell University Press, 2000), 3.
17. Spurlock, "The Problem of Modern Married Love for Middle-Class Women," 328.
18. "Students Voice Approval of Double Standard of Morality," *The University of Michigan Daily*, 20 February 1936.
19. Beth L. Bailey, *From Front Porch to Back Seat: Courtship in Twentieth-Century America* (Baltimore: The Johns Hopkins University Press, 1988), 123.
20. Ibid, 122.

21. William Chafe, *The American Woman,* (New York: Oxford University Press, 1972), 105.
22. Groves, "When He Comes A-Courting," 12.
23. William F. Bigelow, *The Good Housekeeping Marriage Book: Twelve Ways to a Happy Marriage* (New York: Prentice-Hall, Inc., 1938), v.
24. Phyllis Palmer, *Domesticity and Dirt: Housewives and Domestic Servants in the United States, 1920–1945* (Philadelphia: Temple University Press, 1989), 91.
25. Wandersee, *Women's Work and Family Values,* 57.
26. "Study of Marriage, Family Is Need in Education Today," Donald H. Cooper, *The George Washington University Hatchet,* 7 December 1937.
27. Terman criticized investigators for being biased in their research about married life, stating that sociologists wanted to measure the impact of marriages on societal welfare, psychologists looked at marriages effects on mental health, while moralists examined the impact of marriage on character and eugenicists measured its impact on racial constitution. Lewis M. Terman, *Psychological Factors in Marital Happiness* (New York: McGraw-Hill, 1938), 7.
28. "Marriage Parley Will Extend Over Weekend," *The Mount Holyoke News,* 12 March 1937.
29. "Nearly Half of the Student Body is Dissatisfied" *The University of Michigan Daily*, 29 April 1938.
30. Paul Popenoe, *Modern Marriage: A Handbook for Men* (New York: The MacMillan Company, 1940).
31. "Courses in Marriage," *The University of Michigan Daily,* 23 January 1935.
32. "Marriage Lectures" *The Mount Holyoke News,* 5 May 1939.
33. Ibid.
34. Ibid.
35. Ibid.
36. These statistics bear out with a notable amount of student newspaper column space used to describe recent engagements and weddings of students and alumni. A columnist for *The George Washington University Hatchet* noted that, "Prosperity must be returning if one may judge by the marriages and engagements announced this summer." "A Letter to Annabelle," *The George Washington University Hatchet,* 24 September 1935. Other headlines included: "Cupid Busy at Pre-June Marriage Arrangements" *George Washington University Hatchet,* 5 June 1935; "Wedding Bells Steal Our Coeds; GW Men Get Married Too" *George Washington University Hatchet,* 25 June 1935; "GW-ites Still Embarking Upon the Sea of Matrimony" *George Washington University Hatchet,* 30 July 1935; and "Co-eds, Men Crowd Path to Altar—Students, Alumni Elect Marriage in Increasing Numbers" *George Washington University Hatchet,* 22 October 1935 which stated that "It seems as if we have had hundreds of weddings here this year and still the lovely co-eds and gallant men of GW march up the aisle in ever-increasing numbers." Statistics from Robert S. Lynd and Helen Merrell Lynd, *Middletown in*

Transition: A Study in Cultural Conflicts (New York: Harcourt, Brace and Company, 1937), 149.

37. The authors of *Middletown in Transition* describe 1935 as the year when many middle-class people began to believe that the Depression was finally over. "One got the impression by 1935 that part of the spirit of minimizing the effects of the Depression was by making public comments that it was over or had never occurred." Researchers witnessed that in 1935 Middletown residents' morale was back up to pre-market crash levels and optimism about the business world was rising. Lynd and Lynd, *Middletown in Transition,* 7 and 22.
38. Allen, *Since Yesterday,* 132.
39. Frederick Lewis Allen argued that undergraduates of the 1930s much "less scornful of their parents and of parental ideas, less likely to feel that family life was a mockery, than the young people of ten years before." Allen, *Since Yesterday,* 135.
40. Rainey, *How Fare American Youth?,* 144.
41. Leland Foster Wood, *Making A Home: A Study of Youth, Courtship and Marriage* (New York: Abingdon Press, 1938), 27.
42. "Recovery and Social Conditions," *American Journal of Sociology,* 42: 878–886 as cited in Stouffer, 110.
43. The grinding sense of frustration generated by these circumstances was expressed by a young man who had recently graduated from college and was working as a clerk for $10 a week: "Hell! What's the use of my even thinking of getting married, let alone tying myself up in an engagement. I'm stuck! There's no future for our generation, and there's nothing we can do about it. I don't expect to marry—can't hope to on this sort of job." Lynd and Lynd, *Middletown in Transition,* 148. Young women described marriage as a means to break out of their parents' home and control too. Marriage represented an escape, "the only escape she can conceive of from her family. The husband as the rescuer from this tedious, restricted household is the only possible hero of her dreams." Ethel S. Beer, "The Social Life of the Business Girl," *Social Forces* 17 (1939): 546–550.
44. Allen, *Since Yesterday,* 132.
45. Samuel A. Stouffer and Paul F. Lazarsfeld, *Research Memorandum on the Family in the Depression,* (New York, NY: Social Science Research Council, 1937), 79. reprinted by Arno in with title *Studies in the Social Aspects of the Depression* (New York, NY: Arno, 1972). Stouffer and Lazarsfeld explain that hundreds of thousands of families doubled up during the Depression. The Real Property Inventory that was conducted in 64 cities during January 1934 found that about "2% to 15% of families were doubled up, with the greatest doubling up in the southern cities." 79
46. Ibid.
47. "Students Voice Approval of Double Standard Of Morality," *The University of Michigan Daily,* 20 February 1936.
48. Lynd and Lynd, *Middletown in Transition,* 150.
49. Ibid., 150.
50. Modell, *Into One's Own,* 132.

51. Ibid., 133.
52. James L. McConaughy, "Now That You Are Engaged," *The Good Housekeeping Marriage Book: Twelve Ways to a Happy Marriage,* William F. Bigelow, Ed. (New York: Prentice-Hall, Inc., 1938), 21.
53. "Student Conference," *The Howard Hilltop,* 13 May 1936.
54. Ibid.
55. Experts, like Paul Popenoe, bridged the gap between the academic and the popular. He traveled the United States presenting serious lectures at colleges about how to chose a mate and have a stable marriage while also producing mainstream pamphlets with titles like "Are You Husband Hunting?" and "Why Don't You Make Him Propose?"
56. Harvey Kalish, *Why Not Get Married?* (New York: E.P. Dutton & Company, 1937).
57. Paul Popenoe and Roswell Hill Johnson, *Applied Eugenics* (New York: The MacMillan Company, 1933), 181. One of the main missions of the Institute of Family Relations was to offer a "premarital conference" that included studies of personal and family history, tests of temperamental compatibility between potential partners, physical examinations and thorough educational preparation for marriage. Popenoe explained to readers that the lessons had a eugenic mission, but that the students did not need to be told that was the case.
58. Ibid.
59. Rainey, *How Fare American Youth?*, 137.
60. Lynn Y. Weiner, *From Working Girl to Working Mother: The Female Labor Force in the United States, 1820–1980* (Chapel Hill: University of North Carolina Press, 1985), 101.
61. Betsy L. Nies, *Eugenic Fantasies: Racial Ideology in the Literature and Popular Culture of the 1920s* (New York : Routledge, 2002), 46.
62. Ibid.
63. Ibid.
64. Stephen Jay Gould commented on the men who constructed theories about the "fit" and "unfit" by stating that: "Interestingly, most of the men who built biodeterminism in the 1920s recanted their own conclusions during the liberal swing of the 1930s, when Ph.D.'s walked depression bread lines and poverty could no longer be blamed on stupidity." Stephen Jay Gould, *The Mismeasure of Man* (New York: W.W. Norton & Company, 1996), 29.
65. Nies, *Eugenic Fantasies,* 46.
66. "Our Graduates," *The Mount Holyoke News,* 10 March 1939.
67. Ibid.
68. Frances Bruce Strain, *Love at the Threshold: A Book on Dating, Romance and Marriage* (New York: D. Appleton-Century, 1939), 115.
69. Elizabeth Eldridge, *Co-Ediquette: Poise and Popularity for Every Girl* (New York: E.P. Dutton, 1936), 124–5.
70. "Etiquette for Undergraduates," *The University of Michigan Daily,* 18 March 1936.
71. Popenoe, *Modern Marriage,* 24.

72. Strain, *Love at the Threshold*, 115.
73. Kalish, *Why Not Get Married?*, 104–5.
74. Ibid.
75. Laura Hutton, *The Single Woman: Her Adjustment to Life and Love* (New York: Roy Publishers, 1935), 3.
76. Wandersee, *Women's Work and Family Values*, 104.
77. Hutton, *The Single Woman*, 3.
78. Ibid.
79. Ibid.
80. Ibid.
81. Nancy Cott describes how government programs and policies focused on enforcing "economic usefulness" of marriage with husbands as the providers and wives as the dependents. Nancy Cott, *Public Vows: A History of Marriage and the Nation* (Cambridge: Harvard University Press, 2000), 157.
82. Rosa Lee Hill, *How to Attract Men and Money: An Intimate Revelation for Women Past Eighteen*, (Meriden, Connecticut: Ralston Society, 1938), 3.
83. Lee M. Gregory, *Win Him If You Want Him* (New York: Hillman-Curl, Inc., 1937), 12.
84. Lisa Lowe, *Immigrant Acts: On Asian American Culture and Politics* (Durham: Duke University Press, 1996), 56.
85. Stanley G. Dickinson, "It Pays to be Happily Married," *The Good Housekeeping Marriage Book: Twelve Ways to a Happy Marriage*, William F. Bigelow, Ed. (New York: Prentice-Hall, Inc., 1938), 144.
86. Ibid, 146–7.
87. Ibid.
88. "A Business Creed for School and College Girls," written by Benjamin R. Andrews from Teachers College at Columbia University, quoted in Adelaide Laura Van Duzer, *Everyday Living for Girls* (Philadelphia: Lippincott, 1936), 253.
89. "Students Voice Approval of Double Standard Of Morality," *The University of Michigan Daily*, 20 February 1936.
90. "Undergraduate Marriages," *The Mount Holyoke News*, 15 May 1936.
91. Willard Waller, "The Rating and Dating Complex," *American Sociological Review*, Volume 2, Issue 5, October 1937, 729.
92. "Dean Porter States Amherst Policy about Student Marriages in 'Red Book' Symposium," *The Amherst Student*, 24 October 1935.
93. "Undergraduate Marriages," *The Mount Holyoke News*, 15 May 1936.
94. "Dean Porter States Amherst Policy about Student Marriages in 'Red Book' Symposium," *The Amherst Student*, 24 October 1935.
95. "New Policy Allows Vassar Girls to Marry and Remain In College to Complete Regular Four Year Course," *The Amherst Student*, 4 October 1934.
96. "Undergraduate Marriages," *The Mount Holyoke News*, 15 May 1936.
97. Ibid.
98. McConaughy, "Now That You Are Engaged," 19.

99. Wandersee, *Women's Work and Family Values* , 117.
100. Eleanor Roosevelt "Should Wives Work?" *The Good Housekeeping Marriage Book: Twelve Ways to a Happy Marriage,* William F. Bigelow, Ed. (New York: Prentice-Hall, Inc., 1938), 43.
101. Ibid., 52.
102. Palmer, *Domesticity and Dirt,* 13–14.
103. "Job or Marriage?" *The Mount Holyoke News* 11 December 1936.
104. Lois Scharf, *To Work and To Wed: Female Employment, Feminism, and the Great Depression* (Westport, CT: Greenwood Press, 1980), 26.
105. Van Duzer, *Everyday Living for Girls,* 234–5.
106. Historian Alice Kessler-Harris notes that issues involving male and female roles were "allowed to pass unnoticed for generations because they affected mostly poor, immigrant, and single women" were brought to the forefront of national discourse when they began to affect members of the white middle class. Alice Kessler-Harris, *Out To Work: A History of Wage-Earning Women in the United States* (New York: Oxford University Press, 1982), 254.
107. In reality, men were invading traditionally female spheres of employment in record numbers. In *To Work and To Wed,* Lois Scharf explains that during the 1930s, "Men made considerable inroads into bastions of female employment, despite continuing complaints of overabundant numbers, low status and poor pay." Men still took on jobs as teacher, librarians and social workers. Scharf, *To Work and to Wed,* 91.
108. Hutton, *The Single Woman,* 3.
109. "'College Girl is Willing to Sacrifice,' Harlow Reports in C.A. Talk on Marriage Problem," *The Amherst Student,* 29 April 1937.
110. Weiner, *From Working Girl to Working Mother,* 101.
111. Ibid., 109.
112. "Job or Marriage?" *The Mount Holyoke News,* 11 December 1936.
113. "The Youth Problem," *Life,* 6 June 1938, 56–57.
114. "Youth in College," *Fortune,* June 1936, 156.
115. Ibid.
116. "Should Women Work?" *The George Washington University Hatchet,* 12 May 1938.
117. Ibid.
118. Wandersee, *Women's Work and Family Values,* 104.
119. Ibid.
120. "Modern Campus Belle Differs From Predecessors: College Miss Now Invades All Realms Of Activity, Combines Careers" *The University of Michigan Daily,* 15 October 1936.
121. Ibid.
122. Ibid.
123. Cott, *Public Vows,* 173.
124. Ibid.
125. Martin, *How to Win and Hold a Husband,* 5 and Hildegarde Dolson, *How About a Man?* (New York: J.B. Lippincott Company, 1938), 13–14.

126. Palmer, *Domesticity and Dirt*, 93.
127. Linda W. Rosenzweig, *Another Self: Middle-Class American Women and Their Friends in the Twentieth Century* (New York: New York University Press, 1999), 83.
128. Ibid.
129. Ibid.
130. "Modern Campus Belle Differs From Predecessors: College Miss Now Invades All Realms Of Activity, Combines Careers" *The University of Michigan Daily*, 15 October 1936.
131. Elsie A. Pierce, "College Women After Husband, Not Learning, Figures Prove," *The University of Michigan Daily*, 15 January 1936. One longitudinal study of college students found that women who dropped out of college without earning a degree often made more money than women who graduated, "but their choice of husbands was less fortunate and their lives lacked the richness" of women who graduated. "Graduating from College in the 1930s: The Terman Genetic Studies of Genius," Carol Tomlinson-Keasey and Charles Blake Keasey, *Women's Lives Through Time: Educated Women of the Twentieth Century*, Kathleen Day Hulbert and Diane Tickton Schuster, eds. (San Francisco: Jossey-Bass Publishers, 1993), 89.
132. "Marriage, Graduate Work and Professions Are Foremost Among Students' Future Plans," *The Mount Holyoke News*, 19 November 1937.
133. "American Youth—1940," *The George Washington University Hatchet*, 30 April 1940.
134. "College Women After Husband, Not Learning, Figures Prove," *The University of Michigan Daily*, 15 January 1936.
135. McConaughy, "Now That You Are Engaged," 14.
136. Scharf, *To Work and to Wed*, 94.
137. Cott, *Public Vows*, 167.
138. Ibid, 168.
139. "Psychologist Tells Co-Eds to Go Slow In Getting A Man," *The University of Michigan Daily*, 30 November 1932
140. Ibid.
141. Young women who had jobs that paid well had better bargaining positions in the marriage market, they could afford to take their time in choosing a future mate. Elaine Tyler May, *Great Expectations: Marriage and Divorce in Post-Victorian America* (Chicago: The University of Chicago Press, 1980), 3.
142. "Marriage Parley," *The Mount Holyoke News*, 11 December 1936.
143. Ibid.
144. "On the Education of Women," *The University of Michigan Daily*, 17 March 1936.
145. "Put Men in the Kitchen Say Girls," *The George Washington University Hatchet*, 11 October 1938.
146. "Women's Sphere Widens With Added Pressures," *The Mount Holyoke News*, 23 March 1939.
147. "Can You Cook? Sew? College Men Prefer Domestic Brides," *The University of Michigan Daily*, 19 May 1936.

148. Popenoe, *Modern Marriage*, 64.
149. Martin, *How to Win and Hold a Husband*, 5.
150. Gregory, *Win Him If You Want Him*, 12.
151. Ibid., 13.
152. Martin, *How to Win and Hold a Husband*, 5.
153. Kalish, *Why Not Get Married?*, 15.
154. Ibid., 16–17.
155. Ibid.,14.
156. Hutton, *The Single Woman*, 19.
157. Martin, *How to Win and Hold a Husband*, 50.
158. Roland Marchand, *Advertising the American Dream: Making Way for Modernity, 1920–1940* (Berkeley: University of California Press, 1985), 103.
159. The following poem, which demonstrates some of the anxieties young women were experiencing regarding earning a degree, having a job or finding a man appeared in the column "Beyond the Blue," *The Mount Holyoke News*, 8 November 1939.

    They sent me off to college
    To make a lady of me.
    I crammed my head with knowledge;
    Oh, I was smart as smart could be.
    Then home I came a-trooping,
    Diploma in my hand
    To find that while I'd got my learning
    Someone else had got my man.

160. Hill explained that the ability to attract marriageable mate hinged on a woman's proclivity to make an accurate self-analysis of her own personality. Essentially, women were told to look at themselves through eyes of others in order to learn how to sell themselves in the most pleasing possible manner. In Hill's estimation the qualities of a pleasing personality included: flexibility, harmony with self, effective showmanship, magnetic hand shake, appropriateness of clothing, posture and carriage of body, tone of voice, sincerity of purpose, choice of words, poise, keen sense of humor, unselfishness, facial expression, positive though, enthusiasm, sound health, imagination, tactfulness, versatility, listener, speak, personal magnetism, good sport, promptness of decision, courtesy, ability to say no pleasingly, beauty parlor habit, habit of smiling, spirit of romance, democratic. Rosa Lee Hill, *How to Attract Men and Money: An Intimate Revelation for Women Past Eighteen* (Meriden, Connecticut: Ralston Society, 1938).
161. Terman, Lewis M., et al. *Psychological Factors in Marital Happiness* (New York: McGraw-Hill, 1938).
162. Frank Hobart Cheley, *Our Social Assets: How To Make the Most of Them* (New York: The University Society, 1936), 6.
163. Gregory, *Win Him If You Want Him*, 16.
164. Helen Harrison, *Developing Your Personality* (New York: Reader Mail, Inc. 1936), 26

165. Kalish, *Why Not Get Married?*, 27.
166. Ibid., 30.
167. Elmer U. Gross, LL.B., *Meet Your Mate the Modern Way: A Present-Day Practical Solution To An Age-Old Personal Problem* (Boston: The Christopher Publishing House, 1940), 38.
168. Maryellen Maher Lombardi *The Inter-Trait Rating Technique* dissertation (1938) and Mrs. Emma McCloy Layman *An Item Analysis of the Adjustment Questionnaire* dissertation (1937).
169. "Miss Elizabeth Arden Speaks on Personality; NY Beauty Expert Emphasizes Importance of Appearance in Our Personality Development," *The Mount Holyoke News*, 13 November 1936.
170. Dorothy Hoover Downs, *How To Get Your Man and Hold Him*, (New York: A.L. Taylor, 1936), 12.
171. Dolson, *How About a Man?*, 13–14.
172. Ibid, 103.
173. Ibid, 104.
174. Frances Angell, *Compete!* (Philadelphia: Dorrance & Company, Inc., 1935), 34.
175. Ibid.
176. Gregory, *Win Him If You Want Him*, 12.
177. Martin, *How to Win and Hold a Husband*, 9.
178. Janice A. Radway, *A Feeling for Books: The Book-of-the-Month Club, Literary Taste, and Middle-Class Desire*, (Chapel Hill: University of North Carolina Press, 1997), 129. Janice Radway defines a commodity as an "object that could fulfill particular needs and desires and then be discarded."
179. Angell, *Compete!*, 40.
180. Ibid.
181. Ibid.
182. "Bachelor Boys in Limelight; Scheming Sirens Reveal," *The George Washington University Hatchet*, 16 April 1935.
183. Downs, *How To Get Your Man and Hold Him*, 14–15.
184. Angell, *Compete!* , 40.
185. Emily Post, *Etiquette: The Blue Book of Social Usage* (New York: Funk & Wagnalls Company, 1937), 374–5.
186. Strain, *Love at the Threshold*, 102–3.
187. Ibid, 103.
188. Ibid.
189. Ibid.
190. Angell, *Compete!*, 40.
191. "Co-Eds Might Emulate Lassies Who Took Leap Year Seriously, *The University of Michigan Daily*, 26 February 1936.
192. Ibid.
193. "University Men Breathe Easily; Leap Year Over!" *The George Washington University Hatchet* 2 February 1937.
194. "What Coeds Want," Otto McClarin, *The Howard Hilltop*, 27 February 1940.

195. Ibid.
196. Harrison, *Developing Your Personality*, 27.
197. Wandersee, *Women's Work and Family Values*, 114.
198. "Beyond the Blue," *The Mount Holyoke News*, 19 May 1939. *The Mount Holyoke News* ran numerous stories about the career paths of their alum, yet the boastful tone and sneering sarcasm toward Smith students was reserved solely for articles about dating, engagements and weddings.
199. "Marriage, Graduate Work and Professions Are Foremost Among Students' Future Plans," *The Mount Holyoke News*, 19 November 1937.

Bibliography

NEWSPAPERS

The Amherst Student, Amherst College, Amherst, Massachusetts.

The George Washington University Hatchet, The George Washington University, Washington, DC.

The Howard Hilltop, Howard University, Washington, DC.

The Mount Holyoke News, Mount Holyoke College, South Hadley, Massachusetts.

The University of Michigan Daily, The University of Michigan, Ann Arbor, Michigan.

PRIMARY SOURCES

Angell, Frances. *Compete!* (Philadelphia: Dorrance & Company, Inc., 1935).

Angell, Robert Cooley. *A Study in Undergraduate Adjustment* (Chicago: University of Chicago Press, 1930).

Angell, Robert Cooley, Lowell Julliard Carr, and Charles Horton Cooley *Introductory Sociology,* (New York: Charles Scribners Sons, 1933).

Baird's Manual of American College Fraternities (Menasha, Wisconsin: The Collegiate Press, George Banta Publishing Company, 1949).

Banning, Margaret Culkin. *Letters to Susan* (New York: Harper & Brothers Publishers, 1936).

Beech, Gould. "Schools for a Minority," *Survey Graphic,* October, 1939, Vol. 28, No. 10.

Bigelow, William F., Ed. *The Good Housekeeping Marriage Book: Twelve Ways to a Happy Marriage* (New York: Prentice-Hall, Inc., 1938).

Bowman, Henry A. *Marriage for Moderns* (New York: McGraw-Hill, 1942).

Cavan, Ruth. *Building a Girl's Personality* (New York: Abingdon Press, 1932).

Chamberlain, John. "Our Jobless Youth: A Warning," *Survey Graphic,* October 1939 (New York: Survey Associates, Inc.) Vol. 28, No. 10.

Cheley, Frank Hobart. *Our Social Assets: How To Make the Most of Them* (New York: The University Society, 1936).

Davis, Maxine. *The Lost Generation: A Portrait of American Youth Today* (New York: The MacMillan Company, 1936).

Dickinson, Stanley G. "It Pays to be Happily Married," *The Good Housekeeping Marriage Book: Twelve Ways to a Happy Marriage,* William F. Bigelow, Ed. (New York: Prentice-Hall, Inc., 1938).

Dolson, Hildegarde. *How About a Man?* (New York: J.B. Lippincott Company, 1938).

Downs, Dorothy Hoover. *How To Get Your Man and Hold Him,* (New York: A.L. Taylor, 1936).

Eldridge, Elizabeth. *Co-Ediquette: Poise and Popularity for Every Girl* (New York: E.P. Dutton,1936).

Eldridge, Elizabeth. *Etiquette For Teens* (New York: Home Institute Incorporated, 1937).

Gallup, George and Saul Forbes Rae. *The Pulse of Democracy: The Public-Opinion Poll and How It Works* (New York: Simon & Schuster, 1940).

Gregory, Lee M. *Win Him If You Want Him* (New York: Hillman-Curl, Inc., 1937).

Gross, Elmer U. *Meet Your Mate the Modern Way: A Present-Day Practical Solution To An Age-Old Personal Problem* (Boston: The Christopher Publishing House, 1940).

Groves, Ernest R. "When He Comes A-Courting," *The Good Housekeeping Marriage Book: Twelve Ways to a Happy Marriage,* William F. Bigelow, Ed. (New York: Prentice-Hall, Inc., 1938).

Hacker, Louis M. *American Problems of Today: A History of the United States Since the World War,* (New York: F.S. Crofts & Company, 1938).

Harrison, Helen. *Developing Your Personality* (New York: Reader Mail, Inc., 1936).

Hill, Rosa Lee. *How to Attract Men and Money: An Intimate Revelation for Women Past Eighteen,* (Meriden, Connecticut: Ralston Society, 1938).

Hill, T. Arnold. "An Emergency is On!" *Opportunity: Journal of Negro Life,* September 1933, Vol. 11, No. 9.

Hockenbury, Myron D. *Make Yourself A Job: A Student Employment Handbook* (Harrisburg: Dauphin Publishing Company, 1936).

Hutton, Laura. *The Single Woman: Her Adjustment to Life and Love* (New York: Roy Publishers, 1935).

Kalish, Harvey. *Why Not Get Married?* (New York: E.P. Dutton & Company, 1937).

Layman, Emma McCloy. *An Item Analysis of the Adjustment Questionnaire* dissertation (1937).

Lombardi, Maryellen Maher. *The Inter-Trait Rating Technique* dissertation (1938).

Lynd, Robert S. and Helen Merrell Lynd, *Middletown in Transition: A Study in Cultural Conflicts* (New York: Harcourt, Brace and Company, 1937).

Martin, Lucille. *How to Win and Hold a Husband* (Los Angeles: Bantam, 1940).

McConaughy, James L. "Now That You Are Engaged," *The Good Housekeeping Marriage Book: Twelve Ways to a Happy Marriage,* William F. Bigelow, Ed. (New York: Prentice-Hall, Inc., 1938).

Popenoe, Paul and Roswell Hill Johnson, *Applied Eugenics* (New York: The MacMillan Company, 1933).

Popenoe, Paul. *Modern Marriage: A Handbook for Men* (New York: The MacMillan Company, 1940).

Post, Emily. *Etiquette: The Blue Book of Social Usage* (New York: Funk & Wagnalls Company, 1937).

Rainey, Homer P. *How Fare American Youth?: A Report to the American Youth Commission and the American Council on Education,* (New York: D. Appelton-Century Company, 1937).

Roosevelt, Eleanor. "Should Wives Work?" *The Good Housekeeping Marriage Book: Twelve Ways to a Happy Marriage,* William F. Bigelow, Ed. (New York: Prentice-Hall, Inc., 1938).

Stouffer, Samuel A. and Paul F. Lazarsfeld, *Research Memorandum on the Family in the Depression,* (New York: Social Science Research Council, 1937).

Strain, Frances Bruce. *Love at the Threshold: A Book on Dating, Romance and Marriage* (New York: D. Appleton-Century, 1939).

Stratton, Dorothy Constance. *Your Best Foot Forward: Social Usage for Young Moderns* (New York: McGraw-Hill, 1940).

Terman, Lewis M., et al. *Psychological Factors in Marital Happiness* (New York: McGraw-Hill, 1938).

Towner, Wayland D. "The Case of Youth vs. Society," *Journal of Social Hygiene,* October, November, December 1935, Vol. 21, 331–348.

Van Duzer, Adelaide Laura. *Everyday Living for Girls* (Philadelphia: Lippincott, 1936).

Waller, Willard. "The Rating and Dating Complex," *American Sociological Review,* Volume 2, Issue 5, October 1937, 727–734.

Waller, Willard. *The Family: A Dynamic Interpretation* (New York: Cordon, 1938).

Weaver, Robert C. "The New Deal and the Negro: A Look at the Facts," *Opportunity, Journal of Negro Life,* July 1935, Vol. 13, No. 7.

Wieman, Regina W. *Popularity* (Chicago: Willet, Clark & Company, 1936).

The Woman's Press, *Courageous Living in Times of Crisis* (New York: The Woman's Press, 1933).

Wood, Leland Foster. *Making A Home: A Study of Youth, Courtship and Marriage* (New York: Abingdon Press, 1938).

Woodward, Elizabeth. *Personality Preferred!: How To Grow Up Gracefully* (New York: Harper and Brothers, 1935).

SECONDARY SOURCES

Allen, Frederick Lewis. *Since Yesterday: The Nineteen-Thirties in America, September 3, 1929—September 3, 1939* (New York: Harper & Brothers Publishers, 1940).

Allen, Frederick Lewis. *The Big Change: America Transforms Itself, 1900–1950* (New York: Harper & Brothers Publishers, 1952).

Ascher, Carol. "Selling to Ms. Consumer," *American Media and Mass Culture: Left Perspectives,* Ed. Donald Lazere (Berkeley: University of California Press, 1987).

Bailey, Beth L. *From Front Porch to Back Seat: Courtship in Twentieth-Century America* (Baltimore: Johns Hopkins University Press, 1988).
Baritz, Loren. *The Good Life: The Meaning of Success for the American Middle Class* (New York: Alfred A. Knopf, 1989).
Beasley-Murray, Jon. "Value and Capital in Bourdieu and Marx," *Pierre Bourdieu, Fieldwork in Culture,* Ed. Nicholas Brown and Imre Szeman (Lanham, MD: Rowman and Littlefield, 2000).
Bird, Caroline. *The Invisible Scar* (New York: D. McKay, 1966).
Bourdieu, Pierre. *Outline of a Theory of Practice* (Cambridge: Cambridge University Press, 1977).
Bourdieu, Pierre. *Distinction: A Social Critique of the Judgment of Taste,* Translated by Richard Nice, (Cambridge: Harvard University Press, 1984).
Bourdieu, Pierre. "Social Space and Symbolic Power," *Sociological Theory*, Volume 7, Issue 1, (Spring 1989), 14–25.
Bourdieu, Pierre and Passeron, Jean-Claude. *Reproduction in Education, Society and Culture,* Translated by Richard Nice (London: Sage, 1990).
Bourdieu, Pierre. *The Field of Cultural Production: Essays on Art and Literature* (New York: Columbia University Press, 1993).
Brenner, Johanna. "On Gender and Class in U.S. Labor History," *Monthly Review,* (New York: Monthly Review Press) Vol. 50, No. 6, November 1998.
Butler, Judith. *Gender Trouble: Feminism and the Subversion of Identity* (New York: Routledge, 1990).
Cancian, Francesca M. *Love in America: Gender and Self-Development* (New York: Cambridge University Press, 1987).
Cate, Rodney M. and Llyod, Sally A. *Courtship* (London: Sage, 1992).
Chafe, William. *The American Woman,* (New York: Oxford University Press, 1972).
Chesler, Phyllis. *Woman's Inhumanity to Woman,* (New York: Thundermouth Press/Nation Books, 2001).
Conkin, Paul K. *The New Deal; The Crowell American History Series* (New York: Thomas Y. Crowell Company, 1967).
Cott, Nancy. *Public Vows: A History of Marriage and the Nation* (Cambridge: Harvard University Press, 2000).
Davis, Clark. "The Corporate Reconstruction of Middle-Class Manhood," *The Middling Sorts: Explorations in the History of the American Middle Class,* eds. Burton J. Bledstein and Robert D. Johnston, (New York: Routledge, 2001).
Denning, Michael. *The Cultural Front: The Laboring of American Culture in the Twentieth Century* (New York: Verso, 1996).
de Swaan, Abram. *The Management of Normality: Critical Essays in Health and Welfare* (London: Routledge, 1990).
Ehrenreich, Barbara and John. Eds. "The Professional Managerial Class," *Between Labor and Capital* (Boston: South End Press, 1979) 5–45.
Ehrenreich, Barbara. *Fear of Falling: The Inner Life of the Middle Class* (New York Pantheon Books, 1989).
Elder, Glen H. *Children of the Great Depression: Social Change in Life Experience,* 25th Anniversary Edition (Boulder, CO: Westview, 1999).

Fass, Paula S. *The Damned and the Beautiful: American Youth in the 1920s* (New York: Oxford University Press, 1977).
Feldstein, Ruth. *Motherhood in Black and White: Race and Sex in American Liberalism, 1930–1965* (Ithaca: Cornell University Press, 2000).
Frank, Ashley "Liberalism as Intellectual Leadership," *The Philosopher,* Volume LXXXVI, 1998.
Giddings, Paula. *When and Where I Enter: The Impact of Black Women on Race and Sex in America* (New York: Bantam Books, 1984).
Gordon, Lynn D. "Race, Class, and the Bonds of Womanhood at Spelman Seminary, 1881–1923," *History of Higher Education Annual* Vol. 9 (1989).
Gould, Stephen Jay. *The Mismeasure of Man* (New York: W.W. Norton & Company, 1996).
Horowitz, Helen Lefkowitz. *Campus Life: Undergraduate Cultures from the End of the Eighteenth Century to the Present* (New York: Alfred A. Knopf, 1987).
Jones, Jacqueline. *Labor of Love, Labor of Sorrow: Black Women, Work and the Family, From Slavery to the Present* (New York: Vintage Books, 1986).
Jones, Stephen R.G. *The Economics of Conformism* (New York: Basil Blackwell Inc., 1984).
Kammen, Michael. *American Culture, American Tastes: Social Change and the 20th Century* (New York: Knopf, 1999).
Kessler-Harris, Alice. *Out To Work: A History of Wage-Earning Women in the United States* (New York: Oxford University Press, 1982).
Kessler-Harris, Alice. *In Pursuit of Equity: Women, Men, and the Quest for Economic Citizenship in 20th-Century America* (New York: Oxford University Press, 2001).
Kimmel, Michael. *Manhood in America: A Cultural History* (New York: Free Press, 1996).
Kopytoff, Igor. "The Cultural Biography of Things: Commoditization as Process," in *The Social Life of Things: Commodities in Cultural Perspective,* Ed. Arjun Appadurai (Cambridge: Cambridge University Press, 1986).
Kyvig, David E. *Daily Life in the United States, 1920–1939; Decades of Promise and Pain* (Westport, CT: Greenwood Press, 2002).
Larson, Magali Sarfatti. *The Rise of Professionalism: A Sociological Analysis* (Berkeley: University of California Press, 1977).
Leach, William. *Land of Desire: Merchants, Power and the Rise of a New American Culture* (New York: Vintage Books, 1993).
Lowe, Lisa. *Immigrant Acts: On Asian American Cultural Politics* (Durham: Duke University Press, 1996).
Lupton, Ellen. *Mechanical Brides: Women and Machines from Home to Office* (New York: Cooper-Hewitt National Museum of Design Smithsonian Institution and Princeton Architectural Press, 1993).
Marchand, Roland. *Advertising the American Dream: Making Way for Modernity, 1920–1940* (Berkeley: University of California Press, 1985).
Margo, Robert A. "Employment and Unemployment in the 1930s," *The Journal of Economic Perspectives,* Vol. 7, No. 2 (Spring 1993).

Marx, Karl. *Capital: A Critique of Political Economy,* Translated by Samuel Moore and Edward Aveling; Edited by Frederick Engels (New York: The Modern Library, 1936).

Matt, Susan J. "Frocks, Finery, and Feelings: Rural and Urban Women's Envy, 1890–1930,"*An Emotional History of the United States,* eds. Peter N. Stearns and Jan Lewis (New York: New York University Press, 1998).

Matt, Susan J. *Keeping Up with the Joneses: Envy in American Consumer Society, 1890–1930* (Philadelphia: University of Pennsylvania Press, 2003).

May, Elaine Tyler. *Great Expectations: Marriage and Divorce in Post-Victorian America* (Chicago: The University of Chicago Press, 1980).

May, Elaine Tyler. *Homeward Bound: American Families in the Cold War Era* (New York: Basic Books, 1988).

McElvaine, Robert S. *Down and Out in the Great Depression: Letters from the Forgotten Man* (Chapel Hill: University of North Carolina Press, 1983).

McElvaine, Robert S. *The Great Depression; America, 1929–1941* (New York: Times Books, 1984).

McGovern, James R. *And a Time for Hope: Americans in the Great Depression* (Westport, Connecticut: Praeger, 2000).

Mills, C. Wright. *White Collar: The American Middle Classes* (London: Oxford University Press, 1951).

Modell, John. *Into One's Own: From Youth to Adulthood in the United States, 1920–1975* (Berkeley: University of California Press, 1989).

Modell, John. "Dating Becomes the Way of American Youth," from *Essays on the Family and Historical Change,* Leslie Page Moch, Ed., (College Station: Texas A & M University Press, 1983).

Nelson, Dana D. *National Manhood: Capitalist Citizenship and the Imagined Fraternity of White Men* (Durham: Duke University Press, 1998).

Nidiffer, Jana. "Crumbs from the Boy's Table: The First Century of Coeducation," *Women Administrators in Higher Education: Historical and Contemporary Perspectives,* Eds. Jana Nidiffer and Carolyn Terry Bashaw (Albany: State University of New York Press, 2001).

Nies, Betsy L. *Eugenic Fantasies: Racial Ideology in the Literature and Popular Culture of the 1920s* (New York : Routledge, 2002).

Nuwer, Hank. *Wrongs of Passage: Fraternities, Sororities, Hazing and Binge Drinking,* (Bloomington: Indiana University Press, 1999).

Packard, Jerrold M. *American Nightmare: The History of Jim Crow* (New York: St. Martin's Press, 2002).

Palmer, Phyllis. *Domesticity and Dirt: Housewives and Domestic Servants in the United States, 1920–1945* (Philadelphia: Temple University Press, 1989).

Palmieri, Patricia A. "Women's Colleges," *Women in Academe: Progress and Prospects,* Mariam K. Chamberlain, ed. (New York: Russell Sage Foundation, 1988).

Pease, Otis. *Responsibilities of American Advertising* (New Haven: Yale University Press, 1958).

Planyi, Karl. *The Great Transformation* (Boston: Beacon Press, 1957).

Radway, Janice A. *A Feeling for Books: The Book of the Month Club, Literary Taste and Middle-Class Desire* (Chapel Hill: University of North Carolina Press, 1997).

Roediger, David. *The Wages of Whiteness: Race and the Making of the American Working Class* (New York: Verso, 1991).

Rosenzweig, Linda W. *Another Self: Middle-Class American Women and Their Friends in the Twentieth Century,* (New York: New York University Press, 1999).

Rothman, Ellen K. *Hands and Hearts: A History of Courtship in America (*New York: Basic Books, 1984).

Rotundo, E. Anthony. *American Manhood: Transformations in Masculinity from the Revolution to the Modern Era* (New York: Basic Books, 1993).

Scharf, Lois. *To Work and To Wed: Female Employment, Feminism, and the Great Depression* (Westport, CT: Greenwood Press, 1980).

Seidman, Steven. *Romantic Longings: Love in America, 1830–1980* (New York: Routledge, 1991).

Shumway, David R. "Something Old, Something New: Romance and Marital Advice in the 1920s," *An Emotional History of the United States,* eds. Peter N. Stearns and Jan Lewis (New York: New York University Press, 1998).

Smith-Rosenberg, Caroll. *Disorderly Conduct: Visions of Gender in Victorian America* (New York: Oxford University Press, 1985).

Spurlock, John S. "The Problem of Modern Married Love for Middle-Class Women," *An Emotional History of the United States,* eds. Peter N. Stearns and Jan Lewis (New York: New York University Press, 1998).

Stearns, Peter N. "Consumerism and Childhood: New Targets for American Emotions," *An Emotional History of the United States,* eds. Peter N. Stearns and Jan Lewis (New York: New York University Press, 1998).

Sundstrom, William A. "Last Hired, First Fired? Unemployment and Urban Black Workers During the Great Depression," *The Journal of Economic History,* Vol. 52, No. 2 (June, 1992).

Susman, Warren. *Culture as History: The Transformation of American Society in the Twentieth Century,* (New York: Pantheon Books, 1984).

Terkel, Studs. *Hard Times: An Oral History of the Great Depression,* (New York: Pantheon, 1970).

Tomlinson-Keasey, Carol and Charles Blake Keasey, "Graduating from College in the 1930s: The Terman Genetic Studies of Genius," *Women's Lives Through Time: Educated Women of the Twentieth Century,* Kathleen Day Hulbert and Diane Tickton Schuster, eds. (San Francisco: Jossey-Bass Publishers, 1993).

Tyack, David and Elisabeth Hansot, *Managers of Virtue: Public School Leadership in America, 1820–1980* (New York: Basic Books, Inc., 1982).

Tyack, David, Robert Lowe, and Elisabeth Hansot, *Public Schools in Hard Times; The Great Depression and Recent Years* (Cambridge: Harvard University Press,1984).

Van Gennep, Arnold. *The Rites of Passage* (Chicago: University of Chicago Press, 1960).

Veblen, Thorstein. *Theory of the Leisure Class: An Economic Study of Institutions* (New York: B.W. Huebsch,1899).

Walker, Pat. "Introduction," *Between Labour and Capital* (Boston: South End Press, 1979).

Wandersee, Winifred D. *Women's Work and Family Values, 1920–1940* (Cambridge: Harvard University Press, 1981).

Ware, Susan. *Beyond Suffrage: Women in the New Deal* (Cambridge: Harvard University Press, 1981).

Ware, Susan. *Holding Their Own: American Women in the 1930s* (Boston: Twayne Publishers, 1982).

Weiner, Lynn Y. *From Working Girl to Working Mother: The Female Labor Force in the United States, 1820–1980* (Chapel Hill: University of North Carolina Press, 1985).

Weininger, Elliot B. "Class Analysis and Cultural Analysis in Bourdieu," *Economic Sociology European Electronic Newsletter,* Vol. 4, No. 2 (March 2003).

Westin, Jeanne. *Making Do: How Women Survived the '30s* (Chicago: Follett Publishing Company, 1976).

White, Kevin. "The New Man and Early Twentieth-Century Emotional Culture in the United States" *An Emotional History of the United States,* eds. Peter N. Stearns and Jan Lewis (New York: New York University Press, 1998).

Wolcott, Victoria. *Remaking Respectability: African American Women in Interwar Detroit* (Chapel Hill: University of North Carolina Press, 2001).

Wouters, Cas. "Etiquette Books and Emotion Management in the Twentieth Century: American Habitus in International Comparison," *An Emotional History of the United States,* eds. Peter N. Stearns and Jan Lewis (New York: New York University Press, 1998).

Zunz, Olivier. *Why The American Century?* (Chicago: University of Chicago Press, 1998).

Index

F

I

J

K

L

M

For Product Safety Concerns and Information please contact our EU representative GPSR@taylorandfrancis.com
Taylor & Francis Verlag GmbH, Kaufingerstraße 24, 80331 München, Germany

www.ingramcontent.com/pod-product-compliance
Ingram Content Group UK Ltd.
Pitfield, Milton Keynes, MK11 3LW, UK
UKHW021959180926
475701UK00003B/107
* 9 7 8 0 4 1 5 6 4 8 1 3 4 *